THE WINNERS MANUAL

THE
WINNERS
MANUAL

FOR THE GAME OF LIFE

JIM TRESSEL

WITH CHRIS FABRY

Tyndale House Publishers, Inc. | Carol Stream, Illinois

Library of Congress Cataloging-in-Publication Data

Tressel, Jim.
    The winners manual : for the game of life / Jim Tressel with Chris Fabry.
      p. cm.
    ISBN-13: 978-1-4143-2569-9 (hc)
    ISBN-10: 1-4143-2569-X (hc)
1. Success—Psychological aspects.   I. Fabry, Chris, date.   II. Title.
    BF637.S8T67 2008
    650.1—dc22
                                           2008021255

Printed in the United States of America

14   13   12   11   10   09   08
 7   6   5   4   3   2   1

This book is dedicated to all the difference makers in my life. Of course, my mom and dad, Eloise and Lee Tressel, whom I miss every day. My wonderful wife and friend, Ellen Jeanne, who has unselfishly partnered with me to serve others. And my biggest fans and supporters, Zak, Carlee, Eric, and Whitney. You are the best, and I am so proud of you. I was blessed to have two awesome older brothers, Dick and Dave. Thank you all. I love you!

TABLE OF CONTENTS

FOREWORD BY JOHN MAXWELL

When Coach Jim Tressel asked me to write the foreword for *The Winners Manual: For the Game of Life*, I was honored. Having grown up in Ohio, I am keenly aware of the impact of Ohio State football and the positive influence that the Buckeyes' coach can have throughout the state and the nation. Recommending this book allows me to introduce Jim Tressel and his coaching and teaching philosophy to some people who might not yet have had the opportunity to get to know him.

Over the years, I have had the good fortune to interact with Coach Tressel and the Buckeyes on numerous occasions. I am proud to say that they have used some of my materials in their pursuit of excellence, and I have had the opportunity to speak to his teams during the 2004, 2006, and 2007 seasons. I have also had the privilege of reading the team version of the Winners Manual that Coach Tressel has developed over the past twenty-two years with his teams—the foundation for the book you're now reading. One of my own books, *Talent Is Never Enough*, was inspired by a page in the team's manual that describes qualities that do not take talent but are essential to the ultimate success of a group.

In the time I've spent with the Buckeyes, it has become obvious to me that the coaching staff has a plan for the development of the whole person, the complete student-athlete. I have been with them in the meeting room, the locker room, and on the sideline. The Buckeyes are focused, competitive, caring, loving, tough, and classy. They have a passion to be winners! The young men who play football for Ohio State have a healthy perspective about themselves, which allows them to express their abilities in a highly competitive world, both on and off the field. They truly seek to reach their full potential.

Each chapter in *The Winners Manual* will illustrate a different fundamental that Coach Tressel has identified as essential for winners. You will study the fundamentals through a combination of quotes and anecdotes, culminating in a "personal game plan" that will help you apply the fundamentals to all phases of your life. No matter what "position" you play in life, these fundamentals will serve as great training for your contribution to whatever "team" you're on.

My professional goal is to add value to people's lives every day. Coach Tressel shares the same passion. If you work through the principles in this book and implement them, you will benefit from *The Winners Manual* and have value added to your life that you will certainly want to pass on to others.

ACKNOWLEDGMENTS

Thank you, first and foremost, to all of the men, women, and families of our United States military, past and present. Their unselfish service and sacrifice have allowed us the freedom to safely chase our dreams in this wonderful country and to seek to be winners in the game of life.

Thank you to all the coaches, players, and dear friends who have shared their lives with me for so many years. I have been so blessed to work with you and grow from your loving examples.

Thank you to Joe Malmisur, Andy Geiger, and Gene Smith, extraordinary athletic directors who have given me a chance to serve. To Mark Summers, who has been there for me, on and off the field, since we played together at B-W. And to Doc Spurgeon, who has taught so many people that love makes the difference if you truly want to serve.

Finally, thank you to all of the good people at Tyndale, especially Carol Traver and Chris Fabry, who encouraged me to share these lessons that have affected my life, in hopes that we can make a difference for others.

Jim Tressel

PROLOGUE

"If the game of life ended tonight, would you be a winner?"

I first heard that question asked by Bobby Richardson, the great second baseman for the New York Yankees, when I was a teenager at a Fellowship of Christian Athletes camp. Richardson was an athlete I looked up to tremendously—seven times in the World Series, MVP of the 1960 World Series, selected nine times as an all-star, and winner of five straight Gold Gloves for fielding. He was the epitome of a professional athlete. He exuded excellence. But as much of a hero as Bobby Richardson was to me, the question he asked actually troubled me greatly because I didn't have a good answer. How can you know if you're a winner?

That question has continued to intrigue me throughout my life, and in a way, it has defined my life as a son, a husband, a father, and a coach. I didn't consciously set out on a quest to answer it, but looking back, I can see how much my life has been shaped by that simple question.

To many people, winning is everything. Striving for a conference championship can be a passion that turns into an obsession. Even more, a national championship can be a goal that feels exhilarating. I've seen the positives of setting a goal and pushing a team of players to achieve it, working together and striving for something as a team. But I've also seen the destructive force of that kind of ruthless search and what it can do to young people and the coaches who try to win at all costs. Everyone wants to be a winner, but at the end of the season, only one team will stand at the top of the mountain.

So how can you know if you're a winner in life? Must we redefine the word? And if your life's game ended this second, would you consider yourself a winner? How can you measure such a thing?

The book you're holding is my attempt not only to answer those important questions but also to distill the heart of a nearly four-hundred-page handbook we give to our football players as they enter each new year at The Ohio State University.

THE DEVELOPMENT OF THE WINNERS MANUAL

The Winners Manual originated in 1986 at Youngstown State University, where I had just been hired as head football coach. The first Winners Manual we handed out to our Penguin players was about seventy-five pages long and had a flimsy plastic cover and spiral binding that barely held the pages together. I'm not sure many of those books have stood the test of time, but the contents certainly have.

Every year since 1986, I've added a few quotes or stories, and I've deleted a few. Sometimes I worry that I have too many quotes. But you never know when a guy who is struggling with something in his life will pick up his Winners Manual and notice a quote in there. I'll hear guys talk about a quote that got stuck in their mind, and I'll think, *See, it was worth it to keep that one in there.* Even former players who are now in the NFL call and ask for the latest version of the Winners Manual. They might be in training camp, or they're having a difficult time with an injury, and it seems to offer the boost they need at the moment.

From its humble beginnings, the Winners Manual has developed into a handbook that includes everything my coaches and I think would be helpful for our players to have when they walk in the door on the first day of training camp. Today, the Winners Manual that we give our players and coaches begins with a tribute to our country and includes the Pledge of Allegiance and a section on the importance of the American flag. We even print the text of the Gettysburg Address by Abraham Lincoln.

Next comes a section on Ohio State football, our mission statement, songs such as "The Buckeye Battle Cry," "Across the Field," and "Hang on Sloopy," plus copies of several letters I've come across from great coaches such as Paul Brown and Woody Hayes.

Then we get into what we call The Plan. It's a step-by-step process of personal assessment and goal setting that the players find helpful. We take each player on a journey of success and introduce him to the Block O of Life, which we'll discuss shortly.

After sections covering our preseason and in-season travel and activities, our policies-and-procedures regulations—everything from personal conduct rules to the confidentiality of the playbook—we eventually get to the fundamentals for winners that make up the bulk of the Winners Manual. This is our "tools" section, in which we try to give each player the personal and team tools he'll need to succeed.

For the purposes of this book, we've boiled nineteen fundamentals down to ten chapters. Of course, we can't include all the material from the Winners Manual here, but we've tried to give you the heart of it—the sayings and ideas that have stood out to our players.

Through the years, I've asked for input regarding the contents of the book. Every year, a player or coach will come up to me and say, "Hey, this would be a great addition to the Winners Manual." That's how it began to grow, and as you can imagine, within a few years it expanded from seventy-five pages to a mammoth volume that needed pruning.

The process of addition and subtraction is simple. I have a box in my office in which I collect things I've read or have been given. Every year, in late May or early June, I sort through the contents of the box, looking for new material for the Winners Manual. Then I rewrite certain sections, adding and subtracting, to keep the Winners Manual fresh but also of a manageable size.

I didn't think then, and I don't think now, that we're doing anything revolutionary with this resource. The strength of the tool is that it represents a concerted effort to present thoughts that deserve attention, reinforcement, and practice in our players' lives. I think we've put a little order to it, but most of this material is available in other places in other forms. I like our players to take their Winners Manuals back to their rooms to read during preseason, when they hate the two-a-days and want to quit and go home. Things get difficult during preseason because it's hot, the players are tired, and they just want to get to the games. They're asking, "Why in the world did I come to this place?"

During those times, I hope the guys will leaf through the book and find something refreshing or something that ignites a fire inside to keep them going another day. The thought-provoking wisdom in the Winners Manual gives them a perspective outside of themselves. It may give confidence to someone struggling to measure up. It may spur a player to a greater commitment to The Plan. Four years later, when that player is giving his senior speech, he'll say, "I remember when I was a freshman and I was going to quit. I read this quote, and I want to share it with you because it kept me going and really made the difference for me."

That is my goal with this version of the Winners Manual. If you're struggling with your place in the world, if things have become difficult and you feel like giving up, or if you don't know whether or not you are a winner, I hope that in some small way, this book can be a tool used for good in your life. I want to present ideas, principles, and truths in a way that will encourage you, lift you up when you're wrestling with life, and push you forward and motivate you to be a better person and a more vital part of whatever team you serve.

Over the course of the past twenty-or-so years, I've been rereading a lot of the same messages and quotes and sayings from people who have offered part of their lives and wisdom to me. I'm grateful to be around this game and the people who've allowed me to appropriate much of their wisdom. For me, it all began in my early years, growing up right next door to a football stadium.

THE LIGHT IN THE WINDOW

My father, Lee Tressel, coached at Baldwin-Wallace College, a small, Division III school in Berea, Ohio. Division III coaches weren't paid much back then, but the college gave my father an on-campus house to live in. The house was not only next door to the stadium, it was also right across the street from the athletic center and my father's office. As a result, I got to watch what my dad did every day, to see the impact he had on young people's lives, and to witness how much people enjoyed being a part of the collegiate football experience. I can still remember the feeling of looking out in the evening after dinner, darkness descending, and seeing the light on in the window of his office in the gymnasium, where he was busy making calls to recruits.

I had a chance to play for my father and to see the game from a different angle. Then, after realizing that my dream of playing in the NFL wasn't going to happen, I decided that coaching would be a good way to use the skills I felt God had given me. I was an assistant coach for several schools, and I picked up a little advice here, a little wisdom there, and discovered things that really made sense to me. I vowed if I ever had the chance to be a head coach, I would share the things I'd been taught by these great teachers I had known and loved.

In those days, I was a huge fan of Coach John Wooden of UCLA. I still am. His teams were on an incredible roll in NCAA basketball, and we got to watch them perhaps once a year on television. (Things have come a long way in televised sports since the 1970s.) In order to learn from these great coaches, you couldn't go to a seminar or look them up on the Internet; you had to get a book to study and try to integrate their approaches. I studied Coach Wooden's philosophy—the Pyramid of Success—as well as the work of other coaches who embodied the teachings of my father or the things I strongly believed. You always think you have all the answers until suddenly, you're in charge. So in the fall of 1986, when I became a head coach at Youngstown State, I started compiling the Winners Manual, with the help of my coaches, and each year we've added to it.

I want to make it crystal clear at the outset that what we've experienced and developed is an accumulation of lessons learned from others. I have been extremely blessed to work for Jim Dennison at Akron, Tom Reed at Miami of Ohio, Dick MacPherson at Syracuse, and Earle Bruce at Ohio State and alongside some of the finest assistant coaches in all of college football. When I was at Youngstown State and had a little more time every year than I do now, I would spend a week each year studying other coaches at places such as the University of Washington, Florida State, the University of Texas, the University of Colorado, Baylor University, and the Air Force Academy, as well as the San Francisco 49ers and other schools and organizations. I examined these schools and teams from top to bottom and scrutinized everything they did. Even if I got just one little nugget from that week away, I felt that it was worth it for me. So I want to make sure you understand that I'm not standing on some mountaintop casting down all my wisdom to the people in the valley. I'm sharing the fruit of the good fortune I've had of being around wonderful people and having great experiences.

THE HEART OF THE WINNERS MANUAL

Throughout the years, the Winners Manual has taken various shapes and sizes. We add and delete items as needed, and that has become an organic process used to fit the players' personalities and the situations of our teams each year. But there are a few constants. Every Winners Manual, no matter what the layout happens to be, has the word *TEAM*—which stands for Together Everyone Achieves More—above every other word on the cover of the book. That's not just a symbol. It is the substance of everything we do, everything we talk about, and everything we try to instill in our players. We talk about it a lot, because in all we do, TEAM always comes first.

One of the concepts our players hear about each year, no matter how many years ago they played for us, is the idea of having an "attitude of gratitude." That's a good place to begin, because the concept of living gratefully, and the other ideas you'll read about, are not original with me or with any of the men and women I've been fortunate enough to work with over the past three decades. So many people have contributed to the tools in this book—what we'll call the Big Ten Fundamentals. These teachings have been passed down by my father, coaches I've known and read about, and players who have taught me a lot about winning and losing, life, love, and giving. So before I go any further, I want to pay tribute to them and express my gratitude for the input they've had in my life.

Bottom line, this is the system we've used at Ohio State for the past seven years and the system we came up with at Youngstown State in 1986. It's a people-building tool that helps players become the leaders they desire to be. And you're going to read plenty about football in these pages. But in a great sense, this is not a book about football as much as it is about life.

It's also important for you to know that this *isn't* a book that has all the answers. I'm a bit hesitant about sharing "keys for a successful life," because I don't pretend to have all the keys or even to know where some of them are. My original title for this book was *A Winners Manual*, because I don't want to be perceived as someone who thinks he has all the answers.

Having said that, I really believe this approach helps develop a whole person, not just a great football player. That's our goal—to see someone walk through the door as a freshman and walk out the door four or five years later as a well-rounded student, player, son, friend, and citizen.

Because I have learned a lot more from losing than I've ever learned from winning, I'm going to show you a lot of the mistakes I've made and grown from. You're also going to read stories about players who chose "team" over "self" and were rewarded greatly for their attitude.

It would be the height of arrogance for me to say that this is the only way to a "winning life." That's not my purpose. My goal is to honestly set forth some principles that I've seen work in the relationship between a coach and a player, principles that motivate people to reach for goals that may seem a bit out of their grasp and to embrace a life of success and satisfaction that many people seem unable to achieve.

One more thing I want to clarify about our students. In no way do I want to give the impression that players come into our program morally deficient or with no development in their character, we give them a "magic book," and suddenly they've gone from delinquent people to shining examples of humanity. That's just not the way it is. The players who come to The Ohio State University are some of the best in the country. They're great kids who have already had a lot of input from parents, extended family, and other coaches. Mentors have, many times, poured their lives into these young men, so they come to us with rich life experiences, and they are people with great character and conscience. What we offer them is a four- or five-year program that focuses on each of them as a person. They grow and develop in the crucible of Buckeye football, which is not an easy thing to do. We're giving them more tools to help them develop and putting them in learning situations that take them further down the same road they've been on for eighteen years. They have many of the basics already ingrained in them, but we offer a reinforcement of the importance of those things that crystallizes their thinking.

That's where you come in. No matter where you are in your development, whether you're a young person starting out or you're already in your retirement years, if you want to personally progress in your life and become a team player with those around you, I think this book will help. It is intended as an interactive tool for anyone—coaches, teachers, parents, businesspeople, or anyone else who has influence on others. If you struggle with the concept of purpose in your life and with setting tangible, realistic goals, I believe this book can be a pivotal point in your development.

HOW TO READ THIS BOOK

When we get together each morning in preseason to go through the Winners Manual, we have what we call our Quiet Time. We start in our team meeting room—a large lecture hall—and each player has his Winners Manual along with his defensive notebook or whatever is on the schedule next. Try visualizing this: one hundred or more guys of every size and shape, from three-hundred-pound linemen to tall, thin receivers, all with their heads down, scribbling something they're grateful for in their manuals and reading the section assigned for the day. After they jot down something they're thankful for, they're able to use the next eight to twelve minutes of quiet to help them develop their inner person.

The great thing about this exercise is that every person will come away with something different from the exact same material. It's so amazing what will strike them. I usually ask a question about what they've read, in order to get some feedback so that the other players can hear how their teammates see a statement or story. After they get comfortable, I don't have to call on anyone; they simply raise their hands and describe something that happened in a game or in practice or in class that struck them as relevant to what they've just read.

A guy will raise his hand, and as he's sharing, I'm thinking, *I've known this kid since I sat in his living room with his parents, and* that quote *spoke to him?* It's an awesome process to go through each day, and I learn way more than the players do every year.

I can't be there in your home to hear your perspective, but figuratively you can raise your hand and respond to something you've read and write it down. That's why we've developed Questions for Reflection at the end of each chapter. These are designed for your own soul-searching and to help you grapple with the real-life issues you face each day. You might even get with a group of people and walk through these chapters. You'll be surprised at how much you'll learn from others if you do.

The final section of each chapter is called Your Personal Game Plan. Here, we take each section of the Block O of Life and lead you in specific ways you can grow in that area. Whether it's your health, your career pursuits, your family, or another part of your purpose or goals, this will be the most practical part of the book. Try not to skip over those sections, but don't let them overwhelm you either. You might concentrate on only one section of the Personal Game Plan on a given day or during an entire week; that's all right. Relax and let the material soak in and help you grow.

THE GAME PLAN OF THIS BOOK

This version of the Winners Manual has been designed with three sections. We present Part 1 to you as The Game Plan. This section lays the groundwork for all of the fundamentals. We talk about success as a journey and about having a plan, goals, and dreams—that's the beginning of the process.

We also deal with the basic blueprint of our program, which we call the Block O of Life. When you understand the six components of the O, the difference between your purpose and your goals, you'll be ready to move on to the Big Ten Fundamentals. But keep in mind that throughout the book, you'll refer to the Block O often, returning to it chapter by chapter—in the content of the chapter as well as in Your Personal Game Plan.

Part 2 describes the Big Ten Fundamentals, a series of chapters on the bedrock building blocks of attitude, discipline, excellence, faith and belief, work, handling adversity and success, love, responsibility, team, and hope. These are not meant to be read in one sitting and put back on the shelf. My guess is that you may read one quote and have to stop for a while. Or you'll want to tear out a page and give it to a friend who's struggling in that area.

Part 3 features some of the most important people in my life. We call this section Game Changers. These are the stories of people who have poured their lives into mine. They have personally inspired me and helped me put life on the field into perspective. I can only hope that in sharing their stories, you, too, will be inspired to embrace life as they have.

Finally, in the Epilogue, I'll tell you more about the question we began with: "If the game of life ended tonight, would you be a winner?" The answer to that question is vitally important.

Throughout the book, I'll refer often to our football Winners Manual, the handbook we give to our players at Ohio State. The first 30 percent of that handbook contains game schedules, practice schedules, guidelines for good media relationships, and other "inside" information that we keep just between our players and coaches. The "guts" of the book, however—the part that can really help focus your life and make you a better person no matter what type of team you're on—you'll find here, in the book you're holding.

I've always been the kind of person who is looking for that little bit of guidance that can help me in my passion to do God's will or find my purpose. When I attend a coaching clinic, I'm there soaking it all in, looking for a gold nugget I can take back and implement. Similarly, I've searched for books and other tools to help me along the way. My hope for you is that this book will prove to be a useful tool that will help you move toward your purpose and the accomplishment of your goals. If any part of this manual clicks for you and helps explain some things about life, if you pick up one thing that will help you move forward, then it was worth writing.

Over the years, I have read several books and heard several messages that have been pivotal in my life. The speech by Bobby Richardson comes to mind, as well as the writings of Coach John Wooden. If reading this book becomes a pivotal moment for you and opens your eyes and heart to things beyond what you have previously thought were important, then we've really scored. It'll be a true winner.

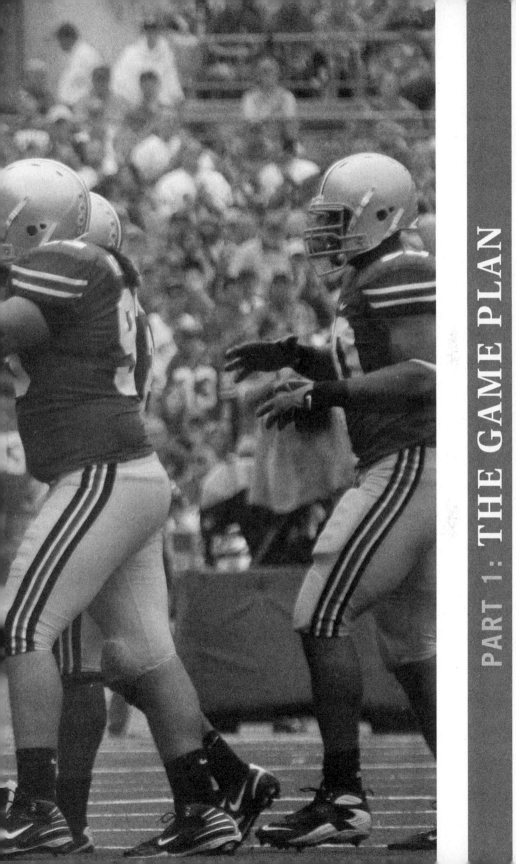

CHAPTER 1

THE JOURNEY OF SUCCESS

DECIDE YOUR PURPOSE, SET YOUR GOALS

If you do the things you need to do
When you need to do them,
Someday you can do the things you want to do
When you want to do them!

DEVELOPING VISION

The first step in creating an improved future is developing
the ability to envision it.

- Vision *will ignite the fire of passion, which fuels*
  our commitment to do whatever it takes *to achieve*
  excellence.
- Vision *allows us to transform dreams of greatness into*
  the reality of achievement through human action.
- Vision *has no boundaries and knows no limits. Our*
  vision *is what we become in life.*

Fame usually comes to those who are thinking about
something else.

OLIVER WENDELL HOLMES

Rejoice in our confident hope.
Be patient in trouble,
And keep on praying.

ROMANS 12:12

Success is a journey that we all take, and it affects every phase of our lives. In order to thrive during that journey, we have to have a clear view of what success is, what it isn't, and what it will take to achieve it. In this chapter, we will discuss a method we use with our players at Ohio State to help them understand what personal and team success is, and to help them set goals, pursue their dreams, and come up with a life plan for moving forward.

Many people define success by how much money they make or how far up the corporate ladder they can ascend. Coaches or athletes can define it in terms of championships, winning records, or great individual statistics. Championships and wins are fine goals. I want Ohio State to be the last team standing at the end of the year, no question about it. We tell the players that we're going to work like crazy on our team goals, and if they don't want to be champions, they're probably on the wrong team. But we also help them devise plans for how to obtain the goals they desire as individuals. We encourage our players to pursue the NFL, if that's what they want to do. But if a player says, "I really want to excel at football, but I feel that medicine is my life's calling," we help that player map out a plan to make it to medical school. It might be medical school, law school, or some other career path, but we want to help every player achieve his goals.

Goals are important, but it's important to understand that people are not *defined* by their goals and whether or not they reach them. A win or a loss does not make you or me a better or worse human being. This is where, in our society, we've so easily lost perspective on the truth about *who we are*. We have to separate who we *are* from what we *do*. With our players, it's vital to distinguish between "purpose" and "goals," as you'll see when we introduce a concept called the Block O of Life in the next chapter. Understanding the difference between purpose and goals is essential to understanding the true definition of success.

John Wooden, the legendary UCLA basketball coach, is one of my heroes. In his classic autobiography, *They Call Me Coach,* he defines the elusive quality of success: "Success is peace of mind which is a direct result of self-satisfaction in knowing you did your best to become the best you are capable of becoming."

That's a great definition. First, it takes away any external characterization of success—conference championship, national championship, awards—and puts the responsibility on the individual to define his own success. Trophies, rings, or trips to the White House do not mean you're a success. Success is found in "peace of mind." That was a revolutionary thought to me. I don't have to look to others to tell me whether I've made it. They can't tell me anything about my success, because they have no idea if I have peace of mind. That's a radical shift in thinking and drastically different from basing my success on whether I win or lose. I grew up in a coach's house, and believe me, I can tell the difference between a weekend after a win and a weekend after a loss. But in Coach Wooden's definition, I can rest in the satisfaction of knowing I did my best at becoming my best. That helps me to know if I've done all I can do.

Coach Wooden wrote his definition in 1972, at a time when many people defined success by the kinds of cars they drove, the houses they lived in, what jobs they had, and what material possessions they owned. In other words, it was a lot like it is today. But Wooden's description of success transcends the dictionary definition. It's not the accumulation of material possessions or the gaining of a certain amount of prestige or rank. It's not moving up the ladder at work, becoming famous, or gaining political power. We try to help our guys understand that success is being the best they can be, and feeling good about that, but then going one step further.

FOR THE GROUP

In defining success at Youngstown State and Ohio State, we built on the thoughts of Coach Wooden and added one tiny but powerful idea. We expanded his definition like this: "Success is the inner satisfaction and peace of mind that come from knowing I did the best I was capable of doing *for the group.*"

Success is a team sport. As Woody Hayes said many years ago, "You win with people." When we added "for the group" to Coach Wooden's definition, we helped to focus our players on the *team* aspect of success.

Our purpose in adding "for the group" was to capture the truth that in being our best, we add to those around us. It forces us to define success in terms of what the group needs, what our team needs, or what our society or country needs. You can see the problem of individualism in sports as well as in society. People tend to worry more about how something affects "me," as opposed to how it affects "us." But if we focus on what we ourselves can get rather than on what we can do for the team, we'll miss a great opportunity.

From a personal standpoint, that's why I consider it part of my job to go to hospitals or help out with fund-raisers for various groups. That's part of the opportunity I've been given as a head coach—to make a difference, not just on the sidelines of a football game, but also in a world of hurting people. Success is not only helping myself; it's helping others reach their goals.

However, there's a potential problem at a place like Ohio State. Because so many talented athletes represent our school, some of them could take the approach that the group really doesn't matter. The main concern could be for the individual to make it to the NFL. The player could have a selfish perspective and say, "I need X number of catches. I need X number of tackles. I need more touches at running back so I can get more yards and gain a bigger signing bonus when it's time for the draft." Fortunately, we choose our players wisely, and they buy into the team concept readily, but there's always a temptation to play for themselves rather than for the team.

Fans also present a problem with success because they expect the team to win every game. They'll be upset if we don't win the national championship every year. That's the nature of being a fan, and we appreciate their backing and thrive on the support they give. But winning every game every year is an unrealistic expectation. The truth is, only one team will win the Bowl Championship Series (BCS). Only one team out of thirty-two in the NFL will win the Super Bowl. In life, not everyone can be the top salesman at a company or get the big promotion. Not everyone starts a business and sees it grow and thrive and expand. So we try to help our players avoid tying their definition of success to their performance. This prepares them for their lives ahead and teaches them that though their *performance* connects directly with their *goals,* their *purpose* is tied to *who they are.*

In 2006, we were disappointed, not because we didn't win every game, but because we felt we didn't play anywhere near our ability. We were disappointed in the national-championship game after the 2007 season, not because we didn't play up to our ability, but because we made a couple of costly mistakes against a great team. And when you play a great team in their own backyard, you can't afford to make mistakes.

The difference for us was that our self-image wasn't crushed after those seasons. Our players and coaches had a handle on their purpose. They felt good about their contribution to the team. Even though we didn't achieve all of our goals, we were still successful.

Jerry Jenkins, coauthor of the best-selling Left Behind book series, makes a similar point about the stories he writes. He says, "Regardless of what we write, from books to articles, they should never simply be *about* something. They must always be *for the purpose* of something." So it is with our lives. We were created not just to exist, not just to pass through this world and be *about* something, but to live with *purpose*. Fulfilling our purpose is part of who we are. But what we're about—the goals we set, the dreams we have—is part of what we do.

We must never let goals, adversity—or even success—define us. Those things don't hit at the heart of who we are. We'll talk more about this important concept in the chapter on handling adversity and success, but in the meantime, let me give you an example from the NFL. Dan Marino, the great Miami Dolphins quarterback, was amazingly talented and set a lot of records at his position, yet he never won a Super Bowl. You would hope that Dan Marino doesn't gauge his career by its lack of a Super Bowl trophy. Equally, you would hope that he doesn't hang his worth as a person on those passing records. The reason he should feel good about himself is so much bigger than any record or championship ring. If a person measures his success by his inner satisfaction and the peace of mind that comes from knowing he did the best he was capable of doing for the group, he'll be able to gauge that success correctly.

By any objective standard, Dan Marino was a success, but only he knows for sure. That question has to be answered by the individual, because only the individual knows whether he or she has the inner peace that comes with success.

Many people want to know what goes on in the locker room after a championship win or loss. I don't let cameras into the locker room after the game. Win or lose, that's our time as a team, and I don't feel that we need to have it recorded. It's recorded in our hearts, and that's enough.

After our loss to Louisiana State University in the BCS national-championship game in January 2008, I remember expressing how proud I was of all my players. I was proud of their accomplishments throughout the season. I couldn't help but think back on all the hard work and preparation it had taken to get to that game in New Orleans. There were a lot of people who never thought we would play for the championship that year. I didn't say much about that during the season because I knew our guys believed we would be there. They had great faith in our team and ignored the talk. I mostly told them how proud I was to be part of that team, how hard I thought they had played and prepared, and how well they had represented Ohio State that night. At times like that, you talk a little from the heart about your appreciation for those guys who won't be back. It's their last game as Buckeyes, and that's tough.

The interesting thing about the media is that they're always asking questions about this moment or that moment and what happened when we were all together. But it's not about a moment. The other coaches and I didn't have to pontificate about how we felt about those guys and how much we appreciated them, because every day since training camp, we had been reinforcing that. We didn't have to make "the big speech," because we'd been pouring our lives into those players for four or five years, and the players had been responding to us every day.

Success is an everyday proposition. It isn't defined by a championship game or the day you get your diploma, get drafted by an NFL team, make the big sale, land the account of a lifetime, or get your law degree. Don't get me wrong, those are great days, and we should celebrate those accomplishments. But the key to a successful life is in the journey and the process. It's that emphasis on the *journey* to success that we work on each day, step by step.

I know that sportswriters want something earthshaking to write about—to describe that moment with our team when we're together and the emotions are high. Those reporters want to let the reader get a glimpse inside the locker room. But the truth is, there was a lot that went into those moments of celebration or grief, a lot that happened long before those "locker-room moments." To me, the process is what's most fun in football, and I'm sure it's that way for any profession. The process of going full bore into the season and balancing your purpose with your goals and the family you love and all the things you try to accomplish—it's a daily adventure.

I guess the specifics of what happened in that locker room in New Orleans will have to stay with the team. But you can be sure that those guys knew how their coaches felt about their effort, their passion, and their work. And most of all, they knew how we felt about *who they are.* That night, we didn't do what we wanted to do on the field, but that didn't change who we are.

When we won the national championship at Ohio State in 2002, I used to chuckle at all the talk about how we'd finally pulled off the big win. I tried to get across to the team that we were champions long before we won that game against Miami. Suddenly, the media wanted to talk about our players and how much community service they do and how strong they are academically—just because we won the game. But all of that stuff was going on long before we ever won the championship. It was all part of the process.

It's hard in today's society to keep success in its proper perspective and not base our sense of self-worth on what we do. But if you can get there, it's such a comfort. If we lose a game, we're not losers—that's not who we are. And by the same token, if we win a game, that doesn't make us wonderful people. We achieved our goal, and that has its place, but that success—or any failure—doesn't define us.

The thing we should most enjoy about any endeavor is the road we travel together to get there. I've coached in ten national-championship games, nine as head coach. That's extraordinary. Some people coach their whole lives without making it to the "big game," so I've been very fortunate. Most of the time, at the end of those games—we've won five and lost five—we've experienced a bit of melancholy. You know the group you've just traveled with will never be together again in this same way, and that's a little sad, even if you've won. You're sitting there an hour after all the confetti has fallen; the game is over, and you're looking at someone's empty locker, and you know he's heading to the NFL. A guy across from him is off to graduate school. It's in those times that you see it really isn't about one game. One game is just that—one game.

When we won the final game in 2002, we still needed to work on our academics. We still needed to be involved in the community. There were still sick kids at the hospital who would light up when our players walked into the room to talk with them. Nothing had changed except that we'd won the game.

This perspective translates well to the salesman who didn't make the sale, or to the mom who yelled at her kids and then felt really bad about it. In either case, it was just one incident; it doesn't define who you are.

I guess if I could send a healthy message to anyone who reads this book—whether you're a business owner, you work for a corporation, you're a coach, a player, or a mother of three—it would be that no matter what circumstances are in your past and no matter what obstacles you face in the future, *you can win in the game of life.* You can succeed as long as you define success as the inner satisfaction and peace of mind that come from knowing you did the best you were capable of doing for the group.

In the next chapter, we'll go into more detail about the difference between your *purpose* and your *goals* and how that works in your life. But it's important to know that the journey we're on encompasses the totality of life. We have a family journey, an academic or career journey, and a spiritual journey. With our players, we have a football journey that's closely tied with their health journey. Because success in all aspects of the journey is measured by our inner satisfaction and peace of mind knowing we did the best we could for the group, we want our players to think through what it's going to take to feel successful.

THE GOAL SHEET

Each year, we have the guys fill out what we call a goal sheet (see page 12). On the left side are all the components of the Block O, which we'll explain in the next chapter. The most helpful thing about the process of goal setting is that it makes the players *think*. I love it when they say, "I've never thought about that, Coach. I've never written down any goals in my life." They have these ideas in their heads, they have a vague sense of what they may want to do in life, but they've never taken the time to sit down, think it through, and put it down on paper. There are probably many people who have never gone through that process. They may be successful in a career, but they've never taken the time to really focus on what's most important to them and to see their lives from a more holistic perspective.

In the yearly evaluation process, I'll talk with a player about something he's written down. In the "General Thoughts" section beside the Spiritual/Moral component, it says, "Above all else, I realize that my spiritual beliefs and my moral values will shape my life. I will do what is right!"

If a player writes in that section of his goal sheet, "I want to go to church more," I may look at him and say, "Okay. That's a good goal. But define 'more' for me. What is it? Do you want to go to church once a month? twice a month? every week? This is your goal, not mine." We urge each player to get as specific as possible so that we can evaluate how he's doing with that goal. If the player is a Christian and writes down, "I want to read the Bible more," I'll have him put a number on that. Do you want to read the Bible every night? twice a week? This type of exercise helps a player focus and decide what's really important in that particular area of his life.

The next four sections on the goal sheet are "Short-Range Goals," "How I Plan to Accomplish My Short-Range Goals," "Dreams," and "How I Plan to Accomplish My Dreams." I constantly remind the players that

THE BLOCK O OF LIFE: GOALS

GOALS MUST BE SPECIFIC AND MEASURABLE.

	General Thoughts	Short-Range Goals	How I Plan to Accomplish My Short-Range Goals	Dreams	How I Plan to Accomplish My Dreams
Personal **Family**	The family is the basic social unit of our society. My family is very important to me.	1. 2. 3.	1. 2. 3.	1. 2. 3.	1. 2. 3.
Spiritual **Moral**	Above all else, I realize that my spiritual beliefs and my moral values will shape my life. I will do what is right!	1. 2. 3.	1. 2. 3.	1. 2. 3.	1. 2. 3.
Caring **Giving**	How I function as a total person in society is important. I will give back to my community.	1. 2. 3.	1. 2. 3.	1. 2. 3.	1. 2. 3.
Health **Fitness**	One of the greatest gifts we have is our health. My physical conditioning is a controllable commodity. I will develop lifetime fitness habits.	1. 2. 3.	1. 2. 3.	1. 2. 3.	1. 2. 3.
Your Team	I am part of a great team. I count on my teammates, and they are counting on me. I will achieve great things for the team.	1. 2. 3.	1. 2. 3.	1. 2. 3.	1. 2. 3.
Academics **Career**	I am in school to achieve academically and obtain a valuable degree. I want to grow both productively and profitably in my career.	1. 2. 3.	1. 2. 3.	1. 2. 3.	1. 2. 3.

PURPOSE

GOALS

Name: _____   Date: _____

goals must be specific and measurable. They take the better part of a week to complete this sheet, and when they're through, there's not a white spot on the page because they've written so much.

Once a year, we meet with the players to check their progress toward the goals they wrote the previous year. At that point, they can revise or modify their goals and make them even more specific.

I love reading the goals of our players. They talk about things they'll do after they make the NFL. "I'm going to build my high school a new stadium," or "I'm going to start a foundation back in my hometown so less-fortunate kids can go to college." Those types of things make me proud of our players. They show a lot of compassion. Those types of goals and dreams will give them a better feeling of accomplishment than, "I'm going to buy a Bentley." Now, there's nothing wrong with owning a Bentley if that's something a player would like. But I hope those material possessions don't become his primary passion and come to define him, because he's going to find that after he gets one Bentley, he's going to want two or three or six.

It's important to let our goals spring from our purpose. It makes sense that if we're going to do the best we can do, our best should come from who we really are. If we're self-focused, wanting good things for ourselves alone, that's going to affect the goals we set. If we're focused on others and on what we can do for them and the team we have around us, that will affect our goals as well.

We use the goal sheet to find out what's important to the individual players, and then we build a program they can use that's based on what's important to them. Ultimately, we get to know our players better through this process. We find out about a player's background, what makes him tick, and what he hopes for down the road. It's an exciting process to go through.

I've learned a lot by using the goal sheet with our players. I tell them that my passion is to help them achieve their goals, but I want their goals to encompass all of life and not just football. Inevitably, 80 to 85 percent of our players will have strong spiritual goals.

"I want to be part of a church," one player will say.

Okay, I can help him find a church.

"I want to start reading the Bible," another will say.

That's an easy one. I can help him with some devotional tools.

The bottom line of this exercise is that when players begin to understand their purpose in life, their goals will automatically flow from that. And it's my belief that the harder people work on the whole package of purpose and goals, the better they're going to be for the people around them. I don't have empirical data to back it up, but I believe the more we've helped our young people discover their purpose and set specific, measurable goals for their whole lives, the more games we've won.

Personally, when times aren't good and our team is in a losing streak, I go back to the fundamentals. Over the course of my career, when I've returned to focus on my purpose, it has helped me get more grounded. So if you're a salesman, I promise that if you work hard on your purpose— your spiritual component, your family life, and the caring and giving component—you're going to be a better salesman. Without question, I believe the more you work on the whole, the better you will be at every one of the parts.

If you have a plan for your purpose, I think you'll be a better mother, a better teacher, a better cornerback or left fielder or welder. And the more defined your purpose becomes, the better you will be at your goals. I'm thinking of a dad who might be reading this, and the more he reads, the more he thinks, *I want to be a better father.* Maybe he sees that he's come up a little short on the caring and giving component. As he works on that, his relationship with his children will grow deeper. But he'll find that his relationship with his wife will grow as well. And if he lets that caring and giving spill over into his other relationships, he'll become better at every other aspect of his life.

Have you taken time lately to sit and think about why you're here? How would you respond if I were to ask, "What is your purpose in life?" Out of that purpose will flow the goals, dreams, and desires you want to accomplish. Let me challenge you to utilize the goal sheet we give our players. (You can download a full-size copy of the goal sheet at www.thewinnersmanual.com.) Spend some time going through your short-range goals and how you plan to accomplish them, and your dreams and how you plan to accomplish them. Don't rush through the assignment. Think it through, and see what types of things come out of this worthy exercise.

CHAPTER 2

THE BLOCK O OF LIFE

Nurture your mind with great thoughts, for you will never go any higher than you think.

BENJAMIN DISRAELI

The greater danger for most of us lies not in setting our aim too high and falling short; but in setting our aim too low, and achieving our mark.

MICHELANGELO

Excellence is the gradual result of always wanting to do better.

PAT RILEY

To be what we are, and to become what we are capable of becoming, is the only end of life.

ROBERT LOUIS STEVENSON

IN 1986, when I took my first head-coaching position at Youngstown State, I wanted to be able to articulate wisdom and life principles I had learned from so many people in my life and pass them along to the players. That's where the first Winners Manual originated. A vital part of that first book was the Wheel of Life, an illustration that depicted the categories of life to which all the principles applied. Over the years, we've changed the order a bit and tailored the illustration to help the players more easily understand it, but the Block O of Life that we use today has the same basic components as the original Wheel of Life.

What the Block O does is create a bit of order in my life. I'm out there flailing around, striving to get better at what I do, battling to balance work and family, and trying to stay connected to God and others, and all of that creates a certain amount of chaos. But the Block O helps me crystallize my thinking and makes me more efficient. It's not a magic pill. It doesn't necessarily make my purpose and goals easier to accomplish, but it does make life more *observable*. I can see how I'm doing in each area by looking at the goals I'm setting and achieving—or not achieving.

I've shared the Block O with every youth camp I've ever done. Some of those kids started camp in fifth grade, and by the time they were juniors in high school, I could see their eyes start to glaze over when I stood up to speak. I'm sure they were thinking, *Oh no, here's the old man again with the Block O.*

The *O* is divided into two halves. The top half is the part of our lives we consider our *purpose;* the bottom half represents our *goals.* As coaches, we commit ourselves to making sure that every young man who plays football at Ohio State knows that life is not just about football. We pledge to his mother and father, and whoever else cares about him, that his time at Ohio State is going to be a whole-life experience. We aren't going to diminish the value of playing football—we want that to be satisfying and invigorating—but that's not the only thing he's going to learn.

My job as a coach is to do more than just teach the *X*s and *O*s of the gridiron. I recently heard someone explain how the word *coach* came to be applied to an athletic context. The etymology of the word, at least in part, comes from the old stagecoaches that were used to transport mail, valuables, and people before the advent of motorized transportation. Whether a coach was drawn by a horse or a steam locomotive, it carried or conveyed something or someone from one place to another. If you put yourself into a coach, you knew you would end up at your desired destination.

In the same way, athletic coaches carry players or teams from one point in their development to the place they want to be. I tell our players that the most important thing to me is to see them grow as men. Their spiritual plan, their morals, their values, their work ethic—all of those elements need to be part of who we are, what we talk about, and what we demand from each other as a team.

The "Purpose" Components of the Block O

The top half of the Block O refers to our purpose. Purpose comprises those aspects of life that define who we are as individuals and the kind of people we want to become. We start with Purpose because we know that our spiritual beliefs and ethical values, and our commitment to personal integrity, family, and community, will become the foundation for all of our goals and everything else we do in life. By starting with Purpose, we establish the importance of becoming *whole* people, not just good football players.

PERSONAL/FAMILY

Even though a player is going away to college, his family is still a major part of his purpose. We try hard to make sure that family members are included in what we do. We want to provide opportunities for our players to have time with their families, because that's important in their lives. By staying connected at home, they begin thinking about the future. Are they going to be husbands someday? Will they become fathers? When we discuss those ideas and they begin to ponder the future, it naturally causes them to set goals in those areas.

Our players do a great job of setting goals for having a positive impact on their siblings. Almost all of them who have younger brothers and sisters will mention that on their goal sheets: "I'm going to keep track of my sister and make sure that she knows I care about her." "I'm concerned about my little brother. I need to make sure he stays in school and keeps studying hard."

Family will always be a major part of what we do in our football program. There's even a Web site (www.fpaos.org), created by the Football Parents Association at Ohio State, that connects family members of current and past players and managers. They keep families linked to information, give support, and help answer any questions family members have. We like to think our players are not leaving home behind when they come to Ohio State; rather, they are expanding their families as they embrace their nuclear families and make new relationships.

SPIRITUAL/MORAL

In spite of the negative comments made about today's young people, I find they have a great interest in spiritual things. They're spiritually hungry. I haven't run across many kids who are uninterested in growing in that aspect of their lives. We tell our players that they're going to find opportunities to grow spiritually and learn more about belief systems and that they'll be able to test their own belief systems. A university allows people to come from their own small worlds and join with people of different backgrounds and beliefs. The hope is that they will learn from that diversity, grow, and be challenged. So the faith aspect of a person's life, because it affects everything else and is thus an integral part of his purpose, is right at the top of the Block O.

For some guys, when we talk about having a spiritual plan, it triggers something from the past; something clicks in their minds, and they perk up: "Oh man, what's this spiritual-plan stuff? I'd better find out about this." That's why I don't worry about offending people with discussion of the spiritual aspect of their lives. The university teaches comparative religions and allows students to make up their own minds about the choices out there. It's the same in our football program. We don't push students to believe in any particular way, but we do acknowledge the importance of faith and allow them to explore that aspect of their lives if that's what they desire.

CARING/GIVING

Caring and Giving is the final component of the Block O's purpose section. Here we talk about the fact that our players are blessed. They've been the recipients of a lot of good things—God-given ability, height, weight, speed, coaching, support from their parents, and support from their teammates—and because of all that, they have opportunities to succeed.

Along with great blessing comes great responsibility to reach out and care and make a difference to others. The players have been blessed for a reason—not to hoard their talent but to use it for good. We want to see them pass on to others the blessings they've received. So when they leave Ohio State, I want them to have as part of the fabric of their lives a desire to reach out and connect with other people. When they do, they'll be able to feel good about making a difference.

Spiritual/Moral, Personal/Family, and Caring/Giving complete the top half of the Block O. That's our purpose section. Again, it embodies *who the players are.* This is where they derive their definition of success. No matter how much playing time they get, no matter how many games they win or lose or what their grade-point average is—no matter what happens to them while they're part of our team—if they grow in these areas of purpose and continuously strive to improve, they're going to be successful.

The "Goals" Components of the Block O

On the bottom half of the Block O, we list our goals. This section is what we *do*, as opposed to who we are. We know that football is our players' favorite subject. That's why we're here together, and that's our common bond. We have exceptionally high goals in mind for the group, and those come first in our team goals. The needs of the team always come first, but that shouldn't negatively affect an individual's dreams concerning what he wants to become. We're going to give our players a plan that we believe will help us achieve our team goals and at the same time allow them to achieve their individual goals. It's our job as coaches to show our team what they have to do to grow and develop so they can reach those football goals.

Again, as I mentioned in chapter 1, the more we work on the whole person, the better we will be at every part of the Block O. This axiom translates to the team as well. The stronger each individual on the team is, the better we will be as a whole. So we each strive to be all we can be, not only for ourselves, but also for the good of the team.

FOOTBALL/FAMILY

When I talk about goals, I always emphasize that they must be *measurable*. You need to be able to quantify what you want to accomplish—things such as playing first string, the number of games we'll win, the number of yards a running back will gain, or how far a player will progress on his strength and fitness tests. We do not apologize for having the Big Ten Conference championship and the national championship as goals each year. Our guys want to be bigger, stronger, faster, and in better shape than their opponents, but they have to set that as a goal. It's no secret that if they want to go to the next level, they'll have to run at a certain speed and jump a certain height. Today they might lift 200 pounds, and the goal for the next phase might be to lift 230. Or they may run the 100-meter at 10.5 seconds, and their goal is to get under 10.2. We want everyone to set specific and measurable goals related to the football aspect of their lives. Along the way, we want them to understand what it's going to take to achieve those goals—the difficulty of the challenge, and the characteristics of a champion.

There are some things, however, that you can't measure: You can't quantify kindness and respect. You can't bar-chart a person's thoughtfulness or encouragement. But believe me, you know those things when you see them. And when players begin caring for each other and uniting not just as players but as a family working toward the same goal, that's when I know we have something special.

STRENGTH/FITNESS

There are a lot of reasons why maintaining good health makes sense. For players, it means they're going to be able to participate at practice and in games. If they're in great condition, the time they spend rehabbing from injuries or recovering from the general bruising that happens each week is going to be reduced. But the benefits of good health transcend the time they'll spend as students at Ohio State. Occasionally, I tell our players that good health will be a financial plus for them in the future. Let's face it, with the cost of health care these days, the value of good health is tremendous.

To achieve and maintain optimum health, we must develop good nutritional habits. The players' Winners Manual lists the right kinds of foods to eat, as well as appropriate between-meal snacks. We talk to the players about the amounts of protein and carbohydrates to eat each day, and we advise them to be careful about what they eat just before they go to sleep at night.

We also encourage plenty of rest, because studies have shown that sleep may be a player's greatest performance booster. Getting enough sleep can be difficult when players have an exam the next day and might be tempted to cram for it at the last minute. But that's why it's important that players be disciplined in both their study and athletic schedules so they can do all they need to do.

It's our job as coaches to provide the resources our guys need to stay healthy and build strength. It's each player's job to implement the plan to reach those goals.

ACADEMICS/CAREER

The academic phase is a vital part of our goals section. We know that many people without an academic degree do wonderful things. We would never suggest that having a degree makes someone a better person. But if they have the opportunity to move toward a degree and find something they're passionate about, they'll find themselves with choices that someone without a degree might not have. In our football program at Ohio State, we make as many resources available to our players as possible—all the tutors, all the study sessions, anything they could possibly need to be encouraged to be the best they can be academically.

We also have team academic goals. We want to be a 3.0 football team, meaning that our cumulative GPA as a team will be at least 3.0 (on a four-point scale). We want to lead the league in placing players on the Academic All-Conference Team, just as we want to lead the Big Ten on the football field. Those goals are all measurable.

CUSTOMIZING THE BLOCK O

The six components of the Block O we use are specific to our group of players. I'm sure that if a business or a church staff decided to use the Block O and asked, "What six things do we want to focus on?" they might come up with some different components. We sat down as a staff more than twenty years ago and took a hard look at where we were as a group. We decided that the six areas of the Block O were the ones that would have the greatest impact on college-age players and give them a jumpstart on their short-range development and their long-range dreams, so we try to progress in each one of those areas.

Some players tend to get stuck on the Purpose section. They don't have any idea what their purpose is. Instead of allowing them to become anxious about their purpose—figuring out what they don't know—we help them understand what they *do* know. Each player has a spiritual component to his life. Each player is part of a family. We hope he's also part of making a difference in others' lives by caring and giving. These sections of the Block O will help our players define their purpose and set goals.

The same is true for people from all other walks of life. For example, a mother who stays at home with her children to nurture and care for them has her purpose and her goals more closely aligned than many other people in our society. She may not get much recognition from the outside world, and at times she may despair because of the seeming futility of the mundane things she does every day. But if she sets her sights on her purpose—to raise her children in a loving, caring environment and help them grow into quality people—she'll be able to block out much of the negative input she gets from the surrounding culture.

The problem for many people today is that they've mixed up their purpose with their goals. Some think their purpose is the job they do—but that drops them down into the Goals section. I'm a football coach. That's what I do. But that's not my purpose. Many people will default to the *doing* rather than focus on *being*. Some will define themselves by what they do rather than who they are.

When you meet someone for the first time, invariably the question comes up, "What do you do?" That's a fine question, but rarely have I heard someone ask the more central questions: "Who are you?" and "What defines your purpose?" The challenge is to get people to step back from defining their goals to first define their purpose. How do we do this?

One idea I always come back to is this: "Before I can *do,* I must *be.*" We tell our players that before they can be champions, they must master the things that champions embody. That's where the Big Ten Fundamentals come in, and we'll discuss them in Part 2.

Our players' jobs are to be the best football players and the best students they can be. But as important as those two things are, they are still only what our players *do;* they are not *who they are.* Our task as coaches is to get our players interested in *being* first and letting what they *do* flow out of that. They should strive for their goals out of the overflow of their life's purpose.

This principle translates to individuals in all walks of life. If I sell insurance, manage an office, teach, drive a bus—or whatever else my profession happens to be—my life's purpose comes first (because that reflects who I am), and my profession, my goals, and everything else that I do flow out of that. And here's some good news: It's never too late to realize that you are what you are, not what you do.

EXPANDING AND ENRICHING OUR LIVES

When I organized the original Winners Manual at Youngstown State, I knew I wanted to include all the things I believed were important to the program, not just things directly related to football. I wanted our players to see football within the context of their whole lives.

One aspect that may seem a little out of place in a football setting is community outreach. Can visiting a hospital really make your team better? I believe the answer is yes, and once the players experience it, once they see what kind of difference they can make in the life of one child or of an adult who's very sick, I think they'll catch a vision for it. I've seen it happen many times. Players begin to see themselves as part of a bigger team and blessed beyond measure. The goal of community outreach is not to get good public relations for the team but to expand and enrich our players' lives by expanding and enriching the lives of others.

A young boy who lived about an hour north of Columbus suffered a terrible injury in a lawn-mower accident. When he got hurt, he was wearing an Ohio State football jersey with the number *33* on it, the number of our linebacker James Laurinaitis. When we heard about the accident a couple of days later, it was reported that the boy had cried and cried when the doctors had to cut his Ohio State jersey off of him. When James Laurinaitis heard that, he was at Children's Hospital in a heartbeat. He found that someone had repaired the young boy's jersey and put it back on him, and James was able to spend some time with the boy at the hospital and give him some encouragement.

When the young boy was able to leave the hospital, we asked him to attend one of our practices and meet our players. They took pictures with him, and I wish you could have seen the look on that boy's face, and on the faces of our players. Our guys thrive on things like that because they have a passion to do whatever they can to care for and give to others.

As an organization, we believe in encouraging community service and allowing it to grow. Of course, we have to be vigilant when we talk about the importance of caring and giving in such a busy world. We don't get first downs because we visited a hospital. We don't win games because an injured boy wears our jersey. On the other hand, those activities make our players more complete as human beings. Entering into someone else's pain and being able to help that person gives perspective. And I do believe that well-rounded and complete people are going to make more first downs and win more games.

Consider the "strength and fitness" component of football. Everyone knows that strength and fitness are important to a team. If you're going to reach your football goals, you have to be a physically stronger team. But what about moral strength and fitness, or spiritual strength and fitness?

A player might come to Ohio State with no spiritual background. That's okay. We want to introduce him to a spiritual journey as part of a complete, well-rounded life. We'd like to see him grow in that area. If a player is already far along on his spiritual journey, he can now be one of our leaders in that area and have a positive impact on others.

ORGANIZING YOUR PURPOSE TO ACTIVATE YOUR POTENTIAL

The truth is, as a student I was good at math but a bit challenged when it came to English. I'm not a fast reader, but because my left brain was stronger, I knew that order and precision could help me. I have always been a busy person, wanting to be involved in ninety million things, and the only way I can accomplish that is by being organized. The Block O is a simple illustration that organizes the important components of purpose and goals in a way that makes sense to me. If you see a better way to organize these same principles for yourself, I encourage you to do it. Far be it from me to suggest that my way is the only way. The Block O is merely an organizational structure that has helped me, and it has also worked for others.

In Part 2, we're going to introduce a set of fundamental attitudes and principles that I believe will help you accomplish your purpose and achieve your goals. I call these the Big Ten Fundamentals, though if we were to break down each fundamental into its component parts, we would actually have a total of nineteen. At the end of each chapter, you'll have a chance to flesh out the fundamentals for yourself by recording your reactions to some questions and observations. I'll also give you a Personal Game Plan that will take each component of the Block O and help you make that fundamental a part of your life.

I believe that when we write things down, we begin the process of *activating* the fundamentals in our lives. It's my hope that you'll be able to identify some areas in your life where you need to grow and change. Maybe you'll say, "I really need to work harder at home. I'm leaving all my energy at the office." You might encounter something in the Attitude section that will make you say, "You know what? People have been really good to me, and I haven't thanked them. I really want to reach out and help others the way I've been helped. I need to invest some energy in that."

This approach reflects my desire to get my mind wrapped around the Big Ten Fundamentals. I don't want to just *understand* the concepts; I want those fundamentals to be *active* in my life. We really do need these tools in order to get the job done. But we can have all the tools in the world, and they won't do us any good if we don't know how to use them.

Now, if the fundamentals are the tools we need to get the job done, the Block O is our blueprint. It sits at the center of everything we do. It's the foundation on which we will build everything else we discuss in this book. At the end of this chapter, you'll have an opportunity to fill in your own Block O as your personal blueprint for the game plan of your life.

THE BIG TEN FUNDAMENTALS

Each of the Big Ten Fundamentals is designed to drive you toward either your purpose or your goals. That's what I talk about when I'm sitting down with the family of a player I'm recruiting to our program. As we talk through my philosophy, we may get into a discussion about academics. Occasionally, I'll be sitting with a family in which no one has ever graduated with an academic degree, and they desire a college education for their son because they know it will give him some options in life. I make it clear that earning a college degree is a great goal, but it doesn't make you a complete person. There are millions of people doing wonderful things with a great sense of purpose who don't have college degrees. I tell the families, "I can't promise your son a degree or that having one will make his life perfect. Instead, we want him to concentrate on the top of the Block O—on his purpose. That will help him feel good about who he is, not just about what he does. All this other stuff is icing on the cake."

The big question is not whether you will get a degree; the question is, What are you going to do with that degree after you get it? The same question applies for the player who gets drafted in the first round by an NFL team or the coach who gets a big contract and is now making lots of money. That's great. Congratulations! Now, what are you going to do with all those blessings you've been given? What are you going to do with all that money? How are you going to accomplish the purpose that will give you real fulfillment in your life?

That's why we make a big deal about caring and giving, which are included in chapter 9, where I talk about love. I'll admit that it seems like a strange topic for a football coach to talk about, but loving and caring and giving are vital parts of our purpose.

INSPIRATION AND MOTIVATION

My desire is that this book would be a tool that you can use every day—whether you're a coach, a player, a company vice president, an elementary school teacher, or a stay-at-home parent raising your kids. I hope it will do more than just inspire you. I hope it will motivate you to make some positive changes in your life. Bookstores are full of volumes containing great quotations and inspirational stories, but there's a huge difference between inspiration and motivation. Adages and stories can be inspiring, but what do you do with that inspiration? Motivation, on the other hand, urges you to think, take action, and make changes.

There are several types of motivation. There's *fear* motivation, which says if you don't do something, you're going to be grounded or benched or cut or fired. There's *reward* motivation, which promises a lollipop for obedience or a pay increase for greater performance. But those two types of motivation eventually run out of steam. If a player runs laps long enough, he'll know he can run them, but he'll eventually ask, "What's the point of all this running?"

The third type of motivation stems from *purpose.* It provides understanding. It leads by example. The person who is motivated by purpose says, "Now I understand why I need to be in good shape or be punctual or have a quiet time." Sometimes, we need tools to help us thoroughly understand a motivational principle, and that's what we hope you will find in the chapters that describe the Big Ten Fundamentals.

Players who join our program at Ohio State may not use all the tools right away, but the coaches are planting seeds every day—similar to what a parent or teacher does—and after a player has been with us for a while, he starts to grasp what it's all about.

I'd love for all those seeds to sprout while our players are still in school, but they don't. And that's really not important. What's important is that we plant the seeds and that we help our players consider some things that might help them later on. I love getting calls and letters from guys in their late twenties or early thirties who say, "Coach, I get it now." That's why I think this process has value no matter what your age or stage of life. My goal is to plant a seed, a thought, and let that motivate you to decide what's valuable and what you can use.

The Block O of Life and your goal sheet can be continuously revised. When you were young, you might have thought you wanted to be an attorney, but when you fell in love with writing, you revised your goals and channeled your passion into that other area. Maybe you thought you were going to be a defensive back and ended up a wide receiver. So you revised your goals.

Many people get frustrated when they set out on a particular course and then can't reach the end. But you have to remember that success isn't necessarily doing what you thought was perfect for you when you were eighteen. As you progress through life, you may find that your purpose is a little different from what it was when you started out.

Maybe you were fired from your first job, or you just didn't like it. That doesn't make you a failure. Losing a job, changing your major, facing setbacks—those things don't make you a failure because they aren't about *who you are*.

A WORD ABOUT DREAMS

In chapter 1, we talked at length about success and the journey we're taking to reach our goals. A big part of that journey is dreaming—and I hope you've been able to brainstorm a little about that.

One of the main reasons for writing goals is to get you to think about your life from a different vantage point. When you're young, it's hard to think long-term. Even when you're older, that's a hard discipline. But the main point of the goal sheet is to get you to begin thinking about your life as a whole.

It's fun to read the dreams that some of our student-athletes have. For some, a dream is something that's three years down the road. Others have dreams that are twenty-five years in the future. When we do this exercise as a team, I simply ask, "What do you dream about?"

If a player says, "I dream about playing in the NFL," I'll say, "Okay, great. That's a wonderful dream. If that's your goal, do you know what it takes to get into the NFL?" That's when the real discussion begins. "Here's how fast players at your position run in the NFL. Here's what they weigh. Here's what they can bench." So we take the dream, turn it into a goal, and show our players how to move toward that goal in a constructive way.

Let me ask you the same question: What do you dream about? What is it that you simply can't let go of? What keeps coming back to you time and again, as silly as it may seem, as far off as it may sound? What is it that creeps into your mind when you're thinking about what you'd like to do with your life? It may be something so personal that you haven't revealed it to another living soul. What do you dream about?

As you identify your dream, write it down. Don't let it slip away. After you write it down, turn it into a goal. The goal is the specific objective you're going to work toward. Now, as you move forward, you may find that your dream isn't all that it seemed, and you find yourself being channeled into another area. But that's okay. When a friend of mine was a kid, he dreamed about being a baseball broadcaster. He began working in radio when he was a teenager. As he progressed, he came to realize how much time it required to broadcast baseball and how much that time and travel took him away from the people he loved. In the end, he decided it was an investment he wasn't willing to make. He was more interested in being with his family. But his interest in radio provided him an opportunity to follow a different dream.

After you've written down your dream and your goals, you need to find someone who can help you—someone who's a little further down the road, a mentor, who can come alongside you and help you figure out how to make your dream a reality. Perhaps it's a good friend who knows you well. Perhaps it's someone in your desired profession who can counsel you on the steps you need to take.

Whatever your dream, whatever goals you set, don't allow the skeptics in your life to steal your dream. Some will laugh at your audacity and say that your head is in the clouds or you need a little dose of reality. Don't allow those people to distract you from your purpose.

Now, if your dream is to play in the NFL and you're fifty-two years old, I'm not suggesting you should quit your job and start working out. Of course not. But if you're fifty-two and you've dreamed all your life about being part of an NFL franchise, the possibility of working for a team in some capacity may not be out of reach.

My point is that no matter where you are on your journey, the closer you can integrate your life's purpose with your dreams—and the goals that spring from those dreams—the closer you will be to feeling truly successful deep in your soul.

REGULAR REMINDERS

Any time our players show up for a meeting to watch film or design plays, they see two things on the front wall of the meeting room. One is our team's mission statement, which outlines what we expect from our players and our team. We want to reach our full potential and represent well the storied institution for which we play. The other item is an eight-foot diagram of the Block O of Life. Because the Block O is central to our purpose and our goals, we keep it in front of us at all times. We also give our players a wallet-size card with the same information and with six blank spaces for their specific goals. The Block O diagram is also on the back cover of their Winners Manual.

We believe that in order for us to choose success and follow it wholeheartedly, we must have our purpose and our goals in front of us as often as possible. So as you journey through the rest of this book, I encourage you to keep the Block O of Life in mind. As you read through each fundamental, think about specific ways you can practice that fundamental in your Personal/Family life, in your Spiritual/Moral life, and in the Caring/Giving part of your life. Then incorporate your purpose into specific goals for your health, your "team," and your career.

On practice days, after our players have completed their meetings, they have some individual time to work on specific fundamentals. It might be their stance, their footwork, their eye control, or whatever they believe needs improvement at that point in the season. I hope you'll use the chapters that follow as your fundamental exercises. If you're in sales and you've just made a huge sale that you're excited about, the fundamental for that day might be Handling Success.

During our Quiet Times, I plug in a fundamental that I think might be important for the team that day. Depending on what time of year it is, I can anticipate what might be going on with the players. The first day we're in pads during preseason, I like to use the word *toughness,* because the guys get excited when they're wearing pads and they're going to smack each other. That's okay. We build on that excitement and talk about what toughness really is. Is it getting into a confrontation at a bar and pummeling some guy who takes a swing at you? Or is it standing up and walking out of there?

In the middle of preseason, when it's hot, the players are exhausted, and it's mentally difficult to get into the task at hand, we talk about *enthusiasm:* What does it mean to be enthusiastic? What does enthusiasm do to the team around you?

These football examples can also be applied in a home, church, or business situation. Let's say you're a business owner, and you see that sales aren't going as well as expected. You believe in the company, your ideas, and the people you work with, but you need some encouragement. For that situation, I would suggest you read the chapter on Work and focus on the section that discusses *persistence.*

The week after we open our season, the first Quiet Time might be focused on Handling Adversity and Success, because we've just either won or lost and we need to talk about how we are going to handle it. We have to deal with one or the other.

My point in talking about these things is that this book is not meant to be read just once and put on the shelf. Instead, it's a *manual* that you can refer to time and again, just as our players do. My greatest hope for you is that the fundamentals you're about to learn will truly become a part of your life and will help you achieve your purpose and pursue your goals more intentionally and successfully.

But before you move on to the fundamentals, I'd like for you to complete your own Block O of Life. You know the components we list for our football team. You know that in the purpose section we have Personal/Family, Spiritual/Moral, and Caring/Giving. Those are constants. But what about on the bottom of the O? Perhaps on the left side you want to simply put *Health,* so that you can work on that aspect of your life. In the Football/Family section, you might simply put *My Team.* Or you can be more specific and name your business or organization. In the section on Academics/Career you might simply list your current job. The point is to customize your Block O so it's useful and makes sense for *you*. You'll want to refer to your own Block O frequently as you go through the rest of the chapters.

PURPOSE

SPIRITUAL
MORAL

PERSONAL
FAMILY

CARING
GIVING

GOALS

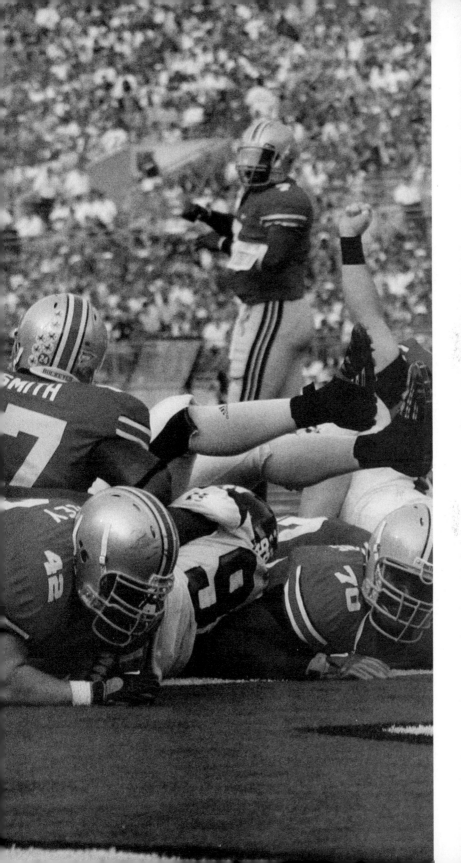

CHAPTER 3

ATTITUDE

The greatest discovery of my generation is that human beings can alter their lives by altering their attitudes of mind.

WILLIAM JAMES

Progress always involves risk; you can't steal second base and keep your foot on first.

FREDERICK WILCOX

Why not go out on a limb? Isn't that where the fruit is?

FRANK SCULLY

Most people are about as happy as they make up their minds to be.

ABRAHAM LINCOLN

I have learned how to be content with whatever I have.

PHILIPPIANS 4:11

I think the final outcome of most football games is affected more by attitude than by talent. I once heard someone say that an upset is really in the mind of the favorite. If the favored team plays to the best of their ability, the underdog probably isn't going to win. But if there's an upset, it's probably because the favorite didn't have the right attitude. A team that has the right attitude and happens to be blessed with the greater talent and ability is not likely to be upset.

As a football team, we have to understand that our thinking affects everything we do. What we're thinking, how we're looking at our situation, is so important. It's not about what the newspapers say. It's not about what Mom and Dad are thinking. They may say, "Oh, you guys are really going to wallop them." Or it could be the other way around: "You guys are going to get killed." But we can't afford to let either of those attitudes creep into our thinking.

It can be helpful, however, to have encouragers who help you believe the best about yourself along the way. I can't tell you how many of our players have said, "My mom kept telling me I could do it. She said I could be anything I wanted to be." The fundamental of *attitude* was practiced and practiced until the player latched onto it. A good attitude can overcome some other limitations, but even great talent can't overcome the wrong attitude.

The Big Ten Fundamentals are difficult to make a part of our daily lives. For example, how do we take the time to be as grateful as we should be? None of us has the perfect attitude we'd like to have. A lot of times I catch myself saying, "I can't believe I was thinking that way." But if we practice the fundamentals and keep reminding ourselves and keep reading the thoughts of great people, we give ourselves a chance to change.

Look at the people quoted in this chapter and throughout the book. These are achievers. They've done extraordinary things. And what I hear them saying to me is that in a great and positive way, I can boil down success in my life to my attitude.

BE WHERE YOU ARE

Voltaire once said, "Paradise is where I am." I love that quote. Our players may not know who Voltaire was or who he played for, but they can learn a great life lesson from him. To me, Voltaire's statement is a lifestyle captured in five simple words.

> **Paradise is where I am.**
>
> VOLTAIRE

I tell people all the time that if I were to have coached at Youngstown State for forty years, I would have been as happy as can be. I didn't have one foot out the door when I was there. I didn't think somebody else had it better. I was in paradise. If you're in paradise where you are—not wishing you were someplace else—that's the right attitude. If you're always wishing you were someplace else, what you'll discover is that the other place has just as many problems and difficulties—maybe *more*—as the place you are right now.

I remember when I was recruiting as an assistant at Syracuse. I used to think, *If I were ever at a place like Ohio State or Michigan or Notre Dame, I'd never lose a recruit, because I'm a wonderful recruiter.* Then I got to Ohio State and—whoa, guess what?— I lose recruits here, too, because there are other good places for young men to go to school and play football.

It's easy to think that somewhere out there is a perfect place where everyone is always happy, has a bigger house, a nicer car, and a more beautiful or handsome spouse. But that's an illusion. A mirage. If we followed Voltaire, we would see that today, right where we are, is the place God has put us—whether it's a mansion or a studio apartment. And if that's true, there can be no better place, because paradise is where we are. It's that kind of thinking—that kind of attitude—that we try to instill in our players at Ohio State.

I arise in the morning torn between a desire to improve the world and a desire to enjoy the world.

E. B. WHITE

YOUR ATTITUDE IS A CHOICE

Attitude is not a formula we can put under a microscope and make it work every time to help us win every game. We're still going to lose from time to time. We're still going to get upset. The salesman is still going to lose a sale. The advertising executive will still strike out on an ad plan. But because our attitude is a choice, I think if we work hard on our objectives and practice our fundamentals, at the end of the day we'll probably be pleased with our number of sales or the effectiveness of our ads or our number of wins. That's what I'd like to get across, because I believe it's true.

The older our players get, the more they realize that it's their choice what they're feeling, what they're thinking, and what approach they're going to take to life. We find that the younger or less-mature players have less of a handle on their attitude and are more reactionary—they're more susceptible to the events of their lives. They'll say things like, "I dropped the ball and Coach hates me; I'm never getting in the game again." Or they'll focus on the referee and a bad call or on anything else that doesn't go their way. In the classroom, it's a professor they think doesn't like football players.

Attitude is not something that comes by instinct. It has to be practiced over and over or relearned over and over. The more our players study and practice this fundamental, the more they believe they can *decide* how they feel. They realize they have *power* over their attitude. Their coach doesn't have that power. Neither does the referee or their professor. How they approach their attitude is *their* choice.

> # The empires of the future are the empires of the mind.
>
> **WINSTON CHURCHILL**

We have to *choose* to have a good attitude. And we have to keep reminding ourselves, in the midst of newspaper publicity or things other people are saying, that *we* are going to be in charge of how we think. That's a powerful principle in the life of a football player, a trash collector, a pastor, a dad, a stay-at-home mom, or someone who works in an office.

Gratitude

> *Spending a little time calculating the number of things that go right is a simple but powerful way to reactivate our sense of wonder and gratitude.*
>
> **RICHARD CARLSON**

I've studied the lives of a lot of different people, people I wanted to be like, and I've found that one common denominator is that they were sincerely grateful for their blessings. Gratitude is one of the attitudes we've tried to instill in our players over the years, and it's one that has had some of the greatest impact on them. I want our players to be continually reminded of how fortunate they are and what they have to be grateful for.

We constantly talk to our players about having "an attitude of gratitude." I think life is a lot more fun if we take stock of our blessings and live in light of them. We all have things we're not excited about and things that don't go the way we want them to, but when we really step back and list our blessings, we find they far outweigh the hardships that seem for a moment to be so earthshaking.

PROMISE YOURSELF . . .

To be so strong that nothing can disturb your peace of mind

To look at the sunny side of everything and make your optimism come true

To think only of the best

To be just as enthusiastic about the success of others as you are about your own

To forget the mistakes of the past and press on to the greater achievements of the future

To share the greater achievements of the future

To give so much time to the improvement of yourself that you have no time to criticize others

To be too large for worry, too strong for fear, and too happy to permit the presence of trouble

---

Because I feel it's important to remind our players about the importance of gratitude, and instill it as an attitude, during their Quiet Time each day, we ask them to write down one thing they're grateful for, regardless of what it is. It's the only thing we make mandatory.

Cultivating an attitude of gratitude is like working on any other fundamental: You have to practice. And it works with football players as well as with other students on campus, business owners, moms at home, and cab drivers. We all need to keep reminding ourselves how fortunate we are.

I hear our assistant coaches talk all the time to their players about what a privilege it is to play at Ohio State. What a privilege it is to be a student at the university. What a privilege it is to play in Ohio Stadium in front of 105,000 people. And what a privilege it is to represent our proud Buckeye tradition.

I've heard a number of stories about members of the military and the Ohio National Guard—both men and women—who have served in Iraq and Afghanistan and who have been asked what they'd like to do as soon as they get back to the States. Many have said, "I want to go to an Ohio State practice or maybe even a game." They talk about how they would get up at 3:00 a.m. when they were overseas, in order to watch or listen to one of our games. They said it reminded them of why they were over there protecting our freedoms. A lot of members of the armed forces attend our games, and we remind our players and coaches how lucky we are that we live in this country and how grateful we are for those who have fought—and are fighting—for our freedom.

> It is impossible to be grateful and unhappy at the same time.

Another one of my favorite quotes is this one: "It is impossible to be grateful and unhappy at the same time." That is a powerful truth. You're either going to be grateful or unhappy. That's your choice. It's difficult sometimes for young people to gain an appreciation for just how fortunate they are, because their world is so new, so young, so fast moving. But it's part of what we try to teach our guys.

When our players talk to a youth group or a recruit, it's interesting to hear how often they mention how fortunate they are. If we do nothing more than help them realize that the hand they've been dealt is pretty good, we've done our job. Of course, they also have to realize that they have a lot to do with how they play that hand, but gratitude is the key.

I am a big fan of Norman Vincent Peale, and I remember an old story told about him. Someone once asked him to name the greatest sin. Now, he could have said a lot of things—there are some terrible sins—but he stopped and thought awhile before responding that the gravest sin a person could commit is the sin of ingratitude. That really stuck with me, because I don't know that we often think of ingratitude as sinful. But it really is, especially when we consider just how blessed we really are.

THE IMPORTANCE OF PERSPECTIVE

I marvel at some people in our country and around the world who possess so little compared with what we have, and yet their perspective is one of thankfulness. They're grateful for something as simple as clean water or a full stomach. That tells me that whether we have little or much, we need to find a way to be grateful for what we do have.

Perspective is so important to understanding how fortunate we are.

THE GLOBAL VILLAGE

If we could shrink the earth's population to a village of precisely one hundred people, with all the existing human ratios remaining the same, the village would include . . .

60 Asians,

12 Europeans,

15 from the Western Hemisphere (9 Latin Americans, 5 North Americans, and 1 Oceanian), and

13 Africans.

Of those one hundred people . . .

50 would be female,

50 would be male,

80 would be nonwhite,

20 would be white,

67 would be non-Christian,

33 would be Christian,

20 would earn 89 percent of the wealth,

25 would live in substandard housing,

17 would be unable to read,

13 would suffer from malnutrition,

1 would die within the year,

2 would give birth within the year,

2 would have a college education, and

4 would own a computer.

For example, every one of our players has a computer. When they hear that only about 4 percent of the world's population owns a computer and they see how out-of-the-ordinary they are to actually have one, it helps them understand and appreciate the fact that their problems aren't as rough as those of others in the world. From there, it's only a short jump to apply the same principle to their everyday lives. Sure, the guy at the next locker has a better car, or he's a starter on the team, or there are scouts looking at him; but in the big picture we are all so blessed, and we need to recognize that and let it work its way into our lives.

> No race can prosper until it learns that there is as much dignity in tilling a field as in writing a poem.
>
> BOOKER T. WASHINGTON

I've been fortunate to be around a lot of grateful people, but the person who really set the bar for me was my mother. Her father was born in the 1860s, so I never met him. His first wife died, and then he remarried and had my mother and her brother. He was fifty-eight when she was born. He had been a teacher at Cleveland East Tech High School for forty years, but when my mother was in eighth grade, he retired and moved the family to the rural community of Ada, Ohio, the home of his alma mater, Ohio Northern University. My mother met my father in Ada when they were in the ninth grade. He was the son of a farmer and lived in that community.

My mother was always so grateful for her heritage and was so proud to be an American. She knew she'd been given so much, and in response she was determined to serve and to do whatever she could.

She decided to become a nurse, and when World War II began, she worked in a factory to help with the war effort. Whatever her country needed, she was going to do.

American history was her passion, and she worked at the Berea Historical Society and did extraordinary fund-raising. Later, she became president of the Ohio Historical Society. She also served for years as an advisor to the education majors at Baldwin-Wallace College.

Mom was also committed to her family. If any of her children ever needed something, she was there to serve. My dad was a busy coach who wasn't around all the time, so Mom found ways to serve in his absence, including stints as the president of the PTA and also the booster club. She typed the practice schedules for my dad's teams, because at a small school the athletic department didn't have money for a secretary. She sewed the players' names on the back of their jerseys at Baldwin-Wallace College for many years. And her service was always motivated by a perspective of gratitude. She was grateful that her husband had a chance to coach and to have an impact on all those young men. Because of her service and her involvement in the community, she was selected as an outstanding citizen in the city of Berea long before my dad was.

> **If you see no reason for giving thanks, the fault lies within yourself.**
>
> TECUMSEH

We think it's important to talk to our players about gratitude and to show them real-life examples. It's one thing to say, "Yeah, thanks, I'm grateful and fortunate," but it's something else entirely to *live* gratefully. That's what my mom did. Every day she asked, "How can I live with gratitude today? Who can I help today?" So when I think of someone who exuded an attitude of gratitude, it was my mom.

Though she was as healthy as she could be her entire life, when she was seventy-six, the doctors discovered pancreatic cancer. She died three weeks before my first game at Ohio State. But even as she was dying, she was grateful and served others.

There's a great researcher at the James Cancer Hospital on our campus, Dr. Michael Caligiuri. He had discovered a treatment for pancreatic cancer that worked in the laboratory. For whatever reason, the pancreas repels chemotherapy, and it has blockers that cut the effectiveness of drugs. Dr. Caligiuri found a way to neutralize the blockers and send the chemicals to arrest the cancer's growth. It had never been tried.

So they came to my mom and said, "Would you like to try this?"

"Sure," she said. "If it works, I get to stay here with the people I love. If it doesn't, I get to go to heaven and be with the people I love. I'm just grateful for the life I've lived, and if this can advance finding the cure someday, let's go."

> # Earth produces nothing worse than an ungrateful man.
>
> ### AUSONIUS

I remember sitting with her two or three days before she died. She said, "Aw, I feel so bad. I'm not coming through for all these people. These nurses are wonderful, and I'm so appreciative of these doctors, but I can't help feeling I'm letting them down."

"Mom, come on," I said, trying to encourage her. But that was the way she was. She was grateful and happy every day of her life. And I can't help but think that a little of her legacy is being poured into our young players now so that they can learn to live gratefully.

LIVING A GRATEFUL LIFE

I think it's a huge wake-up call anytime you take things for granted. When you're a team member, if you ever enter Ohio Stadium and you're not ready to play, it means you're taking for granted the wonderful privilege you have, and you're not really grateful. It means you're not living with an attitude of gratitude. When I enter that stadium, I should be saying, "Wow, how many millions of people would like to be running out on this field right now in front of 105,000 fans and millions of television viewers?"

The same thing goes in the classroom. We tell our players that if we have tutors available and they don't take advantage of that and don't do as well in their classes as they could, that's failing to recognize how fortunate they are.

One thing we do during the preseason to foster an attitude of gratitude is have the guys write a couple of letters. We encourage each player to tell someone he knows how fortunate he is to have that person in his life. I don't know everything the guys write, but I have had some people tell me, with tears in their eyes, how much those letters have meant to them.

I think especially in this age of e-mails and text messages and voice mails, a good, old-fashioned, handwritten note speaks volumes to people. Many of our players get a thousand pieces of mail a day, so they don't even think about this. But take someone who's not getting any mail, and see if that kind of gesture doesn't mean something. It might be a fourth-grade teacher, a mentor, or a former coach. The neat thing about a letter is that you can hold it in your hand and save it in some special place. It can be stashed in a drawer, ready to be pulled out when the person needs a little boost. For our players, writing those letters of gratitude is a great action step.

To determine whether people are living a grateful life, we can look in the classroom or the home or wherever they spend their time. If they're not committed to becoming the best students in the classroom or the best sons or daughters at home, that's a huge warning sign. I think the person who has a right attitude is able to say, "Man, am I lucky to be here! I need to study—I really don't like this class, but I'm so thankful I'm here that I'm going to study hard. Practice is hard, but I'm going to take advantage of every opportunity I have." Constant reminders of how fortunate we are can help us to keep things in proper perspective.

> **We each have a choice: to approach life as a creator or a critic, a lover or a hater, a giver or a taker.**
>
> AUTHOR UNKNOWN

We all have times when we've slacked off at work. That shows we're not grateful for the jobs we have. We've all neglected our relationship with God. That comes directly from a lack of gratitude. We get too busy in our own little worlds and let the pressures around us squeeze us into a mold that's not helpful. I read a great quote by a fourteenth-century Christian mystic named Meister Eckhart. He said, "God is at home; it is we who have gone for a walk." It hit me as soon as I read it that the reason we're out for a walk is our ingratitude. We haven't checked in at home.

Another good illustration of thankfulness is our walk-ons, the guys who come to Ohio State without a scholarship and with no guarantee they'll play or even make the team. They gain so much from our program, and it's probably more comprehensive than what our star players gain. Walk-ons are typically a little less distracted and a little more grateful. They aren't preoccupied with worrying about where they're going from here; they're busy enjoying the opportunity they have right now. Some of our other players have realistic goals of playing in the NFL, and

HAVING THE PROPER ATTITUDE

1. More athletes fail through faulty mental attitudes than in any other way.
2. Attitudes are habits of thinking. You have it within your power to develop the habit of thinking thoughts that will result in a winning attitude.
3. The foundation for the proper attitude consists of developing the habit of thinking positive thoughts.
4. Tell yourself constantly that you can do something, and you will. Tell yourself you can't, and your subconscious mind will find a way for you not to do it.
5. A desire to win and a desire to prepare to win are important ingredients of a winning attitude.
6. Before you can scale the heights of athletic greatness, you must first learn to control yourself from within. Be your own master. Control your emotions.
7. An athlete with a good attitude is coachable. He welcomes criticism, constantly seeks to learn, and avoids criticizing his coach or teammates.
8. True success depends on teamwork, and the winning attitude puts the good of the team ahead of anything else.
9. Whether or not you create a winning attitude is entirely up to you—but nothing is more important to you on your road to the winner's circle.

people are telling them how much money they're going to make at the next level. So, in all fairness, it's harder for them to keep their minds in the here and now. But the guys who have to work hard just to get in the door? You can see it in their eyes every day. They're happy to be part of the team.

THE LURE OF BIG MONEY

I've been coaching for more than thirty years, and in that time I don't think kids have changed all that much, but some parents have. Thirty years ago, parents put as their top priority their son's getting a diploma, becoming a man of good conscience, and growing as a human being. These days, with the possibility of the NFL looming, some parents—not all, but some—see a potential financial windfall. They've been sending their sons to camps, getting them in the best leagues, paying for personal trainers—in short, shelling out lots of money for more than a decade—and now it's time to cash in on their investment.

One of the things I occasionally hear is, "My son needs more touches," which means that they want their son to get the ball more.

Often I respond, "Hey, you've got a great son. You are so lucky. He's a wonderful young man, and he's trying his hardest, both in the classroom and on the field. No matter what he decides to do, he's going to be successful, and he's growing in so many ways. Now I know you're not happy that he's not playing more. It hurts him because he knows it hurts you. But you've got a great kid."

That intensified focus from parents has been a big change over the last couple of decades, and the influx of big money into sports has been a major factor. My dad coached until 1980. The first year he ever made twenty thousand dollars was 1975. In 1978, Woody Hayes's last year at Ohio State, his salary was forty thousand dollars. So the world has changed, and I understand how that can affect one's priorities. But if I could say anything to parents whose sons or daughters have some

> **Nothing is worth more than this day.**
>
> GOETHE

athletic skill, I'd say let them become good people first. Good citizens. Let them be people who care and give and want to be part of a team. Whatever happens after that is gravy.

When my dad was leaving college in 1949, he had a decision to make. He had to choose between going to graduate school or playing professional football. He had been drafted by the Philadelphia Eagles in the second round. You may not believe this, but the pay was about the same for both of those pursuits, and because he had a child on the way, it made a lot more sense for him to go to graduate school than to play in the NFL.

> **Your life is either a celebration or a chore. The choice is yours.**
>
> AUTHOR UNKNOWN

Now, look at that same scenario in today's world. Do you think a guy would rather be a graduate assistant at OSU or go to the NFL? There's no question what he would do. The world has changed, and we're not ever going back to the good old days. That's why I think it's so important to teach gratitude, because the world distracts us from being grateful for what we have. That's why we like to start the day with this fundamental.

THANKS, MOM!

What are most of our guys thankful for? To be honest, I don't look at what they write. But I do know that when the time comes for their senior speeches, their mothers are always right at the top of the list.

With little boys, moms are a huge influence. Every senior who has gone through our program gives a senior speech, and each year the content varies. We give the guys guidelines about what they should focus on, and one suggestion is that they talk about a fundamental that was critical to their development. Another is to talk about someone they consider a hero or a winner in their own lives. Whenever they do that, their moms get mentioned almost every time. I can go down my list of guys: Tyler said his mother was his hero. She worked forty to seventy-two hours a week and yet was always there for him. Dan thanked his mom for her support and said she was the nicest person in the world. Kirk's father died of cancer when he was nine years old. He thanked his mom for her input in his life. Trevor said, "My mom is the backbone of the family." So their relationships with their moms are huge to these guys.

We also talk a lot about real-life issues. I have a list of about thirty, and I have our seniors pick one so that the younger players get a chance to hear them talk about life after football, class attendance, the value of surrounding yourself with good people or getting proper rest, finances, and other practical issues. College kids these days get nailed with credit cards because they get a free T-shirt if they sign up. One guy told me not long ago that he has five credit cards, each with a fifty-thousand-dollar credit line. I just shook my head and said, "What are you doing?" But I can talk to these guys all day. What makes the difference for them is hearing it from the upperclassmen.

Humility

> If we were humble, nothing would change us—neither praise nor discouragement.
>
> **MOTHER TERESA**

The reality for most of our players is that ever since they were in fifth grade, people have been telling them that they're the best. They were picked first on the playground and in Little League. They've been the tallest, the fastest, and the strongest. Everyone looked up to them in high school. Dozens of colleges recruited them.

All of that can be confusing for young people, especially if they want to be part of a team. They've been told all their lives, "You're great. You're special," and then when they get to the team, they're told they have to give themselves up for others.

We think it's important for our young guys to hear about humility,

COLIN POWELL'S RULES

1. It ain't as bad as you think. It will look better in the morning.
2. Get mad, then get over it.
3. Avoid having your ego so close to your position that when your position falls, your ego goes with it.
4. It can be done!
5. Be careful what you choose. You may get it.
6. Don't let adverse facts stand in the way of a good decision.
7. You can't make someone else's choices. You shouldn't let someone else make yours.
8. Check small things.
9. Share credit.
10. Remain calm. Be kind.
11. Have a vision. Be demanding.
12. Don't take the counsel of your fears or naysayers.
13. Perpetual optimism is a force multiplier.

We often use Colin Powell's Rules as a teaching tool for our players. The rules speak to them right where they live every day. They're honest. They're to the point. And they reinforce much of what we're trying to get across.

because they really want to be positive role models. They want to do things right. They've seen people they respect who may not necessarily be humble, and they're trying to figure out what kinds of people they want to be.

> **Humility precedes honor.**
>
> PROVERBS 18:12

We talk a lot about the concept of humility coming before honor. We first have to humble ourselves, whether it's humbling ourselves to become a part of the team, humbling ourselves to become freshmen (after being at the top of the heap in high school), or humbling ourselves to come under the teaching of someone who knows more than we do. There are a lot of ways we humble ourselves, and other ways we get humbled.

Former French president Charles de Gaulle once remarked, "Graveyards are full of irreplaceable men." That quote is a good one for our guys to hear. I don't want to paint them in a bad light, but they've had lots of people telling them they're wonderful, important, indispensable. And most of the guys who come into our program know inside that humility is important, but I'm not sure they fully understand what it really means.

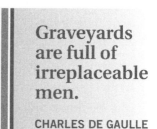

Graveyards are full of irreplaceable men.

CHARLES DE GAULLE

I think of Troy Smith, who had a difficult childhood with different foster parents and a number of schools. He had already had a tough life. We recruited another player at quarterback and recruited Troy for his overall athletic ability, thinking we could mold him into whatever position the team needed. This shows how surprised you can be as a coach. Five years later, Troy won the Heisman Trophy at quarterback and was drafted into the NFL. He said that one of the things that had shaped him through his experience at Ohio State was humility.

SHAPED BY HUMILITY

I'm sure that many of our losses are designed to humble us and shape us into the people we want to be. The truth is, we have to let those times do their work on us. We can fight doing that and try to keep our egos intact, but we may miss out on what we need to learn.

One Bible passage that really captures the essence of humility is Philippians 2:3-4:

> Do nothing from rivalry or conceit, but in humility
> count others more significant than yourselves. Let each
> of you look not only to his own interests, but also to the
> interests of others. (ESV)

We went over that passage just before we left on our trip to New Orleans to play in the BCS national-championship game in January 2008. What struck me was that we are to do nothing out of a sense of rivalry or conceit, but we are to look out for the interests of others.

In football, we can value a player for his speed, or his arm strength, or how he blasts through the line. But ultimately, it's the humble superstar that most guys seem to admire and want to emulate. Humility is a quality worth desiring.

If we are really humble, after a game you won't be able to tell whether we've won or lost. Or whether people are saying nice things about us or criticizing us. The thing that makes me most proud about our players is the feedback I get from people who say the players seem really humble. The way they interact with people when we travel, the way they talk to the media, all of that works together to present a rounded view of who they really are. They're constantly deflecting praise to their teammates and recognizing others for their efforts, and that ties in closely with their attitude of gratitude.

I think it's important to keep the word *humility* in front of our guys. It keeps the bad form of pride at bay. People are confused about the word *pride*. If I asked our team to define it, some would talk about how proud they are of being on the team. Others would talk about the false pride that happens before a fall. Without humility, you're left only with pride. With humility, you also have gratitude.

> # With humility comes wisdom.
>
> PROVERBS 11:2

I try to avoid using the word *pride* because there are so many definitions and it can be confusing. It's a lot like the word *friend*. I've asked players to define what a friend is, and 99 percent of them over the years have said that a friend is someone who's got your back, and if you need him, he'll be there to pop somebody in the nose and fight for you. No player has ever written, "A friend tells you the truth," or "A friend tells you, 'Hey, we have to get out of here.'" If a player whines about his spot on the depth chart, a friend tells him, "You need to start doing this or that better."

So even though some words are more difficult to grasp, everyone knows that the quality of *humility* will draw people to you that you wouldn't necessarily expect. For example, as a Christian, I believe that Jesus is the way, the truth, and the life. But I try not to bash people over the head with that belief or jam it down their throats. Some of my great friends profess a different belief system from mine. For instance, Rabbi Areyah Kaltmann has sent me some awesome messages that I have shared with my teams. I have also had the opportunity to speak at different events for various faith groups. They know where I'm coming from, but I don't think they ever get the feeling from me that what I believe makes me better than they are. I've tried hard to have a humble attitude and present my beliefs as, "Here's what I think."

Some in the Christian community have fractured themselves from society and other religious groups by presenting their messages in a way that seems to say, "We're right, and you're wrong." I like the idea of keeping my faith humble in the context of a university setting. We have unity *and* diversity.

NOT IMPRESSED

Christianity's reputation in America is suffering among the younger generation. In a study of 18- to 29-year-olds conducted by The Barna Group, only 10 percent of non-Christian respondents said they have a "good impression" of Christianity.

Nonbelievers said that present-day Christianity is
Judgmental (87 percent)
Hypocritical (85 percent)
Old-fashioned (78 percent)
Too involved in politics (75 percent)

Many young Christians share their nonbelieving peers' opinions. Half of young churchgoers said they view Christianity as judgmental, hypocritical, and too political. One third indicated it was old-fashioned and out of touch with reality.

(*BARNA UPDATE*, SEPTEMBER 24, 2007)

HAPPINESS AND RESPECT

In this book, and in the Winners Manual we give to our players, there are quotations taken directly from the Bible. We also include truths from other faiths and other wise people—but every statement is there to make us think.

There are two things that give us a chance to have a positive impact on those who agree with us and those who don't. The first one is happiness or joy. If we consistently demonstrate that we're happy or joyful, it's very inviting to people on the outside looking in. They think, *I wonder what makes that guy tick? I wonder what makes him look at life the way he does?* Happiness tears down the walls that separate us and draws people together.

Second, we can earn a hearing from other people by respecting where they are coming from and listening to their perspectives on life. If we repel people with our words and throw up walls, we don't have a chance to dialogue. I get nervous with Christians who are strident with their message and drive a wedge between people. When that happens, it's hard to get those on the outside to even listen to what we're saying. There's clear teaching in the Bible about going out and telling everyone the truth, but it's not quite as clear *how* we are to do that.

> Let your heart be awakened to the transforming power of gratefulness.
>
> SARAH BAN BREATHNACH

I don't ever discriminate against people of another faith or people with no religious faith. I don't give them less playing time. I don't listen to them any less. And that's one thing I hope is also true in your own work or personal life. If you're a business owner, for example, I hope you wouldn't discriminate against a good computer operator just because he or she doesn't see eye to eye with you spiritually.

If we exude happiness and treat other people with respect, then perhaps the more they're around us, the more they'll want to learn about what makes us tick. To me, that's a real strength. I would want the other person to say, "Man, I don't agree with that guy, but I can't argue that he's really happy, and he always treats me well. There's something there I'd like to have."

HUMILITY AND GRATITUDE

An example of a person who combines humility with gratitude is linebacker A. J. Hawk, the great Green Bay Packer and former Buckeye. What made him great at Ohio State was that he did everything you would want a football player or a student or a friend to do. He accomplished a great deal and did it in a humble way. He never asked for the spotlight. In fact, he shunned it. He deferred to his teammates, and it was an interesting phenomenon to watch. His playing ability drew fans, but I think his immense popularity was in large part due to the way he handled himself. He had the chance to leave college early and become a first-round draft choice in the NFL. He didn't even consider it, because I think his built-in humility told him, *I'm not worthy of that right now.*

A. J. also showed how seamlessly gratitude meshes with humility. It always seemed that he was so grateful for the opportunities he'd had at Ohio State, so grateful for his teammates, and so humbled by what we'd been able to accomplish as a team, that he didn't even consider leaving early.

When his senior year was over, the pros were taken by the fact that A. J., who was truly worthy of being a top-ten pick in the NFL draft, was also genuinely humble and appreciative. And I told the Green Bay Packers when they drafted him fifth overall, "Hey, you don't understand what a great relationship this is going to be, because he's the kind of guy that will be so grateful to play in your city, and so humbled by the acceptance he'll get there and the way they'll embrace him. That's just who he is." What a leader he was for his teammates at Ohio State. I've often said in coaching that if your most talented players are also your hardest workers, you've got a chance for real success, because everyone looks up to those guys who produce. And if those top players also have genuine humility, you really have a chance for something special. You can just tell by the way A. J. carries himself that he is one of those guys.

Enthusiasm

Flaming enthusiasm, backed by horse sense and persistence,
is the quality that most frequently makes for success.
DALE CARNEGIE

We have a lot of fun with the final component of attitude: *enthusiasm.* Every time we talk about it, I call on someone different from the team and ask him if he knows the origin of the word. Over the years, I've heard some pretty funny answers. Once, I asked one of the coaches that question while he was still thinking about the word *discipline.*

"Disciple," he said.

The players just howled. Of course, they'll take any shot they can at us coaches if we make a mistake. For six weeks, they were rubbing that one in. And, of course, they thought they were simply showing enthusiasm.

The word *enthusiasm* is a derivative of the Greek word *entheos,* which basically means "full of spirit, full of God." It's our hope that every team member will catch that vision and live, practice, and play in a way that's full of spirit and full of God. That's as enthusiastic as you can possibly be.

We've all been around the type of person that everybody considers "crazy." We say, "That guy is gung ho," or "She never stops. She's always bubbly and seems to be in a different gear from everybody else." The person who lives life at full speed is one who's full of spirit. If you are one of those people, you know that barbs can be thrown your way for being "too perky," "too energetic," or "too positive."

Enthusiastic people seem to have a glow about them—perhaps because they're going a hundred miles an hour. But they're playing with their whole hearts and doing it constantly.

"YOU GOTTA HAVE ENTHUSIASM!"

We like to bring up this fundamental at strategic moments when we know there's going to be a lull. When it's the dog days of August and you've been in training camp for what seems like years, there's no reason to be excited. It's a grind. You're tired, you're sore, you're trying to concentrate, but all you can think about is how hot it is. The guys will have fun teasing me and say, "You gotta have enthusiasm!"

One morning we were talking about enthusiasm, and one of our players, Larry Grant, handed me a piece of paper. "I have one you need to add to the book, Coach," he said.

> None are so old as those who have outlived enthusiasm.
>
> HENRY DAVID THOREAU

This is the way I get a lot of entries for the Winners Manual. Someone will read something, rip it out or write it down, and hand it to me. When Larry gave me his contribution, I taped it in that day, and it's still in there.

> There are three types of people:
>
> Those who make things happen,
>
> Those who watch things happen,
>
> And those who say, "What happened?"
>
> Which one are you?

Those words struck home with Larry because he'd caught the vision that *we* were the ones who were going to make things happen; *we* were going to be enthusiastic and *we* were going to be full of spirit. It's easy to be enthusiastic when you're in a big bowl game or you're playing your archrival. But it's those times when there's not much to be excited about that we bring this one up.

There are certain people around a team who energize it. It doesn't matter what the score is. It doesn't matter what their role is. They might have the least-perceived role of anyone, but they still make a huge difference.

What I've found over the years is that enthusiasm ties in closely with gratitude and humility. People who get enthused have no problem humbling themselves to become part of a team. They can easily sign on to something they believe in. That's what they do. They do everything with spirit and are usually consistently enthusiastic.

There are times when you have to lie to yourself and show a little more enthusiasm than you feel. That's human nature. It's not easy to be enthusiastic about a math class, maybe, but we have to find a way to get excited. That's where a great teacher can make all the difference. We have a math tutor who is unbelievable. I've never seen anyone else energize kids who lack confidence in their math skills like she does—and this is one of the more difficult subjects for today's youth. She has the ability to get them excited about math because *she's* excited. And when someone is full of spirit and full of God about something, it can make learning fun.

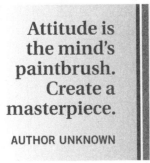

> Attitude is the mind's paintbrush. Create a masterpiece.
>
> AUTHOR UNKNOWN

We have a player that others refer to as "Full Speed." It doesn't matter whether we're walking through a play or running a drill, he's doing it full speed. If he's not supposed to be tackling, he's tackling. If he's going to the locker room for a shower, he's in there and out of there while the other guys are still walking down the tunnel. Players like that can help set the tone for the whole team. Don't ever underestimate the power of an enthusiastic attitude for those around you, no matter what kind of team you're on.

CREATE YOUR OWN ENTHUSIASM

In my first season as head coach at Youngstown State, we were 1-9 heading into the final game of the year. There wasn't much to be excited about, so we had to create our own enthusiasm. We were playing Akron University, and the two schools are about forty miles apart. I had just come from Ohio State, where I'd been an assistant, and I asked one of my former colleagues, Bill Myles, a retired OSU assistant coach, to come talk to my team about what it means to get *enthused* about playing your rival. From the moment he opened his mouth, you could tell that our guys were getting it.

First, Akron was our rival, so it was naturally easier to get fired up about playing them. Second, they had won a bunch of games that year, so we wanted to knock them off. Had we not been playing Akron, it would have been a lot harder, because at the end of a poor season it's hard to raise the level of play with just an appeal to pride. But we won that game, and it was something we built on for the next year and many years to come.

A couple of years later, we were struggling again. We'd had a poor year in 1986, then a really good year in 1987, and then we dipped down again in 1988. We were 2-6 and out of any play-off contention when I asked Chuck Tanner, the manager of the World Series champion Pittsburgh Pirates, to come speak to the team. He lived in Pennsylvania, but only about twenty miles away, and he happened to be coming over to Youngstown anyway, so we invited him to our practice. It was early November in northeast Ohio, which means it was cold, rainy, and dismal. The weather reflected our record. It's not an ideal situation when football is such a strong part of the culture and you're four games under .500.

I'll never forget what Chuck Tanner said, and I'll bet the players on that team still remember his words. He talked to them from a baseball perspective and used a baseball analogy, but as he advanced his theme, it was amazing to see our players respond.

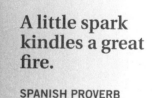

A little spark kindles a great fire.

SPANISH PROVERB

"You have to play Saturday like it's Opening Day," he said.

He was coming from outside the team and hadn't suffered through the six losses. But he gave us a little spark that Thursday. And you could see it in the eyes of our players that they couldn't wait until Saturday.

For the next couple of days, you could hear our guys talking about it and jumping on the idea. You heard it in the locker room and on the field. "We're going to play Saturday like it's Opening Day."

We still had to perform and to execute the fundamentals, but that extra spark of enthusiasm helped us win that game.

It's hard to manufacture enthusiasm, and it's difficult to gauge, but I see it most on the sidelines. There are times when we're looking at the wide view of the field and can see both sidelines. We see the movement there, the excitement, and there's intensity and enthusiasm that can really help the team on the field. We get a feeling of support when we know that people are tuned in to what's happening.

Consider this: Providing enthusiasm just might be your role on any given day. You run out of that tunnel and hear the roar of the crowd. You think it's for you, and then all of a sudden you're just standing on the sideline. But if that's your role that day, to encourage and provide spirit, and you do it with all your heart, it can be infectious. A player comes off the field and maybe he's just made a bad play or his opponent has beaten him. That's your chance. That's the time to energize your teammates.

We watch video taken from high above the 105,000-seat Ohio Stadium, and we can tell when something big happens. You can see the sideline come alive. If the sideline is into it, that's what it means to be full of God, full of spirit. And if your role is to be an encourager, it's just as important as being a starter that day.

I AM ONLY ONE

I am only one, but I am one.
I can't do everything, but I can do something.
And what I can do, I ought to do.
And what I ought to do, by the grace of God, I shall do.

EDWARD EVERETT HALE

At Ohio State, the last thing we do before we charge out of the tunnel and onto the field is recite a poem together: Edward Everett Hale's "I Am Only One." Part of our purpose is to energize the group who will be on the sideline. Whatever your job, that's what you can do. That's what we *need* you to do. And if every man does what he can do, and what the team needs him to do, then we're going to be all right.

It's amazing how you can look at the sideline and know how you're going to do in the game. There's a feeling you get—an energy, a *spirit* of the sideline. It's not measurable, but you can feel it. It's the same thing with enthusiasm.

Enthusiasm really is a way to demonstrate how important your task is to you. When you're tired—it's Wednesday, it's two-a-days, and you're not sure you want to live, let alone be a good teammate—how much enthusiasm you can generate is really an indication of how important this is to you.

Maybe you're on a job that makes you wake up early—you work the early shift, or you teach and you have to drive to work in the cold. That's tough to be enthusiastic about. Or perhaps your spouse has cancer and you have to be at the hospital overnight. I think of Kathy Daniels, the wife of Ohio State assistant coach Joe Daniels, who sat by her husband's bedside for ten straight days. She was exhausted, but it was so important, when Joe would wake up for two minutes, for him to see the enthusiasm, spirit, and love she showed him. And now, Joe is doing great, ready to coach again, because of great doctors and his family's spirit and enthusiasm. That's what enthusiasm is all about, and it is vitally connected to gratitude and attitude and humility. It's a powerful thing to know that someone is on your team with you, rooting and pulling for you. It can keep you going day after day.

QUESTIONS FOR REFLECTION

1. Do you think it's really true that we can alter our lives by altering our attitude? How might this happen in your life?

_____

_____

_____

2. What's it like being around people who are grateful? What about people who aren't grateful? How do they make you feel?

_____

_____

_____

3. Who is the most humble person you know? What aspects of that person's life do you want to emulate today?

_____

_____

_____

4. Do you feel a lack of enthusiasm for some part of your work? Why do you feel that way, and how can you remedy the situation?

_____

_____

_____

YOUR PERSONAL GAME PLAN

1. *Personal/Family:* Think of someone in your immediate family with whom you have a difficult time relating. How could a change of your attitude toward this person help change the climate in your home? What specific thing can you do to help achieve that today?

_____

_____

_____

2. *Spiritual/Moral:* Cultivate your gratitude to God today by making a list of things you're thankful for that you would not have if it were not for God's presence in your life. Share the list with someone you love.

_____

_____

_____

3. *Caring/Giving:* Who in your life has been your greatest "sideline encourager"? Encourage that person with a note or a phone call today.

_____

_____

_____

4. *Health/Fitness:* How might a change of attitude affect the way you care for your body? Put that into practice today by doing something new, or continue doing something to which you've committed.

_____

_____

_____

5. *Your Team:* Is there someone on your team who needs a sideline that's *alive?* How can you show you're full of spirit and full of God for that person today?

_____

_____

_____

6. *Academics/Career:* If an attitude of gratitude takes practice, how can you practice that fundamental with those in your school or work life? Consider keeping a "gratitude notebook" that you can refer to often to help you focus on this discipline.

_____

_____

_____

CHAPTER 4

DISCIPLINE

It is not enough to get things done; they must be done right.

ARTHUR T. HADLEY

Those who work the hardest, who subject themselves to the strictest discipline, who give up certain pleasurable things in order to achieve a goal, are the happiest.

BRUTUS HAMILTON, OLYMPIC DECATHLETE AND COACH

Start by doing what's necessary, then what's possible, and suddenly you are doing the impossible.

SAINT FRANCIS OF ASSISI

As you endure this divine discipline, remember that God is treating you as his own children. Who ever heard of a child who is never disciplined by its father? . . . No discipline is enjoyable while it is happening—it's painful! But afterward there will be a peaceful harvest of right living for those who are trained in this way.

HEBREWS 12:7, 11

IN today's culture, *discipline* is considered a negative, almost foul, word. We associate discipline with a strict, narrow lifestyle in which we're punished if we're not obedient. We tend to think that a disciplined life is restrictive and controlled by some outside authority figure with a sour disposition. In short, we think that a life of discipline means no freedom, no fun, and no joy. But nothing could be further from the truth. The fundamental of discipline will actually help us live more freeing, invigorating lives.

Many people think of discipline as something that's done to us if we're going the wrong way: "Stop that, or I'm going to discipline you!"

Obviously, according to this definition, discipline *is* for people who do something wrong. But the truth is, the reason we're disciplined is that we're loved. Parents discipline their children to point them in a good direction. Coaches are no different. If we understand and utilize the fundamental of discipline, it will help us move *toward* our desired goals in every area of life.

"Why are you on me about my footwork?" a player will ask. "Does it really make a difference how I block this guy?"

The answer, of course, is, "Yes, it *does* make a difference."

Because of a coach's training and experience, he knows that if the players will follow his instructions, they will be more successful in whatever task they're given. So the first thing we try to get across to our guys is that discipline is a positive thing. It's not restrictive or punishing; it's actually liberating.

WHAT IS DISCIPLINE?

The lead quotation in this chapter says, "It is not enough to get things done; they must be done right." That really goes hand in hand with the goals section of the Block O of Life.

A player may have been in the weight room at the assigned time doing squats, but if he's not doing them correctly, if there's something wrong with his technique, he's not getting the most he can out of the exercise. If he's going to meet his goals and play his position effectively, he has to be committed to the process. The coaches will help him do those exercises correctly and give him an opportunity to perfect his craft, but he has to do things right.

> Improving yourself is the best way to help your team.

The great thing about playing sports and being in a group activity like football is that you learn any number of things that will help you later in life. One thing you learn is the discipline of doing a task a certain way and to a certain standard. The payoff is seeing the positive effect of that individual discipline on the team as a whole.

DISCIPLINE

Discipline is "training that is expected to produce a specific character or pattern of behavior."

1. **Bobby Knight:** "a. Do what has to be done
   b. When it has to be done
   c. As well as it can be done,
   d. And do it that way all the time."
2. **Tom Landry:** "Setting a goal is not the main thing. It is deciding how you will go about achieving it and staying with the plan. The key is discipline—without it there is no morale."
3. **Vince Lombardi:** "You teach discipline by doing it over and over; by repetition."
4. **Bob Richards:** "One of the greatest lessons I've learned in athletics is that you've got to discipline your life. No matter how good you may be, you've got to be willing to cut out of your life those things that keep you from going to the top."
5. **Jerry West:** "You can't get much done in life if you only work on the days when you feel good."
6. **Discipline** in football is executing fundamentals and techniques the right way under pressure.
7. **Hebrews 12:11:** "For the moment all discipline seems painful rather than pleasant, but later it yields the peaceful fruit of righteousness to those who have been trained by it" (ESV).
8. **Discipline** implies subjection to a control exerted for the good of the whole, the adherence to rules of policies extended for the orderly coordination of effort.
9. **Discipline:** Do it right
   Do it hard
   Or do it again

The same principle can be seen from the opposite perspective when we consider what mistakes in discipline yield. When a player makes a mistake, jumping offside for example, the entire team is hurt by that five-yard penalty. In the same way, a mistake in the workplace, or in any group, has a rippling effect on the whole organization.

One of the most important lessons you can learn from sports is that it's not about you; it's about the team. You must have discipline in order to affect the team positively.

The word *discipline* comes from a Latin root that means "instruction or learning." A "disciple" is a pupil or student who desires to train by instruction, to follow and learn, and then to repeatedly practice that instruction until he is prepared to *do.*

In the football world, that means practicing your position until you're ready to take the next step and perform in game-time conditions under the scrutiny of 105,000 fans. At an away game, that scrutiny turns to outright hostility. Add to the pressure the fact that millions of fans are watching your every move on television—sometimes in slow motion—and that lined up across from you is a three-hundred-pound lineman who knows how to perform his task as well as, if not better than, you do.

> A champion pays an extra price to be better than anyone else.
>
> PAUL "BEAR" BRYANT

Understanding your role and having the discipline to affect the group translate into whatever you do in the next phase of your life. It's a simple axiom. When one player is penalized, the whole team moves back. To a casual observer, the referee simply moves the ball to a new spot and play resumes, but the penalized player probably just had three years taken off his life because of the stress his mistake created. It's bad enough if the other team's running back charges through the line for five yards. But what really hurts is giving up five yards because someone made a mistake before the ball was even snapped.

I remember as a young coach, during my second or third year at Youngstown State, watching one of my players commit a personal foul. As the yellow flag flew and the official marked off fifteen yards, I stood there incredulous. And I'll never forget what I said to the player as he came off the field. I cringe just thinking about it now. I got in his face and said, "You know what? You're not worth fifteen yards!"

The player slunk to the sideline as I stewed. And then it hit me. I couldn't believe what I had just said to him. I couldn't believe I had demeaned him in front of his teammates. He already felt bad for his lack of discipline on the field, and then I piled on, which was a lack of discipline on *my* part.

Now the truth is, it was a dumb play, and it cost the team. The player needed to learn from his mistake, no question. But I should *never* have said what I did. I needed to learn from it too.

WHEN NO ONE ELSE IS LOOKING

Discipline is what you do when no one else is looking! It's being considerate of the other person. Having good personal habits—you are polite, on time, and take care of business with pride. We must be disciplined as individuals first, and then as a team.

It was late winter of 2006. A. J. Hawk had completed an extraordinary All-America senior season. He was a few classes from completing his degree at Ohio State, and all ten NFL teams that had one of the top-ten draft picks wanted A. J. to visit their city.

This type of attention was uncomfortable for A. J., but he knew it was part of his future, so he agreed to make the NFL visits, with two ground rules: He was not going to miss class, and he was not going to miss any workouts. It was that simple, and he expected the NFL teams to abide by those rules.

> Only a fool despises . . . discipline; whoever learns from correction is wise.
>
> PROVERBS 15:5

There were days when A. J. could be found at the Woody Hayes Athletic Center at four in the morning, completing his workout before departing for yet another NFL city. It was exhausting for him—and for his strength coaches! But the discipline he demanded of himself resulted in his obtaining his Ohio

State degree and his selection by the Green Bay Packers as the fifth player overall in the 2006 NFL draft.

DISCIPLINE IS A DAILY DECISION

When September rolls around and school starts and my players and I are no longer together all the time, I'm not so naive as to think that they'll get up early every day and have their Quiet Time like we did during preseason. But maybe someday they will. Maybe someday they'll realize what that kind of discipline can do for a person who wants to follow a good path.

I believe it was Billy Graham who said, "Those who get up and spend time in the Word to begin the day are not devoid of problems; they're not devoid of discouragement. They just get over it quicker." And that's true. If you can start your day by planting seeds of truth and get those kinds of habits ingrained into your life, you'll succeed at more than just football.

> **Self-discipline is when you tell yourself to do something and you don't talk back.**
>
> W. K. HOPE

We try to relate everything we do on the field to things beyond the game. And it works the other way as well. A situation in life may relate to what happens on the field. If a player is late for class and he makes an excuse about sleeping late, I'll say, "You would never do that in football. You'd never be late for a meeting. You would never miss a practice. You'd die before you'd miss. Even if you're sick and can't even walk, you make it to practice. So what's the difference? You decided that football's important. You have to decide that school's important too."

Everything we do through discipline and habit building, and the pain and sacrifice and rigors of training, enhances the team's performance. And it will pay off down the road. Our guys do a great job with the discipline of maintaining a proper diet. We want three-hundred-pound guys with 15 percent body fat, guys who have a certain vertical leap and can run sprints from sideline to sideline. As soon as they decide that a drill or a habit is important, discipline helps them follow through and actually do what it takes.

Believe me, they quickly see the benefits of disciplined actions and behavior. Two sections of the Winners Manual that we have referred to many times over the years define exactly what we mean by a disciplined player and a disciplined team. I am not even sure where we found these definitions, but they have served us well.

A DISCIPLINED PLAYER . . .

1. Knows the importance of *being on time*.
2. Has learned the value of regular hours and good training habits from working hard in practice.
3. Has learned that the *team* comes before himself. This strengthens his character as he is sometimes called upon to sacrifice for others.
4. Has learned to take orders; in taking orders, he learns how to give them.
5. Knows that discipline is the essence of every successful organization; as a member of the team, he understands the need for it.
6. Has learned that many of these things establish a degree of self-discipline.

A DISCIPLINED FOOTBALL TEAM . . .

1. Doesn't beat itself by mistakes.
2. Keeps penalties to a minimum.
3. Is always ready to play—INTENSITY.
4. Has the guts to come from behind.
5. Rises above adversity.
6. Never, never quits.

DISCIPLINE AND POISE

All the qualities of a disciplined player and team can connect with other worlds outside of football. But I want to show you how these principles worked on the field for us in 2002 with our quarterback, Craig Krenzel.

To play quarterback at Ohio State, a young man must master a set of disciplines we call the Big 3-plus: (1) decision making, (2) no turnovers, and (3) making big plays. Obviously, there are hundreds of things he must do as quarterback, but these three (plus one) are the most important.

Decision making is important because the quarterback handles the ball on just about every play. Everything he does or doesn't do affects the rest of the group, and the discipline he uses in making those decisions has a huge impact on the team's success. So we talk about the discipline of making good decisions and about the importance of disciplined film study that goes into making those decisions.

> You have to have confidence in your ability, and then be tough enough to follow through.
>
> ROSALYNN CARTER

Not turning the ball over is another critical requirement of the job. Throwing an interception or fumbling the football could very well eliminate our chances of winning a game and ultimately, the championship. The team that ends up on the plus side of the turnover margin typically wins the game.

The third requirement for an Ohio State quarterback is that he must make some big plays for us. If he's the man with the ball in his hands, it's up to him to lead the team. So we pound that in and emphasize it. He has to know not only what we are doing with our game plan but also what the other team is doing to try to stop us. A well-prepared quarterback will make some game-changing plays for us.

The "plus" in the Big 3-plus is *toughness.* Whether he has the press beating him up or a defensive lineman smacking him after every throw, a quarterback must be tough. Mentally and physically, quarterback is the toughest position in all of sports.

In 2002, we were undefeated and playing Purdue, a Big Ten Conference opponent. With the clock running down in the fourth quarter, we had fourth down and two yards to go on the Purdue 38. We wanted to get the first down, move the chains, and keep our drive progressing. We called a play that had the primary receiver running a crossing route about four or five yards downfield. As with every other passing play, the quarterback has a primary read on a particular receiver. If that man is covered, there's a secondary read, and if he's covered, there's also a third option. On most plays, we run some clear-out guys, whose routes will draw the defense away from our other receivers.

On that particular down, Purdue called a blitz and brought a lot of pressure, which meant that Craig Krenzel had to make some quick decisions about what to do with the ball. The primary receiver, on his crossing route, was well covered. The secondary receiver on the other side was running an intermediate route, and the defense was tight on him as well. Our third option was a running back who was supposed to get open in the flat, but because of the blitz he had to block someone, so that choice was gone.

Here's where the discipline comes in. Craig had the poise to drop back and assess the situation, even with the blitz coming. He didn't get distracted by the extra men coming at him. He looked at the primary receiver. No go. He looked at the second and third choices. Again, no go. He didn't want to throw the ball into coverage, but he also saw that he wasn't going to be able to run the ball for the first down.

Now, when Purdue blitzed, they played man-to-man in the secondary and just trailed the "clear-out" wide receiver, who was running down the sideline. All of a sudden, our man threw up his hand, indicating he had gained a step on his defender. As Craig checked off his options, he saw the open man down the field and threw him the ball.

The phenomenal thing about that play was that it probably happened in a matter of three seconds. Maybe less. But Craig had the discipline to go through all the options and take the best one.

Now, I have to admit that when he heaved that pass, my first reaction

> It was character that got us out of bed, commitment that moved us into action, and discipline that enabled us to follow through.
>
> ZIG ZIGLAR

was, "What? We just need two yards. Oh no, no. . . ." The percentage chance of hitting the deep ball is not great. We didn't need a touchdown at that point; we just needed a first down. But when the ball was caught in the end zone for a touchdown, my "Oh no," turned into, "Yes!"

After the game the media questioned me and said, "Coach, that was such a great call; it took a lot of courage to call that play with your record on the line."

I kind of smiled, and I was thinking, *I need to explain this.*

What made that play work was a disciplined quarterback who knew exactly what he was looking for and had the poise and discipline to stay with his progression of options until he found one that would work. Because of Craig Krenzel's clearheaded thinking and his ability to lay the ball in there perfectly, our team was still alive in the hunt for the national championship.

Focus

> *The only thing a player can control at golf is his own game; so concern about what other competitors may or may not be doing is both a useless distraction and a waste of energy.*
>
> **JACK NICKLAUS**

Focus is an important component of discipline. In our team Winners Manual, focus has its own section, but here we're going to consider it as a component of discipline.

In 2003, we asked our seniors to define *focus.* Here are a few of their responses:

- Focus is when your mental attention is centered on what you need to do. Nothing else can get into your head.
- Focus is when someone can resist temptation in the present to further pursue a goal in the future.

- Focus means concentrating on your responsibility.
- Focus means total concentration. Committing to something and staying with it until it is done and done right. Never giving up.
- Focus is the ability to concentrate on something by ignoring outside, important forces that can interfere with the task at hand. Taking advantage of all opportunities that facilitate the task and increase the chance of success.
- Focus is disciplined and zeroed in on the goal and only the goal.

Focus is a critical part of discipline, because there are many things going on around us that can draw us away from the singleness of thought we need to accomplish whatever the moment calls for. At Ohio State, we have the good fortune to have distraction issues such as agents bothering players, fans standing outside the practice doors waiting for autographs, other students in class wanting to talk to our players, people calling our players' parents, and 105,000 fans at every home game. The distractions are endless, and it's essential that we cultivate the ability to focus on what's going on right at this moment.

This is where the Block O comes into play, because we know that our guys are enthralled with football, and they practice like crazy. But when that's over and they're supposed to be in class, their focus has to be on that subject. They can't be thinking about practice. Likewise, when a guy is with his girlfriend, he has to be thinking about her, not going over the bad practice he had that day. Wherever we are, that's where our focus needs to be.

BE YOUR BEST WHERE YOU ARE

Focus on the moment is a phrase we use a lot. I know we're not the first ones to have used it, but it's crucial to our success.

The ability to focus on the moment gives you a chance to be the best you can be right here, right now. If you're in the weight room, your lift is your focus. If you're in the classroom, it's that class. If it's a players' meeting to study film from today's practice, the temptation to drift away mentally is strong. The other commitments tugging at you are strong. You have to focus. There are a million distractions during a game—the noise for one. In the Big Ten, you don't use a snap count in most stadiums because you simply can't hear. Your focus includes the peripheral vision necessary to see the ball snapped. Your ability to focus has to be better than the guys' who are playing against you. They're going to try to do things perfectly, and if you're going to compete with them, you have to be right there in the moment.

It's difficult not to daydream and think about the what-ifs and if-onlys of life. Coaches can fall into the trap of thinking about what they'd do if they got a call to be the head coach at a bigger school. It happens to people in business, in the church, and at home—no one is immune.

> Now is everything you have to work with. When you live it fully, it is more than enough.
>
> RALPH MARSTON

I remember my entrance interview at the University of Akron, with Gordon Larson, the athletic director at the time. This was my first coaching job as a graduate assistant. The most helpful advice he gave me was to "keep your rear end and your mind in the same place."

That was in 1975, and I often thought about that advice when we had success and I was rumored to be a candidate for this job or that. People would ask, "I wonder if you're going to go here or there next year?" Fortunately, I would always remember Larson's words. You need to be where you are. And where you are right now is the best place to do as well as you can. That's such a practical exercise, and it will follow wherever you go—in the workplace, at home, and at church, as well as on the football field.

How many times have you been sitting in church or at work and allowed yourself to drift for a moment? How about when you're talking with your children or your spouse? Is your mind racing in some other place? Because we're human, that's going to happen from time to time, but we talk with our players about the ability to regain their focus. When you realize you've drifted, you shake it off, and you get back on task.

TODAY FIRST

In this time of change, help me to be patient, God.
Let me not run ahead of you and your plans.
Give me courage to do only what is before me
And to keep my focus on my responsibilities.
I am tempted to daydream about the future:
However, the future is in your hands.
Thus may I be close to you in all my thoughts,
Accomplish the task before me today,
And do it with all my heart.

FOCUS ON THE MOMENT

One of the coaches I've really respected over the years is Phil Jackson, a former NBA player and coach of the Chicago Bulls during their championship runs in the 1990s. In his book *Sacred Hoops: Spiritual Lessons of a Hardwood Warrior,* he discusses the lessons he's learned from basketball—everything from making sure each player knows he has a vital role on the team to experiencing "each moment with a clear mind and open heart."

> In basketball, as in life, true joy comes from being fully
> present in each and every moment, not just when
> things are going your way. Of course, it is no accident
> that things are more likely to go your way when you
> stop worrying about whether you're going to win or lose
> and focus your full attention on what's happening right
> this moment. The day I took over the Bulls, I vowed
> to create an environment based on the principles of
> selflessness and compassion.

I feel the same way about the Block O as Phil Jackson felt about his approach to his players and life. I don't think it's a coincidence that the harder you work on being a whole person, the better you do with all the individual parts. "Being fully present in each and every moment" is a fundamental we pound on more than anything else—especially during preseason, when it's hot out and we're tired and sore. We break our practices down into five-minute periods, and a practice consists of twenty-four or twenty-five periods. That's about two hours of intensely hard work, and it's hard not to glance up to see how much longer we have. All the players want to do is get to the game, because that's the fun part, but they know they have to stay focused so they *can* play the game.

> Obstacles are those frightful things you see when you take your eyes off the goal.
>
> HANNAH MORE
> (1745–1833)

When our guys come off the field after practice and shower up, they're hungry, but before they can go to dinner, they have to watch practice film. We film everything we do from five different angles, and when the players come off the practice field, they have immediate reinforcement as to what they did well and what they didn't. It's easier for the juniors and seniors to focus on these film sessions because they've been through this for two or three years, but a freshman player, who has never been through meetings and was the best guy on his high school team and never had to listen, is the one who has to work at focusing.

I get e-mails and letters from young coaches, asking for advice on how to get where I am. Now, there are some good books to read, and some seminars, and it's fine to ask the question, but really, the question is not, How do I get where you are? The question is, Where am I now?

When I was at Youngstown State, I told my players that there were more attorneys in our little town than there were Division I football coaches in all of America. So you say you want to be a college coach? Okay. Now here's the competitive side of it: There are only a thousand of them in the whole nation. And to get there, you have to go through a progression. My steps included living in the locker room and eating cold SpaghettiOs from a can when I was a graduate assistant. I made one hundred dollars a month and then worked for five thousand dollars a year. And I consider myself one of the lucky ones.

If I'm talking to a student who desires to be a coach, I'll pull out his transcript. If I see he has a 2.5 grade-point average, I'll say, "Son, you're going to have to improve to get into grad school. If your goal is coaching, you have to focus on what's going on here and now."

Of course, there's overlap here with other fundamentals. If you're always looking for what's next, you won't be looking at your blessings and appreciating all you have. You won't have gratitude. How can you care for someone if you're not listening? If in that moment you don't care enough to be fully present, then you're not focused.

During the 2008 season, one of the most highly anticipated games in Division I will be Ohio State vs. the University of Southern California (USC). There's no question that college football fans around the country will want to watch that game. Some have said that it's the key game of the entire season. My response? Only if we do what we're supposed to do leading up to that game and after it. One of the reasons our guys decided to come to Ohio State is because they get to play in games like that.

That being said, let's go to work. Our focus is not on USC. It's not on Michigan. Our focus is on today and every single day between now and the end of the season. We can't just sit around thinking about one game or another; we have to focus and prepare and plan for how we're going to accomplish our goals.

> The man who succeeds above his fellows is the one who early in life clearly discerns his object, and towards that object habitually directs his power.
>
> EARL NIGHTINGALE

There's no question that when the day arrives to play USC, it's going to be wonderful— as long as we're prepared. If that day comes along and we're not prepared and we haven't done what we needed to do with each moment leading up to it, then we might not like that day. We might want to forget about that day.

You can tell that you're not focused when your brain and your rear end are in two different places. Say you go home to your family but really you're not there, which has happened to me more than once. I have to ask myself when I walk in the door, *Am I going to be focused on this moment? Am I here, or am I back at the office still stewing over what I'm mad about?*

Early in my head-coaching career, I would allow the play of the quarterback to affect how I handled the whole staff, because I was a quarterbacks coach prior to being a head coach. Then, when I became a head coach at a smaller school, I still handled the quarterbacks, in addition to being in charge of the whole group. If my quarterback played well, I was okay with *everybody*. But when my quarterback didn't play well, I wasn't okay with *anybody*, because I was mad.

> It's better to have died as a young boy than to fumble this football.
>
> JOHN HEISMAN

So, how do you work it from a family standpoint so that you're always in the moment with your spouse and your kids? My youngest was teasing me about this not long ago. She'd just seen a movie and said I needed to see it.

"You know the last movie I saw was with you and your sister," I said. "It was *The Rescuers*."

"Yeah, I remember," she said. "I had to wake you up."

It was true. She'd had to wake me up, because I was sitting there just exhausted, and as soon as the movie started I was out like a light. I don't even remember it.

HANGING ON TO THE BALL

On the wall in our coaching office, we keep a quote by John Heisman for the benefit of our running backs: "It's better to have died as a young boy than to fumble this football." Obviously, in football it's important to discuss hanging on to the ball. It's such a fundamental, and it takes concentration and focus. But here's how one of our players applied the same principle to another aspect of his life.

This particular player was a natural on the field, and he loved to carry the football. One of our learning specialists was working with him, and she made him a three-ring notebook with all of his class and tutor schedules. She had a design on the outside with his name on it, and she told him to keep it with him at all times. "Never let it out of your sight."

"I got it," he said. "This will be my academic football. I'll never fumble it."

She was so excited that he had gotten the message. It was that important to him. I think that's why we try like crazy to apply the lessons we learn on the field to the rest of our players' lives. We want them to see the relevance of every aspect of the Block O, and the fundamentals, that can help them today and tomorrow. We think that if we're better in all these areas, we'll inevitably be better as a football team. And I have to believe that the same principles apply at work, church, and home.

QUESTIONS FOR REFLECTION

1. Is it possible to be too disciplined or focused? Explain.

_____

_____

_____

2. Have you thought of discipline in a negative way? How can discipline be a positive thing in your life?

_____

_____

_____

3. How have you seen discipline work in your life or in the life of someone you know?

_____

_____

_____

4. In what arena do you find it most difficult to focus—to be all there every moment? How do you think you could overcome that lack of focus?

_____

_____

_____

YOUR PERSONAL GAME PLAN

1. *Personal/Family:* Do you identify with coming home and "not being there"? If you find it difficult to focus on friends or family after a day at work, what steps can you take to remedy this?

_____

_____

_____

2. *Spiritual/Moral:* Is there a spiritual discipline you'd like to improve on, such as prayer, Bible study, meditation, or stewardship? What specific goal can you set to grow stronger in your faith?

_____

_____

_____

3. *Caring/Giving:* When I lashed out at the player who had committed a penalty, I wasn't focused on what he needed. Is there someone to whom you've been unkind who needs a caring word from you today?

_____

_____

_____

4. *Health/Fitness:* In what area do you need to be more disciplined about your health? What one thing can you begin doing today that will make you a healthier person: Exercising? Eating well? Cutting something from your diet?

_____

_____

_____

5. *Your Team:* Discipline and teamwork go hand in hand. How can you aid your team today by exercising discipline in some area of your life?

_____

_____

_____

6. *Academics/Career:* How have you experienced the disconnect between your rear end and your brain? How can you be more disciplined in the work you've been given to accomplish today?

_____

_____

_____

CHAPTER 5

EXCELLENCE

The quality of a person's life is in direct proportion to their commitment to excellence, regardless of their chosen field of endeavor.

VINCE LOMBARDI

Excellence is not an act . . . but a habit.

ARISTOTLE

Risk more than others think is safe. Care more than others think is wise. Dream more than others think is practical. Expect more than others think is possible.

CADET MAXIM, U.S. MILITARY ACADEMY

Life is often compared to a marathon, but I think it is more like being a sprinter; long stretches of hard work punctuated by brief moments in which we are given the opportunity to perform at our best.

MICHAEL JOHNSON

When you're walking the long hallway that leads to the coaching offices of the Ohio State University athletic department, something intangible strikes even the casual observer. The length of the hallway has something to do with it—it's at least 120 yards long, the same length as a football field including both end zones. Perhaps it has something to do with all the Big Ten Conference championship trophies and the many national-championship trophies that commemorate decades of excellence. Or the numerous pictures of storied coaches and players who have worn the scarlet and gray. It might be the giant O at the end of the hall, made of the same stained glass seen in the front rotunda of Ohio Stadium.

The entire building suggests a single, consistent theme: *excellence.* Excellence in design. Excellence in craftsmanship. Excellence in tastefulness. Excellence in portraying the tradition of Ohio State football. Any recruit who steps into this hallway might ask himself, *I wonder if I could be a part of this success?*

In the same way that a well-constructed building signifies excellence to everyone who sees it, the structure of our lives can pique the interest of those who observe us when we make excellence a central part of our daily quest as individuals.

Here's a good working definition of excellence: "Everybody striving to reach their full potential." As we look at the components of the Block O of Life, we want to increase our excellence and reach our potential in every one of those areas. The process begins by discovering our individual identities, finding our purpose, deciding what we'd like to accomplish, and then creating a plan to achieve that.

> It isn't hard to be good from time to time in sports. What's tough is being good every day.
>
> WILLIE MAYS

Executing a plan to reach our full potential takes a lot of preparation. We must first uncover all the hidden things that can help or hinder our putting that plan into action. Excellent preparation takes tremendous commitment, focus, discipline, and many of the other Big Ten Fundamentals we discuss in the Winners Manual. The willingness to do what it takes to execute that plan will yield excellence, but it doesn't just happen. Achieving excellence requires a great deal of hard work.

EXCELLENCE IN OUR PERSONAL AND FAMILY LIVES

Reviewing the Block O of Life can help us understand what we will gain when we commit ourselves to excellence. For instance, when we consider the Personal/Family component, excellence means understanding the needs of everyone in the family and sacrificing the time and effort it takes to meet those needs. Here again, listening is an important skill and discipline. When we listen, we learn, and we move out of our own comfort zones and into the other person's world. Observing families that have tremendous relationships motivates us to move forward and make the necessary sacrifices and develop the commitment, focus, and discipline it takes to build those kinds of relationships in our own families.

The college years are a time of family transition for our players. Going off to school is probably their first experience away from home. Nevertheless, we must help them craft a plan for excellence in their roles as sons, brothers, grandsons—and ultimately for their future roles as husbands and fathers.

During our goal-setting sessions, it's very rewarding to discuss family goals. Players often talk about making sure they stay connected with their grandparents, who may be elderly. They discuss making their parents proud, performing and behaving in a way that expresses their gratitude for their moms and dads. They mention their dreams of supporting their parents and giving them a different lifestyle to show them how much they appreciate the sacrifices their parents made.

EXCELLENCE IN OUR SPIRITUAL AND MORAL LIVES

When we look at the Spiritual/Moral component of the Block O, pursuing excellence in our spiritual lives means that we seek to know God and create a relationship with him. There are many ways we can do this. Certainly, spending time in prayer is helpful. We can learn to communicate with God, talking with him and pouring out our hearts. In prayer we also learn the greatest aspect of communication: *listening.* Listening with heart, mind, and soul will move us further along the path toward spiritual excellence.

> Only those who have the patience to do simple things *perfectly* will acquire the skills to do difficult things easily.

Reading Scripture is vital in the process, as well as spending time with people who can help us understand what we've read and help us apply it to our everyday lives. Fellowship with others of like mind, either in one-on-one conversation or in a group study—or in the fellowship of a church—can also be helpful. These are fundamental practices that I believe allow us to begin moving toward reaching our potential and achieving excellence in our spiritual lives.

As we crystallize our beliefs and set our spiritual plans in motion, a passion for excellence in serving God will surface. As I have studied and learned from people who embody spiritual excellence, I've noticed some common denominators in those who have pursued this goal.

EXCELLENCE IN OUR CARING AND GIVING

In the Caring/Giving component, it will help us to achieve excellence if we can find areas in which we can reach out and make a difference in other peoples' lives—areas where we can set up our plan to make sacrifices and create relationships, and then spend the time to learn how to serve others in a better way.

We have to understand that on the top half of the Block O—in all those Purpose areas—the excellence we seek is tied to something bigger.

> The foundation of excellence lies in self-control.
>
> H. L. BAUGHER

Excellence doesn't affect just our own lives; it affects the lives of others in our sphere of influence. Our world doesn't revolve around us; it revolves around the group, around the community, and it's in that group setting that our excellence will shine.

In chapter 1, we described the journey of success, and we discussed the importance of having peace and the inner satisfaction that comes from being the best we can be and adding to those around us. In the same way, excellence in our caring and giving occurs when we're doing our *best* for the group, for a purpose much larger than ourselves. We achieve excellence as a by-product of moving forward with the plan we've created—the mission we've set out to accomplish.

The same is true of all our goals. When we set goals for our football team, we first need to study extremely hard, discover our strengths, deal with our weaknesses, study other teams, other coaches, other players, and situations that will show us what it takes to reach our potential.

So much of the groundwork for excellence as a team has been determined and established before we ever set foot on the field of play. What does an excellent football team look like? What does it take to become a championship team? How does a team reach its true potential? What are the factors involved in the overall game plan or the specific duties assigned within the game? What do we have to achieve offensively? defensively? in our special teams? on third down? in the red zone? in short yardage? on the goal line? What practice habits will it take? These questions go on and on, and we're constantly seeking better answers.

Excellence requires planning, commitment, focus, discipline, and the sacrifice of time and energy to move toward our goals. We must discover our talents and then determine how we can best feature those talents as individuals and as a team.

SETTING GOALS FOR STRENGTH AND FITNESS

Many of our guys aspire to play in the NFL. Obviously, they need to study what it takes to become a member of that elite group. Approximately one million kids play high school football in America each year, but that number shrinks to about forty-five thousand at the collegiate level. From there, the chances of moving up to the next level become even slimmer. There are only thirty-two teams in the NFL, each with a roster of fifty-three players. That's fewer than seventeen hundred players who are active in the NFL at any given time. Currently, there are about fifty players from Ohio State playing in the NFL. Those are not great odds for incoming players, so it means they have to learn all they can and implement excellence in every aspect of their training and playing so they can be the best they can be.

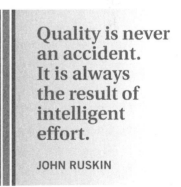

Quality is never an accident. It is always the result of intelligent effort.

JOHN RUSKIN

The NFL looks at a lot of factors when evaluating potential players:

How fast do they run? How high do they jump? How much do they weigh? How many times can they bench-press 225 pounds? The NFL examines all of those details related to strength and speed, as well as the players' grasp of the intricacies of their position.

EXCELLENCE IN ACADEMICS

Students pursuing excellence must seek a subject they have a passion to study. What passion brings them back to the books time and again? Taking advantage of the faculty's knowledge, utilizing tutors and teachers and study opportunities, gaining an ability to learn from books and the Internet, and then applying all of that learning on tests is part of the process. Excellence demands a knowledge of what it takes to go on to a graduate program or to become a doctor or lawyer or to be certified to teach. Once we understand what it takes to excel, we can formulate a plan to achieve it, but then we must have the discipline and focus to roll up our sleeves and accomplish the necessary tasks, being willing to devote the time and energy needed to excel.

> **If you can't win, make the fellow ahead of you break the record.**
>
> AUTHOR UNKNOWN

I remember a mural we had at Baldwin-Wallace College when my dad was the coach. It was the full width of the gymnasium and contained a quote about excellence by Eddie Finnegan, a great track and football coach in the Cleveland area, first at Baldwin-Wallace College and then at Western Reserve University: "It is easy to be ordinary, but it takes courage to excel . . . and we must excel."

That visual reminder became the guiding thought for every athlete at Baldwin-Wallace College—and perhaps for many other students, as well, as they had opportunity to view that giant painting. That's what excellence is all about: the courage to do what it takes to become the best we can be.

It doesn't take much effort to be ordinary. But if God has granted us abilities, we can rise above the crowd by having the *courage* to pursue excellence. And it does take courage to try out for a sport, to sing a song in front of others, or to speak words you've written. Fear of rejection is one of the biggest hurdles in any endeavor, but those who are courageous and take on the challenge will ultimately excel.

"INCREASE IN EXCELLENCE"

The number one expectation within our Ohio State football family is to seek excellence in all phases of our lives. In fact, we identify with the Latin phrase *Macte Virtute* (pronounced *mock*-tay weer-*too*-tay), which means "increase in excellence." We recognize *Macte Virtute* as an imperative statement, a command, to increase in excellence in all we do.

Part of that imperative is making sure our guys understand the difference between our love, care, and concern for them and our desire to help them excel. As we work to help them excel, we're going to critique their performances. Our players' goal sheets state very clearly what they are pursuing in terms of excellence and their specific goals in each area of their lives. Our job as coaches and teachers (and this applies equally to parents and friends) is to help those we love to grow in the areas in which they want to excel, and to give them every opportunity to understand every detail it takes to achieve excellence.

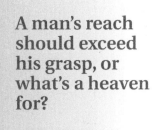

A man's reach should exceed his grasp, or what's a heaven for?

ROBERT BROWNING

Any time we've had a disappointing loss, or even a victory when we didn't play as well as we were capable of playing, we feel disappointment and regret because we know that we could have done better. Our loss to Florida in the BCS championship game that capped our 2006 season was difficult to work through. We knew we could have played better than we did that evening. As the head coach, I felt personally responsible for that, and I found myself constantly reevaluating our performance. What could we have done differently in the game? Were there some aspects of our game preparation that we could have improved? If we had brought certain things to everyone's attention, perhaps we could have solved some problems before they occurred.

Every time we step onto the field and don't do what we're capable of doing, it reflects on our definition of excellence—reaching our full potential. But when we don't live up to our potential, and we didn't in that game against Florida, we can't continue to berate ourselves. We learn from it, and then we store those lessons away so that perhaps some of the errors we made in the past won't be made again.

YOU ARE AT THE TOP WHEN . . .

1. You have made friends with your past, and you are focused on the present and optimistic about your future.
2. You have the love of friends and the respect of your enemies.
3. You are filled with faith, hope, and love, and you live without anger, greed, guilt, envy, or thoughts of revenge.
4. You know that failure to stand for what is morally right is the prelude to being the victim of what is criminally wrong.
5. You are mature enough to delay gratification and shift your focus from your rights to your responsibilities.
6. You love the unlovable, give hope to the hopeless, friendship to the friendless, and encouragement to the discouraged.
7. You know that success (a win) doesn't make you and that failure (a loss) doesn't break you.
8. You can look back in forgiveness, forward in hope, down in compassion, and up with gratitude.
9. You are secure in who (and whose) you are, so you are at peace with God and in fellowship with humanity.
10. You clearly understand that yesterday ended last night, that today is a brand-new day, and it is yours!
11. You know that "he who would be the greatest among you must become the servant of all."
12. You are pleasant to the grouchy, courteous to the rude, and generous to the needy, because you know that the long-term benefits of giving and forgiving far outweigh the short-term benefits of receiving.
13. You recognize, confess, develop, and use your God-given physical, mental, and spiritual abilities to the glory of God and for the benefit of humankind.
14. You stand in front of the Creator of the universe, and he says to you, "Well done, my good and faithful servant."

The list on the previous page was contributed by one of our players a number of years ago. This list illustrates what it means to increase in excellence, especially in the Purpose section of the Block O.

COUNTING THE COST OF EXCELLENCE

When one of our players commits to a written goal, such as gaining admission to medical school, becoming All–Big Ten at his position, being drafted into the NFL, or winning the BCS championship, our first order of business is to help him understand what it will take to attain that level of excellence. Understanding the plan is essential to achieving our goals.

> **Attempt the impossible in order to improve your work.**
>
> BETTE DAVIS

Without question, many of our players have a passion to be drafted by an NFL team. We tell them that the first thing they need to understand is the importance of presenting themselves as young men of excellent character. Second, they must execute to the best of their ability on the game video, week after week, throughout their collegiate career. NFL scouts and coaches evaluate hours and hours of video of every eligible member of a draft class.

On top of all that, the NFL Scouting Combine becomes a deciding factor for eventual draft status. Therefore, our guys need to know what it will take in each and every category to become the best they can be—to excel.

Entering the 2008 NFL draft, defensive lineman Vernon Gholston was generally considered to be a first-round pick. His performance at the NFL Combine and his Pro Day at Ohio State catapulted him into a projected top-ten pick. It was during his team interviews that his genuine character became obvious, and that helped him to become the sixth overall pick in the first round, selected by the New York Jets.

To fully appreciate Vernon's accomplishments, you have to understand the story behind his career. Even though he didn't play organized football until his sophomore year in high school, he used his natural talent and worked hard every single day to increase his excellence in every way. During meetings with the coaches, he sat on the front row, and his ears were always open. Vernon was blessed with a tremendous physical presence, but four key things helped to make him into the football player and person he is today:

1. His willingness to learn and to work hard to improve.
2. His humble attitude toward learning, which showed in his willingness to take instruction.
3. His passion to become the best he could be.
4. His tireless effort to study others who have played his position well.

> I can accept failure. Everyone fails at something. But I can't accept not trying.
>
> MICHAEL JORDAN

Vernon Gholston is a good example of what it means to increase in excellence. He constantly studied himself on film in an effort to take his tremendous physical talent to a higher level. The more he learned about football, the more he wanted to learn. He formulated a plan and then followed through on it. He prepared, sacrificed, and worked hard, and now he's at the point where he can become all he wants to be—an excellent NFL player.

DEFINING EXCELLENCE

If you are seeking to reach your full potential, I would say that you first need to keep in mind that excellence means becoming the best *person* you can possibly be, in whatever discipline or profession you choose. You might be a stellar performer on the field—or in business, or in the classroom—but if you're not living an upright life, or if you haven't paid proper attention to the Purpose components of the Block O of Life, you won't achieve your full potential or true excellence. You must be willing to evaluate yourself as objectively as you can and ask yourself whether you have your priorities in order and whether there's something you could do better.

Of course, we're all human, and there will be times when we won't perform our particular roles as well as we can or as well as we would like. But our *intentions* are just as important as our performance in determining how close we come to reaching our full potential. Even with the best intentions, however, we still must be willing to look at what we could do better.

Sometimes when it comes to seeking excellence, we get caught up in things that are peripheral. A football team might worry about the officials' calls, or how the ball bounced, or other things that are really not within their control. One thing that is *always* within our control—whether it's in football, in business, in our families, or in the church—is our ability to identify what we can do better now and in the future. If we focus on our own contribution—at getting better at what *we* do—we have a much better chance of feeling good about who we are and of moving toward the inner satisfaction and peace of mind that we seek for the good of the group.

> The hallmark of excellence, the test of greatness, is *consistency.*

Excellence takes a great deal of heart, sacrifice, and a willingness to recognize our strengths and weaknesses. And we need to be able to evaluate our strengths objectively and give proper attention to our weaknesses.

For example, I can't sing at all. If I had a passion to be a singer, it would be a long road for me—or perhaps a very short road on *American Idol.* So I probably shouldn't pursue work as a singer, but I have to evaluate my strengths, figure out my talents, and then move toward reaching my potential in the appropriate arena.

There's an important difference between the Purpose section of our lives and the Goals section when it comes to talent and strength. Being a strong, spiritual person who wants a relationship with God does not require a lot of ability; being a strong family person who wants to sacrifice and do all we can for our families, and being a person who cares about others does not take great talent. With some effort, we can all excel in those areas. When it comes to our goals, however, we have to be realistic, evaluate our talents, and then do all we can to become the best we can be.

Coach Jack Johnson, longtime head football coach at Pickerington High School in central Ohio, contributed the following description of excellence:

EXCELLENCE

Going *far* beyond the call of duty,
Doing *more* than others expect,
This is what excellence is all about!
And it comes from *striving,*
Maintaining the *highest* standards,
Looking after the *smallest* detail,
And going the *extra* mile.
Excellence means doing your *very* best.
In *everything!* In *every* way.

JACK JOHNSON

CONSISTENCY: THE HALLMARK OF EXCELLENCE

At Ohio State, the expectations for our football team are extremely high. Anyone who chooses to coach or play for the Buckeyes must understand that clearly. Excellence week in and week out, year in and year out—that is what we seek. And the hallmark of excellence, the test of greatness, is *consistency.*

In order to create that consistency, that excellence, our team must understand *everything* that contributes to a successful team: turnover margin, special teams, running game, run defense, third-down efficiency, red-zone offense and defense, short yardage, and so on.

Understanding your game, your business, and your challenges—and tirelessly perfecting them—are what it's all about.

Dr. E. Gordon Gee, president of Ohio State, is one of the most highly experienced university presidents in the nation. During his thirty-four years in higher education, he has served as president of Brown University, the University of Colorado, and West Virginia University, in addition to a previous stint at Ohio State (1990–1997). He returned to Ohio State in 2007, after two years at Brown and seven years as chancellor of Vanderbilt University. I'll never forget what he said at a press conference shortly after his return. He remarked that what had happened while he was gone was amazing and that OSU was clearly a place of excellence. He expressed his desire to build upon the hard work of those who had put so much into the school, and then he said, "My goal is to take Ohio State from excellence to eminence." That statement was profound, and I made sure we added it to our Winners Manual. Excellence can flow from the highest position of a school or organization and wash downward over individuals and groups. It can also flow upward from seemingly insignificant people who have little rank or position but who take pride in whatever tasks they are given.

> **If you heed your fears, you'll die never knowing what a great person you might have been.**
>
> DR. ROBERT SCHULLER

Use whatever duty you've been assigned today to exemplify excellence, and see what that does for your own peace of mind as well as for the good of your team.

QUESTIONS FOR REFLECTION

1. What can a building or a workplace tell you about an organization's commitment to excellence?

_____

_____

_____

2. Some people respond negatively to the topic of excellence. Why do you think that's so? What could remedy their feelings?

_____

_____

_____

3. What one aspect of your work life comes to mind when you think of excellence? Is it a positive or negative example?

_____

_____

_____

4. Is there something in your life now that you know is not measuring up to the standard of excellence? What can you do to remedy that?

_____

_____

_____

YOUR PERSONAL GAME PLAN

1. *Personal/Family:* It may seem out of the ordinary to think of excellence in terms of your family relationships. But if excellence can be defined as "each person striving to reach his or her full potential," how might this work out in your family today? Is there someone you can encourage toward excellence today?

   _____

   _____

   _____

2. *Spiritual/Moral:* At times, the spiritual aspect of life is referred to as a "resting" in God's grace and goodness. Excellence requires work and striving. How do those two ideas coexist? Does this introduce some tension into your faith? Why or why not?

   _____

   _____

   _____

3. *Caring/Giving:* What does excellence look like in the component of Caring and Giving in your life?

   _____

   _____

   _____

4. *Health/Fitness:* What aspect of your health do you feel you are doing in a way that is not excellent? What would you have to do to change that?

   _____

   _____

   _____

5. *Your Team:* How have you seen someone exhibit excellence on your team? What feeling did it generate in you as you watched? Have you told that person how you feel about his or her example?

_____

_____

_____

6. *Academics/Career:* Learning and advancing in a career takes hard work. Think back over the years to something you've done that you would consider an example of excellence. Who helped you accomplish that goal? Have you told that person how much you appreciate his or her input in your life?

_____

_____

_____

CHAPTER 6

FAITH AND BELIEF

Be courageous! Have faith! Go forward!

THOMAS EDISON

Faith doesn't mean the absence of fear. It means having the energy to go ahead, right alongside the fear.

SHARON SALZBERG

Faith is the confidence that what we hope for will actually happen; it gives us assurance about things we cannot see.

HEBREWS 11:1

The Hall of Fame is only good as long as time shall be, but keep in mind, God's Hall of Fame is for eternity! To have your name inscribed up there is greater more by far, than all the fame and all the praise of every man-made star!

AUTHOR UNKNOWN

The section on Faith and Belief is always one of our team's favorites. When the players give their senior speeches, they often talk about this fundamental as having been a key to their growth and development.

As we've seen in studying the Block O, success is a journey. It is defined not by those outside of us—who give us awards or bestow honor—or even by our winning of championships. The true measure of success is whether we feel good about our ability to contribute to whatever team we're on. Ultimately then, to have a successful journey, we must have the faith and belief that we can and will be successful. It is vital that we be equipped and prepared for the journey and that we constantly remind ourselves of our ultimate purpose.

Faith and belief are not merely tools we use to pull ourselves up by our bootstraps and forge ahead blindly. There's a substance to our faith.

There's an object for our belief. The result is an assurance that *we can do the job* as we interact with others, have our personal quiet times of study, and cultivate the confidence we need to pursue our goals. If we don't have a deep-seated faith and belief in the plan, the preparation, and each other, we won't achieve our objectives.

There are two components to the fundamental of faith and belief: (1) the faith people have in something bigger than themselves and (2) the belief they have in themselves and what they're doing.

Faith is part of the Purpose segment of your life on the Block O. *Belief* is part of your Goals, as you live your life according to your faith.

Faith is who you are. Belief is what you do with your faith.

Many of our players will say that their faith is what gives them confidence. Faith is the rock they lean on as they strive to achieve in all areas of their lives. Ultimately, they're reflecting on their faith and counting on their faith. And it's the practice of their faith, their spiritual plan, that gives them the edge of confidence.

> # Champions believe in themselves even if no one else does.
>
> AUTHOR UNKNOWN

Our players invest a lot of time in their personal faith plans and their spiritual plans. Fortunately, on campus there are a lot of opportunities for them to grow in those areas. Ohio State has programs or groups for every faith tradition to help students grow in their particular faith mission. Many of our guys are leaders on campus, outside of football and their academic pursuits, and they're leaders in helping others grow in their faith. Some are very active in Bible studies or fellowship groups, such as Athletes in Action, Fellowship of Christian Athletes, or Campus Crusade for Christ. Many of our guys complement their own faith journeys by taking leadership roles in faith-related groups and inviting other students to join them.

THE MAIN EVENT

On the day that Joel Penton first came to Ohio State, he set a plan that he was going to be the best football player he could be. He played defensive tackle and really knew how to run hard and put people on the ground. He wanted to excel as a student while he was here as well, but ultimately his number one focus was his faith and his desire to share that with others and lead others. Some guys dream about the NFL. Joel's dream was to be a minister.

In 2006, he was playing as a fifth-year senior, and he had one class left in order to graduate. The previous spring, he had come to me and said, "Coach, I've had the opportunity to go out and share with a lot of youth groups and churches, and it's been great. But I'd like to do something big. I'd like to do something beyond all of that."

"Well, Joel," I said, "what do you have in mind?"

"I want to have a big event. I want to invite people to come and hear what really makes me tick—and what makes a lot of the other guys tick too. I want to plan it, market it, and be responsible for all the details. And I want you to speak." His purpose was to reach Buckeye fans and people in Central Ohio who knew the players in their uniforms but didn't necessarily know anything about them personally. He wanted people to know what was really important to the players outside of football and how faith had made a difference in their lives.

> I think when you move past your fear and you go after your dreams wholeheartedly, you become free. Know what I'm saying? Move past the fear.
>
> L L COOL J

I told him to go for it. But I also warned him of the realities. "It's going to be a lot of work. Plus, there are some things you have to do. Students have every right to talk about their faith on campus, as long as they do it according to the letter of the law."

Joel agreed and set his plan in motion. He wondered if they should have the meeting in a baseball stadium, like some of the Billy Graham crusades. But because they were scheduling the event for October and considering the potential for weather problems during that time of year, they decided to hold it in the St. John Arena on campus.

The arena holds more than thirteen thousand people, and I remember thinking when I first heard about the event that it was going to be tough to get a lot of people out on a Monday night in late October. I wanted to make sure Joel knew that his journey through this experience was the most important part, so I kept telling him, "Joel, you know it doesn't matter how many people actually show up at this. Even if it's just a few hundred, it'll be a success, because you're going to learn a lot through the process."

He'd nod and then come back and tell me they might need to rent two arenas. I'd try to calm him down a little, but he was really fired up about it.

Joel sought out a professor who would allow him to do an independent study and make the production of the event his final class. He would set up the whole thing, do all the marketing, planning, and organizing, all the partnering with other groups, and he would also coordinate the security and support staff. He got a group of students interested in helping, and they started having meetings to work out the details. A lot of Joel's Buckeye teammates expressed interest, and they also partnered with Cedarville University, a private Christian school about fifty miles from Ohio State. Joel's committee got nearly one hundred churches involved, as well as Campus Crusade for Christ, Athletes in Action, and the Fellowship of Christian Athletes.

> **The future belongs to those who believe in the beauty of their dreams.**
>
> ELEANOR ROOSEVELT

Joel invited me to a couple of the meetings, and each month those meetings got bigger. Before long, they filled a lecture hall. Joel told me that they were calling their evening "The Main Event," and he was so excited as the day approached. Again, I reminded him of how much he had learned in the process of developing his idea and that just reaching a few people would make the event a success. But Joel wasn't through with his plan.

He went to the OSU marching band and asked if any of them would be interested in participating. As it turned out, most of them took part. He went to the cheerleaders and said, "If any of you want to be part of this, you're welcome." Virtually all of the cheerleaders were there. Everything was snowballing, and there was no doubt it would be a success from a programming standpoint. The only question was whether anyone would show up.

During the football season, Monday night is a busy night for coaches, and I had told Joel that my priority and main responsibility were to the team and the staff but that I'd be glad to come over and speak for a few minutes. Shortly before the big day, he said to me, "Coach, I know you can't be there for the whole thing because it's an in-season game-plan night, so I'll have a campus police car pick you up."

Our football offices and facility are only about a mile from the arena, so I said, "I'll just drive over myself."

"No, I'll get you there real quick," he said, "and it won't be a mob scene or anything."

I reminded him again that it didn't matter how many people showed up. I probably was afraid he would be disappointed by the turnout. He'd had people handing out invitations at the home game the previous Saturday, and I could tell he was really hoping a lot of people would attend.

As it turned out, attendance was not going to be a problem. The afternoon of the event, we started getting word that people were lining up hours before the doors opened. And Joel was right—I needed that police car to get through the crowd. When I arrived, the program had already started, and when I walked into the arena, I was stunned. The place was *full*. A lot of our student

> To disbelieve is easy; to scoff is simple; to have faith is harder.
>
> LOUIS L'AMOUR

athletes were on stage, they had video inserts and humor, and everything about the evening was done well. In every way, The Main Event achieved the goal that Joel had set: to allow himself, several of his teammates, and his coach to share the role that faith had played in their lives.

As part of the program, volunteers passed out cards for people to fill out if they wanted further information or wanted to be contacted about growing in their faith. As I understand it, thousands of those cards were completed and returned.

It was a real tribute to Joel and his teammates that they were proud of their faith and wanted to share it. And it was great to see young people take the lead like that and have an impact on people's lives. That's true leadership, and it shows what a difference faith can make.

Belief

> *Faith is believing what we do not see. The reward of faith is to see what we believe.*
>
> **AUGUSTINE**

Belief is centered more in the individual, and it represents a strong, internal feeling that suggests, "I can do this." At its core is an ability to move forward because of the evidence the person can see. He or she says, "I believe in the people I'm with; I believe in the preparation I've had; I believe in the plan that's in place."

That kind of thinking deep in the soul is the final piece of the puzzle in our search for a successful journey. Take Joel Penton's Main Event, for example. He had done the dreaming about that night. He really wanted people to take away something special from the event. So he put his plan of action to work, making the details come together, handling the adversity that came his way with different scheduling problems and the weather question. But through all the ups and downs, he had to believe he could do it, that people would come, that he wouldn't get so excited he'd forget his speech, that God would honor the mission, and that Joel would feel good about the journey.

Another good story about belief comes from our 1991 team at Youngstown State. When you're in Division I-AA football, the pinnacle of achievement is to progress to the play-offs and win the national championship. We had been talking about that goal since the first day I got there in 1986. We'd worked hard to build the team. We'd had some losing seasons and some winning seasons in which we went to the play-offs but didn't advance. In 1989, we had advanced two rounds, and we were starting to feel as if we understood what it was going to take to reach the top.

In 1990, we were 11-0 during the regular season and had a great year. We were up at the top of the rankings and then lost to Central Florida in the first round of the play-offs on a last-second field goal. But even in that loss, you could tell that our guys were learning a lot about what it takes to succeed.

We went into 1991 with a good group and every reason for optimism, but after seven games, our record was 4-3. Our prospects for making the play-offs didn't look good. That wasn't the path we'd hoped to take. We thought we were a lot better than that. And to make matters worse, we were getting ready to play

> **We are only beaten when we cease to believe what we can be.**
>
> AUTHOR UNKNOWN

Georgia Southern, which had won a bunch of national championships in the mid to late 1980s and in 1990. They were the standard of excellence at that point. They had begun a football program in the early 1980s and had an extraordinary run to the top. They were virtually unbeatable on their home field at Paulson Stadium.

The night before the game, we were not at the height of our confidence. If we lost the next day, we'd be 4-4, and it would pretty much be over as far as the play-offs were concerned. The team we were playing was tough, and there were a lot of reasons to waver in our belief.

However, at our team meeting, our captain, Kevin Brown, stepped up and gave the best speech I've ever heard on belief. He chronicled all the preparation we had done. He pointed out, position by position, why our team was up to the task ahead. He exuded confidence and challenged every person in the room to believe we could win. And he said, "If you don't believe, there's no way we can be successful against a team like the one we're getting ready to play."

Sometimes something happens in a locker room or at a team meeting or when you're on the road for an away game, and you feel as if there is something going on that is bigger than that particular meeting. There's something happening in the room that you didn't expect, a chemistry that's coming together.

I don't know how long Kevin's speech lasted. Maybe just a few minutes. But I don't think anyone took a breath throughout his entire talk. The message was loud and clear: We would not see any of our dreams come true if we didn't believe. What I learned that night is that our captain believed more than I did. He probably believed more than anyone else in the room did. But he wasn't going to let that room *not* believe.

> Nobody will believe in you unless you believe in yourself.
>
> LIBERACE

The next day, we went out and played an amazing football game. Not only did we have Georgia Southern to contend with and a Paulson Stadium crowd that was quite intimidating, but there was also a 30–40 mph wind blowing throughout the game. Still, with 5:40 left to go in the fourth quarter, we were ahead 19-17.

As the clock continued to wind down, we were faced with a fourth-and-one situation at our own 29 yard line. With all that wind, we knew if we punted the ball, it would go about twelve yards, and Georgia Southern would kick a field goal and win. But if we went for it and didn't make the first down, they'd get the ball right there at the 29, with an even better chance of kicking a game-winning field goal. After talking it over on the sideline, we decided to go for the first down—and we made it.

A few plays later, we again faced a fourth-and-one situation—this time at our own 39. The other team's defense was digging in, trying to stop us. But our guys were ready. We went for it again, and again we made it.

On the next set of downs, things became even more desperate. Instead of having another short-yardage situation, we had something like eight yards to go on third down. But again, our guys rose to the occasion, our quarterback completed a pass for another first down, and we were able to run out the clock without Georgia Southern ever touching the ball during that last 5:40.

That game ignited a spark in our team. We not only won the rest of our games that season, but we were also able to advance in the play-offs. And it just so happened that the national-championship game that year was going to be played in Paulson Stadium at Georgia Southern.

There was a little creek running through the Georgia Southern campus in Statesboro. It was called Eagle Creek, and the talk was always that there was great magic in that water. So on our way out of town to the airport that day after beating Georgia Southern, we stopped the bus, got a jar, and dipped out some of that water. We told the guys we were going to take it back to Youngstown and mix it with Mahoning River water, which was full of steel by-products and industrial waste. We said that it was going to be our magic potion when we came back to Paulson Stadium seven weeks later. We were going to take our potion, sprinkle it on the field, and have our own magic to win the championship.

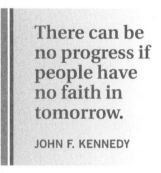

There can be no progress if people have no faith in tomorrow.

JOHN F. KENNEDY

When we made it to the championship game, against Marshall University, we took that odiferous concoction of creek and river water, which was even worse after seven weeks of aging, and poured it on the field. Then we went out and won the game, kicking off a four-year run in which we made it to the championship game every year and won it three times.

Anyone associated with that 1991 team would tell you that Kevin Brown's exhortation about belief was the key to the whole season. Of course, those fourth-down conversions, a good defense, and disciplined play were big parts of it as well, but I don't know that any of that would have been enough without Kevin's reminder about belief. Ultimately, you have to believe in what you are doing in order to be successful and to have a chance to achieve your goals.

THE FOUNDATION OF FAITH

Faith and belief are really two sides of the same coin. Having faith means placing your trust in something much bigger than yourself. Faith is the bedrock of a winner. It's what anchors you. It's the foundation for everything you do, and thus it's part of who you are.

Belief has more to do with what you're trying to accomplish. It's more personal. It's what you *do* rather than who you are. Belief is the outward expression of an inner faith. As we said before, faith is tied to your *purpose,* whereas belief is more a part of your *goals.*

> All I have seen teaches me to trust the Creator for all I have not seen.
>
> RALPH WALDO EMERSON

At Joel Penton's Main Event, I think people were eager to hear from him and the other players because they admired the way our guys carried themselves, the way they played on the field, and the way they worked hard for their success. If Joel and his teammates had not reflected their faith in their goals, in the way they played their hearts out on the field, or how they acted off the field, I'm not sure as many people would have shown up to hear what they had to say. If they had talked one way about their faith but acted another way, people would have seen the contradiction and wouldn't have been as interested in listening.

As it was, the testimony of the lives of those players both on and off the field piqued people's interest. "What is it with those guys? What's important to them? I want to know more." That's what people were saying that night when they came.

I've used "The Guy in the Glass" every year since I began compiling the Winners Manual. But one year, for some reason, it was left out of the final printing. Bobby Carpenter, who now plays for the Dallas Cowboys, came to me during the preseason and said, "Coach, my favorite poem, the one I look forward to reading every year, isn't in the book."

I went to my assistant, Deb, and asked, "What did I do?"

Every year, I try to add a little and edit some things, but I had every

THE GUY IN THE GLASS

When you get what you want in your struggle for pelf,
And the world makes you King for a day,
Then go to the mirror and look at yourself,
And see what that guy has to say.

For it isn't your Father, or Mother, or Wife,
Who judgment upon you must pass.
The feller whose verdict counts most in your life
Is the guy staring back from the glass.

He's the feller to please, never mind all the rest,
For he's with you clear up to the end,
And you've passed your most dangerous, difficult test
If the guy in the glass is your friend.

You may be like Jack Horner and "chisel" a plum,
And think you're a wonderful guy,
But the man in the glass says you're only a bum
If you can't look him straight in the eye.

You can fool the whole world down the pathway of years,
And get pats on the back as you pass,
But your final reward will be heartaches and tears
If you've cheated the guy in the glass.

DALE WIMBROW

intention of keeping that poem in there. And it just shows that there are certain things that can't be anticipated. I have no idea how certain quotes, stories, or poems will speak to these guys, and sometimes even an unintentional omission or change will get their attention.

That preseason, we copied "The Guy in the Glass," handed it to the players, and said, "Fold this up and put it in your book, because we left it out."

THE GAME OF LIFE

The game of life is not played with pads and helmets. It's a day-to-day high-wire act without a net. And the thing that drives us, that pushes us forward step by step and ultimately directs our course, is our faith. Boiled down, faith is who we are on the inside. That's what the guys who spoke at the Main Event wanted to portray—who they really were as men, without the trappings of the uniform and the statistics.

Faith is embodied in our purpose. At the bottom of the Block O, we focus on our ability to journey toward our goals and successfully reach them. The main component of that journey is a belief that we can achieve, that we *will* achieve, and that we aren't plagued by questions about our ability.

> Behind every great achievement is a dreamer of great dreams.
>
> ROBERT K. GREENLEAF

I find with our guys and with groups I talk to that there's often some hesitation in people. *Can I really do this? I know I want to, but can I really do it?* It's a constant mental quiz they're taking every day. Having a deep-seated belief helps so much on the journey, and that belief is bolstered by preparation and practice and constant work on the fundamentals. But even with all the preparation and handling what comes our way, at the end of the day we have to *believe* we can reach our goals, or it's not going to happen.

FAITH IN THE PUBLIC ARENA

I'm asked a lot about living out my faith in the setting of a public university, but I don't think it's any different being a Christian where I am than if I were selling cars or making computers in a factory. My job is a little higher profile than those, but that's the only difference. We all encounter people of different faiths, and we all have a responsibility to be aware of other people's thoughts, feelings, and beliefs. As a Christian, I never want to set myself above another person or infer that *I know and you don't. I get it and you don't.* I always want to have an inclusive

THE MAN WHO THINKS HE CAN

If you think you're beaten, you are;
If you think you dare not, you don't.
If you'd like to win but think you can't,
It's almost a cinch you won't.
If you think you'll lose, you're lost,
For out in the world we find
Success begins with a fellow's will;
It's all in the state of mind.

Full many a race is lost
Ere ever a step is run,
And many a coward fails
Ere ever his work's begun.
Think big, and your deeds will grow;
Think small and you'll fall behind.
Think that you can, and you will;
It's all in the state of mind.

If you think you're outclassed, you are;
You've got to think high to rise.
You've got to be sure of yourself before
You can ever win a prize.
Life's battles don't always go
To the stronger or faster man,
But soon or late the man who wins
Is the fellow who thinks he can.
It's all in the state of mind!

WALTER D. WINTLE

demeanor, yet when it comes down to it, I want other people to ask, "Why does he conduct himself this way? Why does he invest so much in his spiritual plan for his life?" I'm not afraid to answer those questions when someone is curious.

Obviously, when it comes to sharing my faith and my life, some venues are easier than others. I make sure when I give a talk about my faith that I'm not speaking on behalf of Ohio State but that I'm there on my own behalf. I present it as what I happen to believe. Seldom do I speak about my faith unless I've been invited. I don't say, "We're going to have an event, and I'm going to tell you what I believe." Typically a group will ask me to speak—but even then I think it's important to have compassion for what others think and an awareness that there are other schools of thought.

Those outside our belief systems will evaluate whether or not they should consider our beliefs as they observe the way we live. My hope is that when people observe me—whether it's on the job, in the neighborhood, at church, or at the store—they'll see something they'd like to know more about. It's just like Joel Penton and the players who spoke at the Main Event. People had observed those young men countless times on the football field, but Joel wanted people to come and hear what made them tick. And I can tell you that his message that night was no different from what it would have been if he'd had only six people in the room.

> Faith is the bird that feels the light and sings when the dawn is still dark.
>
> RABINDRANATH TAGORE

After the Super Bowl in 2006, Lovie Smith, head coach of the Chicago Bears, spoke at a prayer breakfast in Columbus. I took my seniors to the event because I couldn't fit in everybody from the team. I had one senior who was of another faith, and I didn't want to exclude him. So I asked, "Would you be comfortable going to something like this?" I mean, it was Lovie Smith of the Bears. This guy could end up playing for him someday.

"Oh, Coach, I'd love to come," he said. So he was at the prayer breakfast.

In whatever I do, I go out of my way to include others. The Jewish community in Columbus knows where I'm coming from with my Christian beliefs, but I make a special effort to be a part of their causes and needs because I know the platform I have at Ohio State is helpful to many.

IT COULDN'T BE DONE

Somebody said that it couldn't be done,
But he, with a chuckle, replied
That "maybe it couldn't," but he would be one
Who wouldn't say so till he'd tried.
So he buckled right in, with a trace of a grin
On his face. If he worried, he hid it.
He started to sing as he tackled the thing
That couldn't be done, and he did it.

Somebody scoffed: "Oh, you'll never do that;
At least no one ever has done it."
But he took off his coat, and he took off his hat,
And the first thing we knew, he'd begun it;
With the lift of his chin, and a bit of a grin,
Without any doubting or quiddit;
He started to sing as he tackled the thing
That couldn't be done, and he did it.

There are thousands to tell you it cannot be done;
There are thousands to prophesy failure;
There are thousands to point out to you, one by one,
The dangers that wait to assail you;
But just buckle right in, with a bit of a grin,
Then take off your coat and go to it;
Just start in to sing as you tackle the thing
That "cannot be done," and you'll do it!

EDGAR A. GUEST

I don't say, "No, that's a different faith, and I don't want to help them." I'm happy to do it.

When you think about it, Jesus did the same thing. He often spent time with people who were different, had a different faith, or had no faith. I believe we're called to do what is Christlike rather than say, "I'm a Christian. Look at me." I don't really care about labels.

When I think about what it means to be a Christian, I think it is more about how I live than how I label myself. Jesus once said to his disciples, "If you love me, you will obey what I command" (John 14:15, NIV). Obeying Jesus means doing what he says—but just as important, it means doing what he did. Rather than plaster a big sign around my neck to make sure everyone knows I'm a Christian, I think that Jesus wants me to simply follow his way.

It's the same with coaching: Is my ultimate goal to have my players all call me Coach, or is it to have them hear my teaching and grow through it? I believe Christ is much more interested in our living and growing through his message than he is in our calling ourselves Christians. In our lives, God wants us to love and serve all people, just as it is my responsibility to coach all of my players and not discriminate—for any conceivable reason.

> Our doubts
> are traitors
>
> And make
> us lose the
> good we oft
> might win
>
> By fearing to
> attempt.
>
> WILLIAM SHAKESPEARE,
> *MEASURE FOR MEASURE*

Jim Schmidtke is our Athletes in Action representative. He runs a Bible study for the coaching staff, and I've known him for more than twenty-five years. We had a discussion once when he was deciding whether to send his children to a Christian school or to the public school. Really, both answers are fine, depending on how a family sees its values and its goals, but part of our discussion that day was that if we're all at the Christian school, we're secluding ourselves, which is the opposite of what Christ would like us to do. He wants us to engage the culture and make a difference.

I don't find it uncomfortable at all to live out my faith in a public setting. But I do think it's important to go the extra mile with people who don't necessarily believe what I do. I want them to think, *Hmm, he treats me better than some people who believe what I do.* I think that's a little of what Jesus did with his life.

Belief, to my way of thinking, is taking the faith you have and activating it. You believe in the team, so you play hard. You believe in each other.

You trust the guy in front of you to block the linebacker who's coming to get you. You trust that the guys on your right and left are going to push through the line with all their might to tackle the guy with the ball. But first, you have to believe.

Regardless of what aspect of life you want to name, whether it's about your faith or your family or a work assignment, nothing worthwhile is going to happen unless you believe. That's why when we present success as a journey, we talk about having a plan and dreams. And then we have to go to work on those plans and dreams, all the while handling adversity and success. The key to all that is belief. Belief that we can do the task. Belief that we *will* do the task. Active believing reinforces the other fundamentals and helps make us winners.

QUESTIONS FOR REFLECTION

1. Faith is an inside job that works its way out in our lives, but many people look only at the "doing" of faith (such as going to church, praying, etc.). How has this chapter challenged your thinking about faith and belief?

_____

_____

_____

2. It's one thing to talk about faith; it's another to live out what you believe. Why do you think it's difficult for people to live what they say they believe?

_____

_____

_____

3. Think of a time in your life when a difficult task overwhelmed you. How did a belief in yourself help? Or, how did a lack of belief in yourself hurt you?

_____

_____

_____

4. In the poem "The Guy in the Glass," the writer makes it clear that you are the person you have to please in order to feel successful. Is it difficult for you to look in the mirror for any reason? If so, what can you do to change that?

_____

_____

_____

YOUR PERSONAL GAME PLAN

1. *Personal/Family:* Is there someone in your family who has believed in you no matter what? Why not thank that person today for his or her support?

_____

_____

_____

2. *Spiritual/Moral:* Is there some dream or desire you have regarding your faith, like Joel Penton's Main Event? What steps could you take to make your dream a reality?

_____

_____

_____

3. *Caring/Giving:* Sharing your faith in a gentle way is one of the most caring, giving things you can do. Who is one person with whom you could do that this week?

_____

_____

_____

4. *Health/Fitness:* Is there some goal regarding your health that you have a hard time believing you can achieve? Think about what preparation and action you can put into place this week to reach that goal.

_____

_____

_____

5. *Your Team:* What struggle is your team going through right now? How could your example of belief in the team help change things?

_____

_____

_____

6. *Academics/Career:* Are there academic or career goals about which you feel less than confident? What can you do to remedy that lack of confidence?

_____

_____

_____

CHAPTER 7

WORK

Whenever you start—give it your best. The opportunities are there to be anything you want to be. But wanting to be someone isn't enough; dreaming about it isn't enough; thinking about it isn't enough. You've got to study for it, work for it, fight for it with all your heart and soul, because nobody is going to hand it to you.

GENERAL COLIN POWELL

I've read that I flew up the hills and mountains of France. But you don't fly up a hill. You struggle slowly and painfully up a hill, and maybe, if you work very hard, you get to the top ahead of everybody else.

LANCE ARMSTRONG

Success doesn't come to you . . . you go to it.

MARVA COLLINS

Work is love made visible.

KHALIL GIBRAN

Work willingly at whatever you do, as though you were working for the Lord rather than for people.

COLOSSIANS 3:23

It's important to understand that work is not who you are; it's what you do. Many people get that backward and think their lives are defined by what they accomplish or by what positions they hold. On the negative side, some define their lives by something bad that happened to them or by something negative they did. But you have to go back to the original concept of the Block O and work through all the components to get Work in perspective.

Work is one part of the journey of your life. It's part of your spiritual journey. There are mornings or evenings when you don't want to have your quiet time. And there's probably no harder work than prayer. It can be work just sitting in church or in a fellowship of some sort and listening attentively. Marriage is work. Parenting is work.

Growth in each of the six of components of the Block O requires work. In this chapter, we'll consider the importance of work, persistence, and toughness in life. As you'll see, if you want to leave a mark on the lives of people around you, it takes intentional living.

Much of the Work section in the OSU Winners Manual features quotations from famous people who shed some light on the subject. Some of these quotations have stuck with our players throughout the years, and I'm glad to share them with you throughout this chapter.

> **Even if you're on the right track, you'll get run over if you just sit there.**
>
> WILL ROGERS

No matter what endeavor you pursue in life, if you want to succeed, you're going to have to work at it. As kids, we thought football was pure fun. We'd get a group of our buddies together and find a field to play. Those were fun days. I've always felt there's a lot you can learn about people from how they play. But at some point, if playing football is what you choose to do with your life, there's going to be an element of hardship and toil. Likewise, a musician who chooses to master the piano will tell you that she loves music. But to truly do justice to the instrument, a pianist must practice hours every day, even after she becomes accomplished. Someone who wants to become a writer must take the time to study and learn more about the craft. Many people say, "I know I have a book in me," but until they sit down and put words on the page, it's just talk.

Some guys with a lot of natural talent come into our program at Ohio State and are blown away by the amount of study football takes. These are guys who were always the best players in youth football and in high school, and some have leaned on their talent to make up for any deficiencies in their fundamentals or work ethic. At the collegiate level, and certainly at the professional level, you can't get away with that. It takes a lot of work, a lot of conditioning, lots of repetitions each day, and then building on the knowledge you've gained until you get to a certain level of proficiency. And after you get to that point, it takes even more work to stay there.

Michael Jordan once said, "Coaches or players can say anything they want, but if they don't back it up with performance and hard work, the talking doesn't mean a thing."

That's how success is achieved. You work at it bit by bit, day by day, one step here, another there. You fall, you get up, and you keep going.

WORK IS A LIFELONG PURSUIT

My grandfather was a dairy farmer, and he never took a day off. Those cows had to get rid of their milk every day. My grandfather not only worked hard, but he was also the most spiritual

> Coaches and players can say anything they want, but if they don't back it up with performance and hard work, the talking doesn't mean a thing.
>
> **MICHAEL JORDAN**

man I ever knew. He died at age eighty-seven, sitting in his rocking chair, his Bible in his lap, opened to Psalm 23. I remember when I was an assistant at Ohio State, sitting by my grandfather out on the porch and talking about life. Death didn't scare him at all. He had a heart issue and a bit of cancer, but he was still farming into his eighties. He loved that he was providing people with something important, something sustaining, and he farmed with a passion.

Believe it or not, my grandfather was actually excited at the prospect of death. He knew the answer to the question that Bobby Richardson asked when I was a kid: "If the game of life ended today, would you be a winner?"

Given how much time my grandfather invested in his dairy farm, it would have been easy for him to define himself by his profession. All he did was work. I'm not sure where the concept of a forty-hour workweek came from, but it sure wasn't from my granddad. Nevertheless, he was one of the most well-rounded people I've ever known. He gave to people. He cared. He made time for his family. There's no question you have to find the balance between your work and all those other things.

I'm in my mid-fifties now, and many of my friends are over sixty and still working. I met a woman on an airplane who was sixty-five. She said she had recently retired—and she hated it. She said she loathed the lack of interaction with people, so now she was back to working part-time.

Bruce Beard, a friend and mentor in the pension business, is one of the strongest Christians I know. He studies apologetics at Oxford and is just a brilliant guy. I remember him sitting with my mom and me talking about her future when she was in her sixties. Bruce said, "Even though there are some people who have made retirement a grand dream—'I have four more years until I retire'—there's nothing in the Bible that talks about retirement."

> Stopping a piece of work just because it's hard, either emotionally or imaginatively, is a bad idea. Sometimes you have to go on when you don't feel like it.
>
> STEPHEN KING

Other coaches have certainly taught me a lot about what it means to work. Tom Landry, the famous coach of the Dallas Cowboys, used to say that you need something to believe in, someone to love, and something to do.

Of course, I grew up in a coach's household, watching my dad every day, and the lessons became even more real when I trained under Jim Dennison at the University of Akron, Tom Reed at Miami of Ohio, Dick MacPherson at Syracuse, and Earle Bruce at Ohio State. Those men taught me firsthand how to work hard and work smart.

I worked with a group of assistant coaches night and day. We all dreamed of being head coaches one day, but until then we were going to be the finest assistant coaches in America. Guys like Glen Mason, Gary Blackney, Bob Tucker, Dom Capers, and Mark Dantonio all worked their way to the top and became very fine head coaches.

Naturally, the workers I admire every day are our players and coaches.

They are passionate about their daily tasks, and for them, at times, work looks like it's more fun than fun itself.

I really admire people who have found a seamless transition in life. They've worked for a while, a lot of hours every week. They know what it means to put their nose to the grindstone and get things done. Then there are folks who have worked the eighty- to one-hundred-hour weeks and now want to work only fifty. I say they're the best workforce you can find, because they know who they are and they know they're not the right ones for the hundred-hour jobs. They're not the principals anymore. They're not the football coaches or the teachers, but they still want to be around kids and help them.

I have five guys on my staff whom we call academic encouragers. They're retired educators who work two or three days a week. They're out on campus; they make sure my guys are in class; they sit and build relationships with them, talk about school, talk about football, talk about the ups and downs of life. It's perfect for them because that's what they love to do, and we have a need in that area.

> Work is the foundation of all business, the source of all prosperity,
>   and the parent of genius.
> Work can do more to advance a youth than his own parents,
>   be they ever so wealthy.
> It is represented in the humblest savings and has laid the
>   foundation of every fortune.
> It is the salt that gives life its savor, but it must be loved before it
>   can bestow its greatest blessing and achieve its greatest ends.
> When loved, work makes life sweet, purposeful, and fruitful.
>
> AUTHOR UNKNOWN

WORK IS PART OF THE FABRIC OF OUR LIVES

The truth is, work is really a gift from God. In the beginning, God gave people meaningful work to do. It's part of the fabric of our lives. And I've always believed that anything good in life takes effort. That's why in the

Block O, none of the elements can be accomplished without energy. If you want to keep your body healthy, it takes work. If you want to advance in your career, you have to work at it. Your conscious desire to care and give to others takes work. Your spiritual life takes work. Your family life takes work. And I guess it's an individual decision where you'll invest your time and energy in each of those areas, but my job as the head coach is to make sure that it isn't all about football for my players and coaches. There's a balance between each element of the Block O. I've had guys who have even gotten a little too carried away with community outreach. Athletes can get caught up with the pats on the back and the good feelings. Some people can get so excited about exercise that it becomes the thing that drives them: "I'm going to run that marathon or do the triathlon."

> Success is the intersection where dreams and hard work meet.

There's nothing essentially wrong with those pursuits, but they have to be kept in balance with everything else.

Work is universal. Work is required in all phases of life. You don't inherit a deep spiritual life. You're not going to wake up one day and find you have good relationships with your children or your grandkids. You don't "discover" a good marriage; you have to work at it. But when some people talk about work, their only point of reference seems to be the number of hours they spend on the job—as if that's the only way to gauge it.

KEEPING WORK IN PERSPECTIVE

You hear a lot about the work ethic of NFL coaches. How some will sleep at the office a few nights a week, for example. I'm not sure I believe all that. Some of those stories are legends.

Having said that, I know that coaches can get work out of whack at times. We place far too much importance on our preparation and planning. But all of us have to find our own ways of doing things. There's no question that balance is tough, especially when we love what we do and want to do it with passion.

On the flip side, I'm sure a certain percentage of the population avoids giving an honest day's work. They stare at their computer screens all day and don't do the company's work—and then wonder why there are cutbacks.

One thing we do in the OSU Winners Manual is provide an in-season weekly schedule. We outline rules of personal conduct, and one guideline in particular seems to prevent a lot of problems. We tell our players not to be out past 10 p.m. We tell them, "Nothing good is going to happen after 10 p.m. You might survive it, nothing bad might happen, but nothing good is going to happen either." We also tell our coaches, "Any play you devise, any idea you come up with after ten o'clock is not going to work in the game."

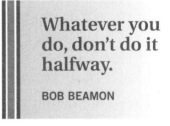

Whatever you do, don't do it halfway.

BOB BEAMON

If you asked our players about us coaches, they'd say, "Those guys are always working." Compared to them, we are, because we're not going to class and football is all we concentrate on. But we try to balance the schedule, and if we work a few late nights, then we take some mornings off.

Some athletes in our society want to get an edge by using performance enhancers. One of our rules of conduct centers on drug usage. We tell the players there will be no sympathy for drug users of any sort. "If you need an upper of any kind to get ready to play," I tell them, "do us all a favor and quit the team. There is no drug that improves an athlete's performance. What improves you is *hard work.*"

It's important to get work in its proper perspective, to see it for the gift it is, and to use it for the good of your team.

HOW DO YOU SEE IT?

Two stone cutters were asked what they were doing.

The first one said, "I'm cutting this stone into blocks."

The second one replied, "I'm on a team that's building a cathedral."

Every guy I've ever coached at Youngstown State or at Ohio State knows about the gazelles and the lions. This is one story they always talk about. And we always tell this story the night before the most challenging day of preseason: the running test.

> Every morning in Africa, a gazelle wakes up. It knows it
> must run faster than the fastest lion or it will be killed.
> Every morning, the lion wakes up. It knows it must
> outrun the slowest gazelle or it will starve to death.
> It doesn't matter whether you are a lion or a gazelle,
> when the sun comes up, you'd better be running!

The running test is challenging because it's just plain hard. It taxes the mind and body with a combination of sprints and endurance. We begin in three groups, the cheetahs, the lions, and the bears. Players line up on one sideline, run the fifty-three yards across the field, touch the other sideline, and run back. The cheetahs have to do it in sixteen seconds, the lions in eighteen seconds, and the bears in twenty seconds. They get a thirty-second rest, and then they do it again. We do the drill twenty times.

The players have to have speed, or they won't complete the drill on time, so there's an aerobic component. And because they have to slow down and change directions at the sidelines, there's an anaerobic component as well. After ten repetitions, we add one second to the completion time and extend the rest time to forty-five seconds.

Now, if you want to talk about work, at the end of the running test those guys know what they're made of. But they also know they're not just running to stay busy. There's a point to all our conditioning work. It's making our players stronger. It's showing them that they have endurance and that they're up to the task ahead of them.

On the journey to success, after we've made all our preparations—the goals and blueprints and dreams—the next step is to work toward those goals. To do that, we need two qualities that are vital to our work: *persistence* and *toughness*.

Persistence

Nothing in this world can take the place of persistence. Talent will not; nothing is more common than unsuccessful men with talent. Genius will not; unrewarded genius is almost a proverb. Education alone will not; the world is full of educated failures. Persistence and determination alone are omnipotent.

CALVIN COOLIDGE

Persistence is the key to the success of any team, business, endeavor, or person. We have a page in the Winners Manual that the guys come back to again and again. It says, "Whatever you do, do it passionately. Failure is an event, not a person. Every obstacle presents an opportunity . . . *if* you're looking for it. Relax! You only fail when you quit."

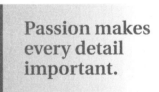

Passion makes every detail important.

G. K. CHESTERTON

A player's career is not defined by one event. A fumble, an interception, or a bad decision that costs the team does not mark him for his career—unless he allows it to. Many people have had something bad happen to them, and they've allowed that *thing,* whatever it is, to define them. Maybe they made a poor decision when they were younger, and now they're living in the shadow of it. It could be a disease, a bad family of origin, or the loss of something dearly loved.

Persistence is a quality possessed by people who want to achieve. If they have a passionate desire to succeed, the goal becomes much more important than the obstacles thrown in their way. They realize that a single event, failure, or circumstance does not define them.

FOCUS ON THE PERFORMANCE, NOT THE PERFORMER

One thing we try to do as coaches—and we fail at this many times—is to evaluate and critique the *performance* and not the performer. That's hard to do. It's a fine line to walk. Our players want us to critique their performance, and they want us to be truthful and tough, because they want to become the best players they can be. But as coaches, we have to make sure that our players know that our critique is about their actions on the field and not about them as individuals. We want our players to receive a critique as coming from someone who loves them, who wants to help them improve, and not to think that they themselves aren't good enough. This isn't about them; it's about their performance. It's a lot like parenting children. When you're correcting your children, you hope that they don't think you're analyzing them as people. You're looking at their behavior and trying to help them, but you're not critiquing them as individuals.

> **Whatever you do, do it passionately. Failure is an event, not a person. Every obstacle presents an opportunity . . . *if* you're looking for it. Relax! You only fail when you quit.**

This principle applies as well to our relationships with God. God loves us, and there's no question he's going to evaluate our behavior. If we're sincere about following him, we're going to evaluate our own behavior and try to change, to align ourselves with his will. But we should never think that our performance will change how God feels about us.

I told a story in chapter 4 about yelling at a player who had committed a personal foul. When I yelled at him, "You're not worth fifteen yards!" one of the things that made that moment so egregious was that I was focused on the player and not on his performance. I still can't believe I said that. The message I sent that day was as far off the mark from what I believe and how I should have acted as I could get. But at the same time, I have to see my own performance as a coach that day as an *event.* I'm not a failure because of that one instance when I lost my cool.

Failure is an event. That's a difficult concept for a lot of our players to grasp, because they've had so much success at other levels of competition. But it's true. Failure is an event—it's not personal.

LEARNING FROM FAILURE

Each year, I get a lot of cards and letters from people who write me long, heartfelt messages: "Coach, I just wanted to tell you how sorry I am about the loss in such and such a game. You must be devastated." Stuff like that. Well, I read those letters, and I appreciate the sentiment. I know the people who wrote them care. And if they're reading this now, I hope they're not mad at me, but I have to say that I have never had a loss as a head coach that devastated me. Now, of course, I'm disappointed that LSU came out on top in the BCS championship game in January 2008. Sometimes I think that we might have had a different outcome if we'd done something different in the third quarter, or if I had told the players about a particular defense LSU was running, maybe they wouldn't have made certain mistakes. Those kinds of things go through your head, for sure. But I'm not personally devastated by that loss.

Flip it around. When we win a big game, I get letters and e-mails and notes about our being at the pinnacle of the sport and about how my career has great meaning and blah, blah, blah. Yes, winning the big one is great. It's a wonderful feeling to see the confetti coming down and the joy of the players, and it's great to be able to share that with your family and know that all the hard work you've put in for a whole season has paid off. But honestly, I don't feel any different about myself during the presentation of the trophy than I did before the game.

It can be difficult to keep that perspective, however, because the sportswriters and interviewers focus simply on whether you won or lost. You're either a good guy or a bad guy. To me, that's what persistence is about. Persistence takes the focus away from the performance and puts it on the process. Okay, that play, that business plan, that decision you made didn't work. You didn't sell as many books or burgers or whatever you were trying to sell. But in those situations, *you* are not a failure. The bad things that happened didn't make you a failure. Those were simply *events,* not reflections on you as a person.

After a loss or a disappointing performance, go back to the problem, analyze it, ask what you can learn from it, figure out how to do it right and how you are going to visualize doing it right the next time. Remember, the fact that you didn't achieve the desired outcome doesn't mean *you* are a failure. It simply means that the plan you had in place didn't work, so you have to get better. If you don't improve, you may no longer be employed—but that doesn't make you a failure either. Everything that happens—good and bad—should motivate you to be *persistent*. When things don't go your way, back up and start over. Learn what you can do to improve, and get back in the game.

> The way to get started is to quit talking and begin doing.
>
> WALT DISNEY

TWO TYPES OF PERSISTENCE

There are two types of persistence. In the first type, we start having doubts and aren't sure about ourselves or about the plan we've set forth, but we press on anyway. We may not be certain about our ability, but there are some factors inherent in what we're doing that propel us forward.

The second type of persistence comes from something deep inside us. Persistence isn't just what we do; it's a part of who we are. If we're this type of person, it doesn't matter what the score is, what our record is, or what obstacles are in front of us; we're living a lifestyle that says, "We're not giving up." We have a plan, and we're going to persist. Period.

I would say I'm characterized more by the second type of persistence than the first. I can't think of many times when I've been ready to toss it all in. Maybe I'm too naive to know when to quit. Or perhaps it's a gift God has given to me through the years.

I grew up observing the quality of persistence in my father. He was methodical in his work, slowly building from one year to the next, and stayed at one place, Baldwin-Wallace, for twenty-three years. He'd have one year that was good and then two that were very average. In those days, you could build a program slowly, over time. I'm not sure that if he were coaching today, they'd let him work that way. I was at Youngstown

State for fifteen years, which at that level is pretty unusual. I attribute that longevity to persistence.

Today, people are on the move a whole lot more. Seldom do you find a person who stays in one place for very long, and I suppose there are a million reasons for that. The world isn't as patient today; we have fast cars and microwaves, and we want things right now. In a world that values results over everything else, we need to be persistent to pursue and achieve our goals.

We're no longer just competing regionally or nationally—we're competing with the whole world in a growing global economy. We can have our legs taken out from under us pretty quickly these days. So we have to adapt and learn and *persist* if we want our work to move forward.

ANYTIME YOU FEEL LIKE QUITTING . . .

Whenever the going gets tough, encourage yourself with the following example of persistence:

- He failed in business in '32.
- He ran for the state legislature in '32 and lost.
- He tried business again in '33 and failed.
- His sweetheart died in '35.
- He had a nervous breakdown in '36.
- He ran for state elector in '40, after he regained his health.
- He was defeated for Congress in '43, defeated again for Congress in '48, defeated when he ran for the Senate in '55, and defeated for vice president of the United States in '56.
- He ran for the Senate again in '58 and lost.

Even after all his failures, this man refused to quit. He kept trying, until in 1860 he was elected president of the United States. By now you know that this man was Abraham Lincoln.

WHEN PERSISTENCE PAYS OFF

One player at Ohio State who exemplified persistence was Antonio Smith. He came to the team in the fall of 2002 as a walk-on. He had grown up in the inner city of Columbus and was a pretty good player in high school, but he hadn't been recruited at a national level. When Ohio State offered him an engineering scholarship, he decided to go to his hometown school and try to make the team.

During his first couple of years, you could count on the fingers of one hand how many times he played in the regular season. Still, he worked hard, did what we asked of him, and occasionally had the opportunity to play on one of our special-teams units. Antonio was five feet nine, which isn't tall for his position, so he was up against some big odds and some great talent.

Before his final season, when he filled out his goal sheet, he wrote down that one of his goals was to earn a football scholarship. I called him in and told him he'd earned it. We had given him a shot to play defensive back, and he was now competing for a starting position.

> One man with courage makes a majority.
>
> ANDREW JACKSON

Spring conference is the time each year when our players sit down individually to talk with the coach, and I have a chance to help them with their goals and plans. The players and I talk one-on-one about what the team needs and expects from them, and I hope to plant some seeds in the areas of purpose, goals, and values. During the spring conference before Antonio's senior year, we discussed many things, including goals and expectations.

Antonio was a great young man in the community—a really special kid who was great with outreach—and I attribute a lot of that to his grandmother who raised him. At the end of a player conference, sometimes I say, "Hey, I've done most of the talking; now let me hear from you." This time I said, "We've gone over your goals. Is there anything else I can help you with?"

"Two things, Coach," Antonio said. "On one of those Friday nights before an away game, I'd like to share my faith with the team. And because I'm a senior, I'd like you to consider me to give one of those talks."

At our away games, when we have our chapel service the night before the game, one of the players will talk to the team, because we don't really have a chaplain. The subject can vary. It might be about the game, or it could be about the player's faith or whatever else he wants to share. We always let a senior lead those nights.

"Okay, let me jot that down," I said. "What's the other thing?"

He thought a minute. "I really have a goal of being the starting cornerback on the NCAA video game." He was talking about the Xbox or PlayStation game that matches the uniform numbers of some of the real players from individual college football teams with the numbers on the players at each position in the game.

I sat back and looked at him. "Hey, Tone, I don't know how they decide who to put on there."

"I don't know either, but I thought you'd have something to do with it," he said.

I shook my head. "I don't have anything to do with that. I guess maybe they assess things after spring practice or the regular season, for each of the teams."

"Okay, that's just one of my goals," he said.

When the season came along, I didn't know for sure whether Antonio would be a starter for us. But because he was so dependable and consistent—and throughout his collegiate career he had been trying to become the best he could be and contribute to the team—we gave him a starting slot. And then he ended up having one of those storybook years. He started all thirteen games and finished second on the team in tackles, with seventy-one. He was a candidate for the Thorpe Award—awarded to the best defensive back in college football—and was named first-team All–Big Ten. It was amazing. If you had told me a few years earlier that Antonio would have that type of success, I wouldn't have believed you. But he had tremendous persistence. He just wouldn't give up. He earned his engineering degree and received a lot of job offers, but he decided to sign as a free agent with the Indianapolis Colts.

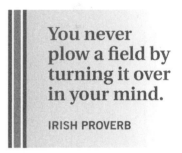

You never plow a field by turning it over in your mind.

IRISH PROVERB

And guess which number was used for one of the starting OSU cornerbacks on that video game? Antonio Smith's number *14*!

Toughness

Everyone has a plan until they are hit.

EVANDER HOLYFIELD

Football players at Ohio State know the truth of Evander Holyfield's words.

You're going through the game, doing everything right, running your patterns, blocking, doing what you're assigned to do, following the plan.

And then you get hit.

Hard.

You can't breathe.

You see stars.

And when the breath starts coming again, you begin to feel the pain, just in time to get hit on the next play, and the next, and the next.

> I hated every minute of training, but I said, "Don't quit. Suffer now and live the rest of your life as a champion."
>
> MUHAMMAD ALI

We talk a lot about toughness with our players—but it's a toughness that transcends being able to take a hit on the field. True toughness comes from courageous actions and applies to every aspect of the game of life. We have to be tough enough to make good decisions—decisions we know are right, even in situations where the right thing may not be the most popular choice. This type of toughness may very well be the hardest thing for young athletes today.

Here are some of the decisions our guys have to make. Someone offers them drugs for free, just to try. Someone else offers them a lot of money in exchange for tickets to a big game. Another person takes them aside and says, "Hey, I can get you twenty dollars for every autograph you sign." And this is only scratching the surface—there are countless other temptations out there. These decisions are the most difficult thing about playing in the limelight at Ohio State. It's not the practices and the running tests and the two-a-days that will break players down. It's the moral and ethical challenges that test their conscience.

> **The secret is this: Strength lies solely in tenacity.**
>
> LOUIS PASTEUR

Really, that's the toughest part about life in general, isn't it? Suppose you're stocking shelves and somebody says, "Hey, why don't you just take a few of those and we can sell them. Nobody's going to know." What do you do? You can either make the right decision, or you can say, "Yeah, this company makes enough money. They won't miss a few of these."

It might be tempting for business owners to fudge on their taxes. After all, "The government gets enough of our money."

On the football field our players get tired; they get sore; maybe they pull a muscle or get a cramp. In extreme cases, they might break a bone. They have to be ready to handle those things, sure, but their greatest challenges will often be found in life off the field. When players are enjoying time with their friends and someone says something derogatory, confronts them, or challenges their manhood, they have to make a decision about whether they're going to stand up to that person and do something that might make them feel good for the moment but will have lasting repercussions.

Or maybe a group wants to go one direction and in a player's gut he knows he shouldn't be doing that. Maybe it's alcohol or drugs or a young woman in the dorms—whatever the social atmosphere is at the moment. The courage he has at that moment to do the right thing will affect the trajectory of his whole life.

Doing the right thing when the pressure's on is a lot tougher than any football practice, and it will have an impact on players' lives a lot longer. Real-life decisions are the tough things. So we make it clear to our players that their toughness off the field will affect their lives even more than decisions they make on the field.

TRAGEDIES AND TRIUMPHS

Often, the most difficult challenges in life are situations that we can't explain. When life really punches you in the gut, you find out how much toughness and courage you truly possess. I had no idea how difficult things could be until I got a late-night phone call in January 1996, when I was coaching at Youngstown State.

DREAM BIG

If there were ever a time to dare,
to make a difference,
to embark on something worth doing,
it is now.
Not for any grand cause, necessarily—
but for something that tugs at your heart,
something that's your aspiration,
something that's your dream.

You owe it to yourself to make your days here count.
Have fun.
Dig deep.
Stretch.

Dream big.

Know, though, that things worth doing seldom come easy.
There will be good days.
And there will be bad days.
There will be times when you want to turn around,
pack it up, and call it quits.
Those times tell you that you are pushing yourself,
That you are not afraid to learn by trying.

The caller said there had been some kind of altercation outside the home of Jermaine Hopkins, one of our players, and that shots had been fired. While everybody else was running for cover, Jermaine, for some reason, had walked out onto the porch and was killed.

Here was a young man who was perhaps our most popular player. An All-American defensive end, he had set a school record for sacks in 1994 and contributed to two national-championship teams, in 1993 and 1994. He was our captain and a great friend to the entire team.

He was also the nicest guy in the world. He was preparing to graduate

Persist.

Because with an idea,
determination, and the right tools,
you can do great things.
Let your instincts,
your intellect,
and your heart guide you.

Trust.

Believe in the incredible power of the human mind.
Of doing something that makes a difference.
Of working hard.
Of laughing and hoping.
Of lazy afternoons.
Of lasting friends.
Of all the things that will cross your path this year.

The start of something new brings the hope of something great.
Anything is possible.
There is only one you.
And you will pass this way only once.

Do it right.

AUTHOR UNKNOWN

in the spring with a degree in hospitality management. His dream was to open a restaurant and help his parents. On that night in January, he had cooked for some of his friends and put out a little spread at his house. He was practicing his craft and had invited a bunch of the guys over to eat after a party earlier in the evening. Now he was dead, the victim of a senseless shooting.

The guys who were at Jermaine's house had taken him to the hospital, and we sent them back to the stadium to wait. Once Coach Ken Conatser and I knew that Jermaine had died, we called his parents from the hospital and then went over to the stadium to talk to the players.

We thought the safest thing was to take them over to the police station, which was not far away, because emotions were running pretty high. A lot of the guys thought they knew the identity of the shooter, and they wanted to go after him. So we were in a holding area, all of us in the same room, when we told them that Jermaine had passed away. When they heard the news, there were guys running, trying to get out of the room. I grabbed one kid, who was Jermaine's best friend, and tried to calm him down. He was a big guy, and he just about broke my back. The sorrow and anger in that room were extraordinary.

> Opportunity is missed by most people because it's dressed in overalls and looks like work.
>
> THOMAS EDISON

That night, my own words came back to me. I had warned my players that things would be harder for them off the field than on it. In the days that followed, we met as a team and grieved. We had terrific support from area clergy, counselors, and university administrators. We let people spill out their emotions and say what they felt. I think we were all able to get some things said and talk it out, but I'm not sure a person ever completely heals from something as devastating as that.

Losing games is hard. Seeing a player get injured and watching his dreams die is a huge challenge. But I'll tell you, helping that team understand that Jermaine wasn't going to be with us anymore was the most difficult and toughest thing I've ever had to deal with. Losing the LSU game for the national championship? That was a tough loss, but it doesn't even come close to the pain of losing a great player, friend, and teammate. That kind of event puts everything else into perspective very quickly. I can't imagine going through anything more painful.

After Jermaine was laid to rest, we retired his number (58), and the university set up a scholarship in his name. Even in death, he was able to give to others.

> I will never look at a firefighter the same way again. What is in someone, hundreds of them, to compel them to run into a burning building while everyone else is running out, just to save people they don't even know? Their bravery has become part of our collective national legacy. Their bravery dignifies us all.
>
> BILL HYBELS

In the spring of 2006, we encountered another difficult situation, this time at Ohio State. During spring practice, Tyson Gentry, a third-year sophomore walk-on from Sandusky, Ohio, who was both a punter and a wide receiver, got hurt on a passing drill. He was running a crossing route, a routine play, but when he caught the pass and was tackled, he landed kind of funny. It didn't look like a big deal, and everybody headed back to the line, but Tyson didn't get up. When the coaches got to his side, he wasn't moving at all. He couldn't feel anything from his neck down.

We canceled the rest of practice. I talked with the other players about the injury and then went over to the hospital to be with Tyson. As it turned out, he had a fracture of the C4 vertebra, about where the neck goes into the shoulders. The doctors fused the surrounding C3 and C5 vertebrae together, and today Tyson has movement in his arms and some of his upper body. His goal now is to walk again.

These types of life challenges cause us to reflect on all the Big Ten Fundamentals, especially the fundamental of faith. When life is suddenly coming at you quickly and overwhelming the football component, you need to have the whole person developed, because it isn't just about football. Tyson Gentry understands that, and I'll talk more about him in the chapter on heroes and winners.

The disappointment about Tyson's injury never ends. The feeling of loss over Jermaine's death is always there. But these situations show us what's important and force us to handle every day with persistence and toughness.

QUESTIONS FOR REFLECTION

1. How many people do you know who have fallen into the trap of defining themselves by what they do rather than by who they are? Is there an experience in your life that you feel is defining you right now?

_____

_____

_____

2. Think of someone you truly admire who is successful professionally and also has deep relationships. What is one thing you can do regarding your work to be more like that person?

_____

_____

_____

3. What has been the toughest experience of your life? How did you get through that experience, and how did it affect you?

_____

_____

_____

4. How is persistence linked with passion? Can you be persistent about something for which you feel no passion?

_____

_____

_____

YOUR PERSONAL GAME PLAN

1. *Personal/Family:* How are you doing with balancing your family and work? Talk with your family members, and get their response to this question; then take action on that information.

_____

_____

_____

2. *Spiritual/Moral:* Knowing that our spiritual lives take work, what can you do today that shows you're willing to work at digging deeper into this area?

_____

_____

_____

3. *Caring/Giving:* If you have previously defined your life by some negative experience, today can be a turning point. What one thing from your past could you let go of today? Is there someone hurting whom you can help today?

_____

_____

_____

4. *Health/Fitness:* What do you need to be persistent about regarding your health today?

_____

_____

_____

5. *Your Team:* Who on your team is going through a tough time? How can you reach out and walk alongside that person through this season?

_____

_____

_____

6. *Academics/Career:* Are there people at your workplace or on your team that you admire for their persistence? Tell them how much you appreciate their example, and ask them what motivates them to be persistent.

_____

_____

_____

CHAPTER 8

HANDLING ADVERSITY AND SUCCESS

I asked God for strength, that I might achieve.
I was made weak, that I might learn humbly to obey.
I asked for health, that I might do great things.
I was given infirmity, that I might do better things.
I asked for riches, that I might be happy.
I was given poverty, that I might be wise.
I asked for power, that I might have the praise of men.
I was given weakness, that I might feel the need of God.
I asked for all things, that I might enjoy life.
I was given life, that I might enjoy all things.
I got nothing I asked for—but everything I had hoped for;
Almost despite myself, my unspoken prayers were answered.
I am, among men, most richly blessed!

AUTHOR UNKNOWN (OFTEN ATTRIBUTED TO AN UNKNOWN CONFEDERATE SOLDIER)

With champions, success is never unexpected; it's a natural
result that comes from continuous, unselfish, unrelenting
determination to win; never letting down, never letting
outside influences into the game.

HARVEY MACKAY

Dear brothers and sisters, when troubles come your way,
consider it an opportunity for great joy. For you know that
when your faith is tested, your endurance has a chance
to grow. So let it grow, for when your endurance is fully
developed, you will be perfect and complete, needing
nothing.

JAMES 1:2-4

I have learned more from losing than I've ever learned from winning. As a head coach, an assistant coach, and a player, I learned more from the the defeats than the victories. When you compare the value of the two, it's not even close. The takeaway value of loss is so much greater.

The same has been true for every team I've ever coached. We have learned more over the years from losing than from winning. And the knowledge we have gained from those losses has helped us win more games. That may sound strange, but every coach and player reading this knows exactly what I'm talking about.

On the journey of success, we begin with plans, goals, and dreams. Once we have those figured out, we get to work. In the process, we invariably face hardship and struggle, as well as triumph and achievement. But whether we face success or adversity, we can learn how to not just "handle" it but to *take advantage* of it. If we want to succeed in life, we must learn how to make the most of both victory and defeat—because we're certain to encounter both along the way.

In my opinion, it's a lot more difficult to handle success than adversity. That's because of a natural human tendency to rest on our laurels when we've done well. If we get punched in the nose, we have an instinctual desire to fight back. If we're knocked down, we get up ready to respond in kind. And if we don't do well during a day's work, we steel ourselves and say, "I'm not going to let that happen tomorrow." When the going gets tough, our internal survival instinct compels us to press on and make things better.

> Great character is the cumulative result when great pain and great disappointment intersect in a man with a teachable spirit.

But I'm not sure that instinct works the same way when we've been successful. I've seen this happen to teams and individuals, and I've experienced it myself. When we get accolades and people tell us how great we are, instead of responding with humility and getting back to work, our tendency is to agree with what we're hearing. We say to ourselves, *Well, we've certainly arrived. We have this thing figured out now. We're something, all right.* When we get puffed up and believe our own press, we're ripe for a fall.

In this chapter, we'll deal with both sides of the coin—adversity and success—because each has a great bearing on the outcome of our lives.

At age four—my pre-sweater-vest days.

We were a football family right from the start. From left, my brothers, Dick (kneeling) and Dave; my mom, Eloise; my dad, Lee; and me, shortly after Dad took the job as head coach at Baldwin-Wallace College.

My parents, Lee and Eloise, have always been a great inspiration to me. They taught me the true meaning of selflessness, hard work, and dedication.

Looking on from the sidelines at Youngstown State.

Waiting to take the
field before a game
at Youngstown State.

My daughters, Carlee and Whitney, and me during a frigid
national-championship parade in Youngstown, January 1992.

Running onto the field before the game:
OSU vs. Northwestern, September 22, 2007.

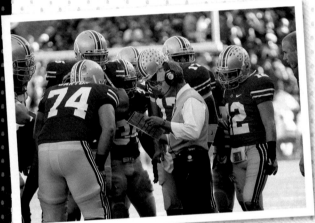

Going over a few
plays during a timeout:
OSU vs. Michigan State
October 20, 2007.

Talking with quarterback Justin Zwick between plays:
OSU vs. Cincinnati, September 4, 2004.

Tyson Gentry is definitely one of my heroes. Ty suffered a broken neck on an otherwise routine passing play during spring practice in 2006. Despite his injury, Ty's attitude has remained positive, and he is confident he'll walk again. I don't doubt it for a minute.

Troy Smith and me on Senior Day 2006.

Patting linebacker A. J. Hawk on the helmet as Bobby Carpenter (#42) looks on: OSU vs. Northwestern, November 12, 2005.

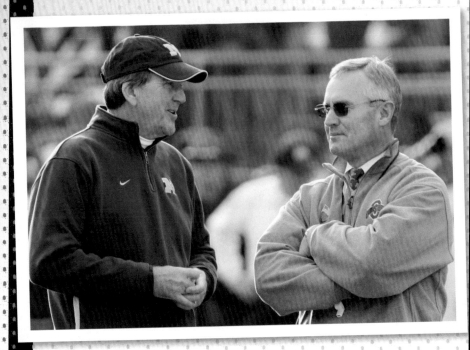

It has been a great honor to be a part of the Ohio State–Michigan rivalry, one of the greatest rivalries in all of sports. Coach Lloyd Carr is one of the best I've ever coached against.

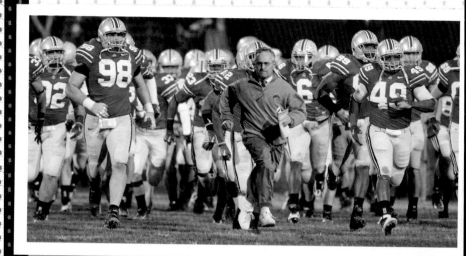

It's easy to get pumped up to play Michigan. Here we are coming back out onto the field after halftime against the Wolverines at home, November 18, 2006, a game we won 42–39.

A tradition that our players have established is to meet on the 50 yard line to pray together as a team. Here we are after a home game against Indiana in 2004.

Holding up the 2006 Fiesta Bowl trophy after we defeated Notre Dame 34–20.

Handing the national-championship trophy to defensive tackle Kenny Peterson after we defeated Miami 31–24 in the 2002 Fiesta Bowl, OSU's first national championship in thirty-four years.

ADVERSITY IS INEVITABLE—SO BE PREPARED

Adversity comes to us all—it's only a matter of when. The real question is not *whether* we'll face adversity but how we will respond to it when it comes. If our attitude is one that embraces learning and growing, we'll treat adversity as a stepping-stone to the success we desire, rather than see it as an insurmountable obstacle. But if we have a negative attitude and become defensive at the first hint of criticism or begin to blame others for our mistakes, we'll miss the opportunity to develop into the types of people we want to be.

When we're successful, when we do something well and everyone's telling us we're wonderful, it can be difficult to maintain the proper attitude. Our natural reaction is to bask in the glory, when what we ought to be saying is, "If you think *that* was good, watch *this*. This will be even better." But it's difficult not to get caught up in the celebration and think, *Yes! I was right. I did have this all figured out.*

We have to be able to make the most of both the positives and the negatives. There will be days when everything goes right and days when

How do you act when the pressure's on
When the chance for victory is almost gone,
When Fortune's star has refused to shine,
When the ball is on your five-yard line?

How do you act when the going's rough,
Does your spirit lag when breaks are tough?
Or, is there in you a flame that glows
Brighter as fiercer the battle grows?

How hard, how long will you fight the foe?
That's what the world would like to know!

Cowards can fight when they're out ahead.
The uphill grind shows a thoroughbred!
You wish for success? Then tell me, son,
How do you act when the pressure's on?

it all falls apart. We'll have stretches where really good things happen, and other stretches when we can't even remember the good things. Other times we will have a mixture of the two.

This Big Ten Fundamental is one that makes a lot of sense to our players because it's a constant in their lives. If they get hurt on the field, they have to learn how to handle it. They have to work at rehabbing their injuries. If they want to get back into playing condition, they have to come back not only physically but also mentally. When a tough loss comes their way, they have to handle the media scrutiny and the feelings that accompany criticism—some of it on-target. If a player gets demoted to second team, he has to work through those changes and try to win back his starting spot.

It's sensible and logical for our guys to understand that's the way life is in sports. It's reality, and they have to learn how to walk through the tough parts. There are some great quotes and reminders in the Winners Manual to encourage them during the process. And every player knows that even if things aren't difficult at the moment, they will be soon enough.

> **Our greatest glory is not in never failing, but in rising every time we fall.**
>
> CONFUCIUS

It's a little more difficult on the success side of the coin because we normally don't think of success as a challenge. But how many stories have you heard about people who have enjoyed some success, only to see it snowball into something bad in their lives? I really believe that handling success is harder than facing adversity. I'm not sure that our country has handled its affluence and "success" well at times. Sometimes our churches don't handle it well. We get off track a little bit to celebrate, and before we know it, we've forgotten the mission and the goal.

There's a fine line between enjoying our success and resting in our accomplishments. If we can't be happy about the success we've achieved, or be content with it, when are we ever going to relax? We'll always be chasing the next championship and never be satisfied, and that's no way to live. We must learn how to celebrate our success without being caught up in it.

THE POTENTIAL PITFALLS OF SUCCESS

The media have a habit of asking which team was my favorite or which win was my most important. Honestly, I've never stepped back and said, "You know, I constantly think of that '91 championship team." Certainly, there are times when I'm in more of a reflective mood and I think about a particular team and some great wins. But usually I'm concentrating on the current team and how to mold them. When you've got a group of kids ready to train and a lot of things to accomplish, you don't have much time to let success suffocate you.

In 1991, CBS televised the Division I-AA national-championship game between Youngstown State and Marshall. We were up against a good team that included Troy Brown, who has since won some Super Bowls with the New England Patriots. Troy was a standout on that Marshall team.

With about a minute to go in the game, we were up 25-17 and had a fourth-down situation with the ball deep in our own territory. We knew that if Troy Brown was playing up on the line, he was going to try to block the punt. So we called time out, and I said to our punter, "This is what they're going to do, so just get the punt off." He got off a pretty good kick, leaving Marshall with a long field and not much time left on the clock. They threw one Hail Mary pass that was incomplete, and then the game was over. That was my first national championship, and it made my dad and me the first father/son champions in NCAA history, because my dad had won a national championship with Baldwin-Wallace in 1978.

> There is no education like adversity.
>
> BENJAMIN DISRAELI

I went out to midfield to shake hands with Jim Donnan, the Marshall coach, and it was bedlam on the field, with people running everywhere. A guy from CBS hustled up to me and said, "You have to get to the end zone. We only have a minute left on the air, and we want to present the trophy."

As I was scuttling down to the end zone, another media guy ran up beside me, stuck a microphone in front of me, and said, "Do you think you'll repeat?"

I kind of slowed down and looked at him. "Well, I don't know. We haven't gotten the first trophy yet, and we can't repeat until we get the first one."

That's an extreme example of expectations, but those in the media invariably want to know after the game what we're going to do the next week or the next season. But we don't know yet. First we have to go back and learn from today, from both the failures and the successes. We study the film. We look at what needs to be adjusted, what planning needs to be different, and then learn how to do it the right way. Then we practice, all the time visualizing or rehearsing it until the next time we get to do it. That's the best way to repeat.

> **Success is a lousy teacher. It makes smart people think they can't lose.**
>
> BILL GATES

Microsoft founder Bill Gates has said, "Success is a lousy teacher. It makes smart people think they can't lose." I love that quote because it puts so many things in perspective. When "smart people" think they can't lose, there's an upset brewing. That's when David beats Goliath and the underdog triumphs. It's why many leading companies end up behind in the market. At one time, they were on top of things, happy with their growth and profits, but when someone suggested they needed to change in some way to remain competitive, their leaders said, in one way or another, "No, we're a winning company. We've got our market and our technology; we're not going to change anything." Then, all of a sudden, three other companies are serving the same market better, and the first company is trying to catch up. So when that statement comes from a guy like Bill Gates, who has been so successful, it makes the point even better.

Whenever we hear something in the media about our having "the best defense in the country," or other similar praise, our coaches remind our players what John Wooden, the legendary UCLA basketball coach, said about handling criticism and praise. His words are hanging in the lockers of many of our defensive players. Here's what Coach Wooden had to say about dealing with the "talk" surrounding a team:

COACH WOODEN ON CRITICISM AND PRAISE

I took criticism from outsiders with a grain of salt. I told my players each year, "Fellows, you're going to receive some criticism. Some of it will be deserved and some of it will be undeserved. Either way, deserved or undeserved, you're not going to like it.

"You're also going to receive some praise on occasion. Some of it will be deserved and some of it will be undeserved. Either way, deserved or undeserved, you're going to like it. However, your strength as an individual depends on how you respond to both criticism and praise. If you let either one have any special effect on you, it's going to hurt us. Whether it is criticism or praise, deserved or undeserved, makes no difference. If we let it affect us, it hurts us." . . .

You have little control over what criticism or praise outsiders send your way. Take it all with a grain of salt. Let your opponent get all caught up in other people's opinions. But don't you do it.

Success does things to you that adversity doesn't. It adds more things to your plate. Take this book, for example. If we hadn't won as many games as we've won, no one would care about my definition of a winner or want to know what system we use with our players. No publisher would be interested in marketing a book by a coach who had won 73 games and lost 208. I wouldn't get invited to speak at banquets, and I wouldn't have gone to the White House with my team, as we did after winning the national championship in 2002.

Success also adds a lot of people to your life—from media reps wanting answers, to friends who want tickets to the big game, to others who simply want to be seen with you.

But for everything that success adds to your schedule, it takes something else away. Whether it's from your exercise time, your spiritual time, your family time, or your students' academic time, success takes away time and can distract you from your goals and plans.

It's interesting that adversity has the opposite effect. When you meet with adversity, you can often find yourself alone. No one's calling to ask you to speak at a banquet. No one's interested in your opinion about success. You don't have people clamoring for your time, so you have more time to yourself.

I remember when we went to the national-championship game for four straight years at Youngstown State. That was four straight fifteen-game seasons, counting the regular season and play-offs. It was a great run, and there was such excitement about the team. But then in 1995, one year after we finished 14-0-1 and beat Boise State for our third national championship, our record fell to 3-8, and obviously, we didn't go to the play-offs. Our ticket staff got a break from all the postseason activity. Our equipment manager's season ended earlier. Our administration didn't have to plan trips to the different games.

> A gem cannot be polished without friction, nor man perfected without trials.
>
> CHINESE PROVERB

We didn't have to do commemorative posters and mugs. When the regular season was over, everybody was forced to take a bit of a breather.

Now, I'm not going to lie to you. From an ego standpoint, I hated the fact that we weren't playing in the postseason. And the players who had experienced success in the previous years didn't like it that we were staying home while other teams were still playing. But from a real-life perspective, it was like a breath of fresh air. I had a little more time for myself. I was able to work on other parts of my life rather than be on the treadmill from one award ceremony to the next or from this speaking engagement to that banquet. Of course, I don't want to miss the postseason every year. One year is about enough—for a lifetime!

The following season, we were able to turn things around and go 8-3, and we won the national championship again the year after that. But the point is that, whatever scenario you have with your team, whether you're winning or losing, you have to handle it, learn from it, and grow from it.

I've often said that those championship postseasons are hard because you already have an impossible number of things you need to do. But then a bunch of things are added, and you don't want to miss out on a single one. Let's face it, how many opportunities are you going to have to take your players to the White House? You have to take advantage of that. And of course you'll have a celebration at the stadium to honor your achievement, or maybe a parade through town, but it takes two or three days to plan and execute those events.

> There is no strength where there is no struggle.

My point is that whether you have success or failure, you have a challenge ahead of you. If you've had a good year and you're out recruiting, the prospects may be better, but you're still going to have to deal with the rigorous travel that makes it difficult to take care of some of your needs. You have to adjust, whether the ball bounces your way or not. Everything that happens during the course of your journey is part of life, and you have to adjust.

LEARNING FROM ADVERSITY

When something goes wrong on the field, our tendency is to kick ourselves, or to berate the player who made the mistake. But if we do that, we don't learn from the mistake; we don't use the adversity for ultimate good. To avoid this trap, we came up with a three-step process that ensures we will respond in a positive way to adversity on the field:

1. Learn from it.
2. Learn specifically what the right way is.
3. Practice visualizing the right way until your consciousness accepts a picture of yourself performing correctly.

After every play, I need to take a moment and ask myself, *What just happened? How did they go to that coverage? What's the right thing for the quarterback to do? What play do we need to check for? What route adjustment does the receiver need to make against that coverage?*

After I figure out the answers to those questions, I visualize the right way to do my job and see myself walking through the steps to make that happen.

All of that happens within twenty-five seconds between plays, but it works on the field as well as in the classroom and in life. If you're having a problem in the workplace, if you're having a relationship difficulty with your spouse, if you're off track spiritually, discover what you're doing wrong, learn the right way, and then practice doing it over and over. Performing it correctly with practice is the key to making it part of your daily game plan.

WOOHITIKE (BRAVERY)

Woohitike (wo-oh-hee-tee-keh), or bravery, is one of the central virtues or values of the Lakota Sioux. They believe that we all have it in us to be brave, that each of us can defend the camp when necessary. Life will give us the opportunity, issuing the invitation to the contest, and as time goes on, we will be shaped and strengthened by our challenges. Whether we can win each time or not, we will be tempered by adversity.

The ancient Lakota hunter warriors handcrafted their own bows from seasoned ash wood. There were two ways to acquire the proper wood. The conventional way was to find a young ash tree, harvest it, and let it dry for at least five years. But the hunter warriors were always on the lookout for a mature ash tree that had been struck by lightning. Such a tree had been dried and cured in an instant by the awesome power of lightning, and any bows made from it would be much stronger. Such trees were rare, but they were preferred because they had suffered the ultimate adversity, and ultimate adversity produces ultimate strength.

The "Woohitike (Bravery)" story is one of my favorite pages in the Winners Manual. So often we look at adversity as something we simply need to slog through. I heard of a pastor who believed greatly in the sovereignty of God, that every step of life is ordered and chosen by God. After a particularly tough round of golf, he threw his bag of clubs in the trunk, slammed the door, and said, "I'm glad that's over." Sometimes, even if we believe our steps are ordered, we don't see a purpose in the pain we're going through at the moment.

When we talk about winning, it's counterintuitive to say that adversity is a key component of success, but it's true. That's because it's not the adversity that does the work in us; it's how we respond to that adversity.

In every phase of life, you're going to face opposition. There will be times when your diet is going great, your exercise program is fantastic, and you feel healthy and look great. Every morning, you get up on time, and you've hit a routine that works for you. Then something

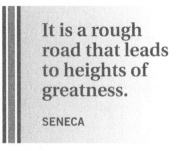

It is a rough road that leads to heights of greatness.

SENECA

happens to derail your train, and the reasons may be legitimate. Your mother gets sick, and you're driving back and forth three hours each way, and you have no time to exercise. And because you're constantly on the road, your diet suffers because you're eating fast food just to survive. That's a reality for many people.

In every phase of life and in every component of the Block O, there will be good pressures and bad pressures on your life. You have to learn how to handle those and respond well. If you're aware of the pressures, if you're *present* and are able to think through what you did wrong (identify), you can also figure out how to do it right (improve), and then practice the right steps to improve (implement). If you follow this three-step process—identify, improve, and implement—you'll not only "cope" with adversity, but you'll also move forward stronger and with more passion toward your goals.

RIDING THE ROLLER COASTER

We finished 2004 at Ohio State pretty strong, but we were a very young team. Looking ahead to the 2005 season, all the pundits and prognosticators were saying we were among the top teams in the nation. Another top-ranked team was Texas, and the Longhorns were scheduled to come to our stadium for the second game of the season. You can imagine how much excitement there was about that game.

We won our first game, and so did Texas, and now the eyes of the sporting world were on Ohio Stadium to see what was about to unfold. Vince Young was the quarterback for Texas, and A. J. Hawk was our premiere defender. It was almost like watching an NFL game, just a year or two early.

It was a beautiful night and a great game. With a little more than five minutes to go in the fourth quarter, we were ahead by six, and we missed a field goal, giving the Longhorns the ball back on their own 33 yard line. The stadium was going berserk, and you couldn't communicate—or even think—because of the noise. Texas was sixty-seven yards away from our end zone, and we had arguably one of the best defenses in the nation, with guys like A. J. Hawk, Bobby Carpenter, Nate Salley, and so many others.

> **Face adversity promptly and without flinching, and you will reduce its impact. Never run from anything and never ever quit.**
>
> WINSTON CHURCHILL

Other than being able to keep the ball ourselves and run out the clock, we were exactly where we wanted to be at that point in the game. If we could stop the Longhorns, we would be able to run out the clock for a win.

Vince Young had played an excellent game for Texas. We probably defended against him better than anyone else did that entire year, but on that final drive, he made a play here and a play there, their running back broke a tackle, and all of a sudden, with only two and a half minutes to go in the game, Young threw a twenty-four-yard touchdown pass, and we were down by a point. On our final possession of the game, our quarterback was sacked in the end zone for a safety, so we lost 25-22. It was a tough loss at home and on the national stage.

It's important to remember that every Saturday, half the teams playing college football lose their games. It's just a fact of life. Our game against Texas in 2005 was a marquee matchup—the second game of the year, number two against number four, and the first time the two schools had ever played each other. With all the buildup and the national television audience, it was a game that everyone wanted to see.

And we lost.

So what did we do? Did we pack up and say, "No way we're going to win the national championship this year. We might as well focus on 2006"?

The question wasn't whether we had won or lost; the question was, What are we going to do now that the situation is clear? How will we respond to that outcome?

Well, we bounced back and won our next two games before heading to Penn State for our first away game of the year. The top picks that year in the Big Ten were Penn State, Michigan, and Ohio State, so we knew we faced a big challenge in Happy Valley. We played a whale of a game but gave up a crucial interception and lost 17-10.

> **The greater the obstacle, the more glory in overcoming it.**
>
> MOLIÈRE

It was a really tough loss for us because we knew we were a good team, but after five games, our record was 3-2, which was not where we thought we would be at that point in the season. We had a lot of seniors with a lot of promise, and a ton of talent on that team, but the results on the field didn't reflect that.

We had set a goal of being Big Ten champions, but the loss to Penn State was a league game. We had wanted to be national champions, but now we were sitting with two losses, so there was no way that could become a reality.

Again, what did we do? How did we react?

The team really came together, and it was marvelous to see the leadership of that group. Guys such as Rob Sims, Santonio Holmes, A. J. Hawk, Bobby Carpenter, Nate Salley, and Nick Mangold really lit a fire under their teammates. Five players on that team would be drafted in the first round of the 2006 NFL draft, and they proved themselves the rest of the season as we reeled off seven wins in a row, beating ranked teams such as Michigan State, Minnesota, and Northwestern and winning a thriller in the final moments against seventeenth-ranked Michigan in Ann Arbor.

Our guys could easily have coasted the rest of the year, focusing on their own stats, making sure they didn't get hurt, concentrating on making it to the next level, the NFL. But they didn't. They wanted to become as good as they could be, and they were going to play every game 100 percent, regardless of our record. They wanted to feel good about their journey.

When the season was over, we accepted a bid to play Notre Dame in the Fiesta Bowl. We won decisively, and I was so proud of that group of guys. They had lost two tough games early in the season and could have let that disappointment spoil their entire year, but they handled it well, and they are revered as much as any group that has ever been through the Ohio State program. It was extraordinary watching them lead and not let the younger players get down.

> In attacking adversity, only a positive attitude, alertness, and regrouping to basics can launch a comeback.
>
> PAT RILEY

They were disappointed, no doubt, but not so disappointed that it kept them from plowing ahead and becoming the best they could be. By the end of the year, no other defense had held Vince Young and the Texas Longhorns under forty points. At the end of our game against Texas, I had told their coach, Mack Brown, "I'm rooting for you guys, because if you can come into our stadium, against our defense, and put together a drive like that, you can go all the way. That was a championship drive."

Though we had to handle disappointment and adversity, the key for Texas was handling their success. And they did that quite well, going undefeated the entire year. But in neither case was the final verdict in, after that second game of the season. We still had nine games to go. And

that's the way it is in life. You're going to have some major disappoint-
ments. And you're going to enjoy some success. You have to face both
with equal tenacity, with equal heart. To me, that 2005 team was a great
example of how to handle adversity. The 2002 team that won every game
was a great example of how to handle success.

STAYING IN THE MOMENT

In 2002, we opened the season against Texas Tech and won 45-21. After
we beat Kent State and seventh-ranked Washington State, we were 3-0.
In the fourth game, we played Cincinnati at Paul Brown Stadium, in a
game we were supposed to win—and we did,
but we probably didn't deserve it. It was as poor
a game as we had played in years.

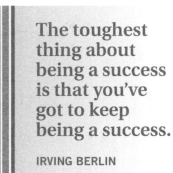

The toughest thing about being a success is that you've got to keep being a success.

IRVING BERLIN

We righted ourselves the next week and,
led by our defense, rolled through the schedule until week eleven, when we nudged Purdue
10-6 in the Craig Krenzel, fourth-and-two,
"great call by the coach" game I described in
chapter 4. The following week, we went into
overtime to defeat Illinois, and the week after
that was a battle royal against Michigan that yielded a 14-9 win. Through
it all, our guys weren't affected by the fact that we were 4-0, 7-0, or 10-0.
They just kept going out, putting their heads down, and making plays.

As we prepared for the BCS national-championship game against
Miami, the defending champions, people were saying we didn't have
a chance because the Hurricanes were just so good. Others were telling our guys that we were the best because of our undefeated record.
Our players did such a great job of handling the pressure. They didn't
waver in their mission; they didn't waver in their preparation and study
and training and getting their rest and eating right. They didn't let success derail what they knew they needed to do. And when it was all said
and done, after four full quarters and two overtime periods, they were
national champions.

I've seen groups that can't handle newfound success, but our guys did a great job of staying in the moment and handling their accomplishments.

I have learned more from losses than I've ever learned from wins, but you can learn good life lessons from both. Don't let adversity or success derail your goals and dreams. Let them propel you forward.

QUESTIONS FOR REFLECTION

1. Do you agree that you can learn more from a loss than from a win? Why or why not?

_____

_____

_____

2. How does having an extremely competitive environment, with the possibility of failure, aid a person's growth?

_____

_____

_____

3. What life situations pop into your mind when you think about adversity and success? What have you learned from both?

_____

_____

_____

4. Has there ever been a situation where you simply wanted to give up but you hung in there? What good things came from that experience?

_____

_____

_____

YOUR PERSONAL GAME PLAN

1. *Personal/Family:* Adversity and success can take a lot of different forms in a family or in your personal life. What success can you envision happening in the future, and how can you plan now to handle the impact on yourself and your family?

_____

_____

_____

2. *Spiritual/Moral:* Adversity can make us think of eternal things, or it can drive us away from God. Has there been a time when either has happened to you? Why do you think you reacted the way you did?

_____

_____

_____

3. *Caring/Giving:* It's sometimes easier to reach out to a person who has gone through difficult times than it is to rejoice with someone experiencing success. Is there someone in either category whom you can encourage today?

_____

_____

_____

4. *Health/Fitness:* Caring for your health means more than just exercising and eating well. What if a debilitating illness were to hit you in the next month? How would you handle that adversity? Are you prepared for that possibility with insurance for your family? How long has it been since you've had a checkup?

_____

_____

_____

5. *Your Team:* How you handle adversity affects your entire team. Do you know someone who has handled success or adversity well? Tell that person how much you appreciate his or her good example.

_____

_____

_____

6. *Academics/Career:* Choose one thing in your career life that you regret. Using the three-step process mentioned in the chapter, write down how you will (1) learn from it, (2) learn specifically what the right way is, and (3) practice visualizing that right way until your consciousness accepts a picture of yourself performing correctly.

_____

_____

_____

CHAPTER 9

LOVE

Be kind to one another, because most of us are fighting a hard battle.

IAN MACLAREN

Life's most persistent and urgent question is: what are you doing for others?

MARTIN LUTHER KING JR.

I may have all knowledge and understand all secrets; I may have all the faith needed to move mountains—but if I have no love, I am nothing. I may give away everything I have, and even give up my body to be burned—but if I have no love, this does me no good. Love is patient and kind; it is not jealous or conceited or proud; love is not ill-mannered or selfish or irritable; love does not keep a record of wrongs; love is not happy with evil, but is happy with the truth. Love never gives up; and its faith, hope, and patience never fail. Love is eternal.

1 CORINTHIANS 13:2-8, TEV

You never know where you're going to get a good idea that will follow your career and undergird everything you're trying to do. When I first saw the quote by Albert Einstein that is now a permanent fixture on the wall of our coaching offices, I was actually visiting Ohio State with my son Zak. I was head coach at Youngstown State at the time, and Zak was dead set on attending Ohio State. He didn't need to visit a hundred schools; he knew where he wanted to go.

As we were going through an orientation sequence, touring the campus and finding out more about Zak's field of study, we wound up in an engineering presentation. The professor put up a slide on the screen, and this quote by Albert Einstein flashed in front of us: "Concern for man and his fate must form the chief interest of all technical endeavors. . . . Never forget that in the midst of your diagrams and equations."

I was probably the only one in the room who had this thought: *Oh my goodness, does that ever speak to football coaches!* Now, I was there as the father of a prospective student. I was sitting next to my son, looking at four years of tuition and room and board, but suddenly I was spellbound. I felt as if I had been searching for treasure for years and I'd finally stumbled onto it. That quotation hit me right between the eyes. I wasn't thinking at all about football when we walked in, but I could see those words fitting perfectly into the world of football.

> Concern for man and his fate must form the chief interest of all technical endeavors.... Never forget that in the midst of your diagrams and equations.
>
> ALBERT EINSTEIN

Over the years, I've shared that quotation with thousands of football coaches who have attended my clinics. It's the kind of essential truth that I think is important for us to recognize, and it's really the heart and soul of what this book is about.

If we get so caught up in the *X*s and *O*s; so focused on the mechanics of the game and making sure every athlete is at his optimal weight and strength; and so committed to preparing every detail we need to win but leave out a concern for our players and their fate, then all our technical endeavors in football will mean nothing. If we focus solely on winning and set aside the loving care of individuals, we place our team and ourselves at a disadvantage.

I've observed the truth of this principle from afar—and sometimes from a little too close. We can have all the makings of a championship team, all the coaching talent in the world, and all the top recruits from around the country, but without the hidden component of love and concern for our fellow team members, we're going to come up short.

PURPOSE BEFORE GOALS

As human beings, we were not made only to achieve things. That's why goals are not at the top of the Block O. Our goals flow from the purpose of our lives. In the Purpose section, you see three headings: Personal/Family, Spiritual/Moral, and Caring/Giving. That whole section of the Block O is about *relationships*. The Personal/Family component is about our relationships with ourselves and with those closest to us, our families. The Spiritual/Moral component is about our relationships with God and with our fellow members of the human race. The Caring/Giving component then expands our relationships to encompass everyone with whom we come in contact. From the moment we're born to the moment we die, life is about relationships.

> Love cures all people—both the ones who give it and the ones who receive it.
>
> DR. KARL MENNINGER

True winners in the game of life will not look merely at goals and achievements. True winners who are part of a winning team will care more about the people beside them in the trenches than they will about the trophy at the end of the journey. True winners will have compassion for their teammates and desire the good of others as well as their own.

This concept is essential to establishing a team that will pull together through the hard times, because the hard times will come. Will adversity fracture the team and pull it apart, or will those difficulties cement the individual members of the team into a cohesive unit?

LOVE AND DISCIPLINE

Dr. Pat Spurgeon, a retired English professor from Georgia Southern University, is a great friend of mine. He has been part of more national-championship teams than anyone I know. He has talked to our players over the years about the concepts of love, caring, and giving. He has told my players and me time and again that in order to be champions, every team needs two basic components: *love* and *discipline*. And if we have love, the discipline will follow, because players who love each other don't want to let the team down. They'll do anything within their power to make the team better.

THE HALLMARK OF CHAMPIONS

> *It is well to be a gentleman, it is well to have a cultivated intellect, a delicate taste, a candid, equitable, dispassionate mind, a noble and courteous bearing in the conduct of life; these are the connatural qualities of a large knowledge; they are the objects of a University.*
>
> JOHN HENRY NEWMAN, *THE IDEA OF A UNIVERSITY*

I have attempted, attempt, and will continue to attempt to live my life by these principles.

All coaches talk about the importance of everyone placing the team before the individual, and "big team, little me" is important, but to stop at this point is to miss the most critical part of the message.

These same coaches almost always talk of sacrifice; it is a privilege. If the giver looks at the giving as a sacrifice, the giving will never be total and absolute.

It is only when the giver looks at the giving as a rare privilege to be entered into with enthusiasm and joyousness that the giving is total and absolute and will carry the greatest impact.

We speak here of the joy that he who loses his life shall gain it.

When the giver gives with all his heart and soul, he begins to understand the nature of love because *love is giving*. The greater the giving, the greater the love.

It is the total and absolute giving of one's self with enthusiasm and joy that separates the exceptional from the excellent. This giving becomes the highest expression of love.

If we hope to reach the top of the mountain, all of us must happily present the gift of our love through the absolute giving of ourselves to our comrades on the journey.

This love is the hallmark of champions!

In this chapter, I've leaned more on a single source—Dr. Spurgeon's teaching—than in any other chapter because I believe he's the one who has most helped our players bond with the idea of the importance of love. He contributed the article on the previous page to our Winners Manual, and it remains an annual favorite.

LOVE AND COMMITMENT

One of Doc Spurgeon's favorite sayings is "There is no joy the world can give like that which comes from joining good men in common purpose."

Every year, at every college that fields a football team, young men will come together with a common goal. At Ohio State, the goal is to win the Big Ten championship and then the national championship.

True love will find an outlet in service.

BILLY GRAHAM

How can a team achieve its goals? Each separate unit—offense, defense, and special teams—must learn its schemes, work on its disciplines, and practice its plays, but none of those activities will lead to attaining the goal if the players don't love one another. If they're not bound together by more than a simple desire to win, their striving will be losing. I'm not knocking the desire to win—that has to be there—but the overriding question is this: Does your team love?

What does the word *love* mean?

It's certainly not the mushy emotion that commonly passes for love in our society.

Love is the deep sense of commitment that each player has for every other player; the feeling of commitment that each player has for every coach—and vice versa; and the feeling of commitment that each coach has for every other coach. If each of these three relationships is not based on love, the team will not achieve its full potential.

Of course, this sense of commitment includes feelings or emotions, but feelings by themselves are not enough. Those feelings—those commitments—must then be followed up with commensurate *action*. When a team decides that it's going to do something, that it's going to strive for a common goal, if the players and coaches are not willing to put everything they have on the line to make that goal a reality, the team is going to fail. And the reason they'll fail is that sooner or later they'll come up against a team that's willing to play that way—to put it all on the line.

Now, if a team does that, if they go the extra mile and show love and commitment among coaches and teammates, does it guarantee they'll win the conference championship or the national championship? No. But it *will* assure that they have given their very best for the good of the team.

> When we come face to face with God, we are going to be judged on how much we loved.
>
> MOTHER TERESA

Doc Spurgeon talks a lot about poems and stories. He's an expert on Shakespeare, so he tells us about King Lear and his daughters as well as other characters from Shakespeare's plays. One poet he quotes often is T. S. Eliot, who said that the greatest problem of the modern world is the inability to make a commitment. That sentiment is the theme of Eliot's poem "The Love Song of J. Alfred Prufrock," whose subject cannot make a commitment. It is also a central theme in "The Waste Land," Eliot's epic poem written a few years after the end of World War I. The modern world is seen as a wasteland, in part because people can no longer commit to anything.

The inability to make lasting commitments is even more prevalent in our day than it was in Eliot's. Look at the divorce rate. Look at the breakdown of the family. Many people who walk away from their families have been living in a romanticized world where everything is supposed to be good and they're supposed to be happy. They haven't learned that there will be tough times and that those tough times can actually draw people together. They confuse fantasy with reality. They repeat the vows "for better or for worse," but they can't comprehend the true meaning of the statement. They can't put it to work in their lives. If there's a bump in the road, they run for someone else. And unfortunately, they find themselves in the same situation with the other person. There will always be bumps in the road; we have to get past them together.

Commitment is the key to every relationship. Whatever team you're on, whether it's a marriage, a family, a work team, or a sports team, in order to achieve whatever goals you've set, you must be bound together by a love that exhibits itself in extreme commitment and the laying down of one's life for the common good.

The failure to commit ourselves is evident in so many aspects of our society. People want to be "cool" rather than committed. They want to be esteemed and lifted up. But you can't focus on being cool if you want to be a champion. You have to be willing to cry. You have to be willing to love. You have to be willing to commit.

> **Commitment is the key to every relationship.**

When I became head coach at Ohio State, Doc Spurgeon told me about a friend of his who had been watching Ohio State's games on television. His friend's assessment of our performance was that we had played only one half of one game that season in a halfway decent fashion.

"You want me to tell you what the problem is with Ohio State?" the man asked Doc Spurgeon. "They think you win tough games with talent. You don't win tough games with talent. You win tough games with toughness. And the way you get tough is through love."

LOVE MAKES THE DIFFERENCE

Here's a story that illustrates how love makes the difference in the performance of champions. When Youngstown State played Eastern Kentucky the week before the national-championship game, a defensive lapse near the end of the game put us in a desperate situation. With about two minutes to go, Eastern Kentucky completed a screen pass and scored a touchdown that put them ahead. There's no question that the game appeared to be slipping away.

We had a linebacker, Reggie Lee, who was devastated because he blamed himself for the touchdown. He was on the sideline with a world

GIVING WHEN IT COUNTS

Many years ago, when I worked as a volunteer at Stanford Hospital, I got to know a little girl named Liza who was suffering from a rare and serious disease. Her only chance of recovery appeared to be a blood transfusion from her five-year-old brother, who had miraculously survived the same disease and had developed the antibodies needed to combat the illness. The doctor explained the situation to Liza's little brother and asked him if he would be willing to give his blood to his sister. I saw him hesitate for only a moment before he took a deep breath and said, "Yes, I'll do it if it will save Liza."

As the transfusion progressed, he lay in his bed next to his sister and smiled, as we all did, seeing the color returning to her cheeks. Then his face grew pale and his smile faded. He looked up at the doctor and asked with a trembling voice, "Will I start to die right away?" Being young, the boy had misunderstood the doctor; he thought he was going to have to give his sister *all* of his blood.

of hurt on his back. He knew he had let his teammates down, and that left him on the brink of despair.

We got the ball back, and on the ensuing possession, one of our wide receivers, Darnell Bracy, made an incredible catch—it was an unbelievable play—and ran the ball in for a touchdown. We won the game. Our guys were celebrating, caught up in the emotion and the realization that we were going to the championship game.

As Doc Spurgeon would say, on that one play, Reggie Lee learned what love really means.

The night before the title game, we had our final meeting to review the game plan. We were all grateful to be in a position to play for the championship, and the mood was positive. Then Reggie Lee stood up and faced his teammates. I don't remember his exact words, but he said something like this: "Doc used to say that we have to lay it all on the line. I always thought that was sappy. I figured it was just his way of trying to motivate us."

Big tears came to his eyes and trailed down his cheeks. The room grew silent as the emotion overcame that tough linebacker. "But after last week, I can honestly say I know what he meant. And I want every one of you to know that tomorrow afternoon when we play, I'm putting it all on the line."

Darnell Bracy had picked up his teammate with that touchdown score. Reggie had gone from despair to hope in one play. He had seen the effects of love firsthand, and in that meeting he wasn't ashamed to embrace it.

A skeptic might say that the receiver wasn't catching that ball out of love; he just wanted to win the game. You're right to say that Darnell wanted to win, but there was no "just" about it. Love has a way of making unexpected things happen. Love can transform a team of players with less than stellar talent into a tightly knit group that can perform above its level of ability.

"PLAY BETTER THAN YOU ARE"

One of Doc Spurgeon's favorite sayings to players and teams is this: "All I ask is that you play better than you are. As an individual and as a team, play better than you are. You may not win. But that's all I'm asking. And for you to play better than you are means you're not playing just for yourself. You're playing for that man on each side of you, on the other side of the ball, your coaches, the people cheering you on. You will forget being tired. You will not be tired. You will play better than you are. But you cannot do that unless you have love."

Two quotations on the walls of our staff meeting room remind us every day why we're here. They narrow our focus on the difference we're trying to make, because when we're immersed in the minutiae of a football season, it's easy to get off track. One of those quotations is the Albert Einstein quote I mentioned at the beginning of the chapter: "Concern for man and his fate must form the chief interest of all technical endeavors. . . . Never forget that in the midst of your diagrams and equations."

> **All I ask is that you play better than you are.**
>
> DOC SPURGEON

On the other wall, in equally large print, is this statement: "They don't care how much you know until they know how much you care."

I've seen this concept work itself out every year in our interaction with players, especially the younger ones. They're wondering if what we've told them about our approach is really what's going to happen. We've talked about their purpose and how important it is in the Block O of Life. We've discussed their goals and mapped out a plan to help them reach those goals. When they see that we really mean what we say, you can tell by the look in their eyes how much it means to them.

> They don't care how much you know until they know how much you care.

Our guys want to win more than anything. But when it comes down to it, it's not the Xs and Os that have the most impact. Anyone with a working knowledge of football can teach a player how to block or how to set up in the pocket for a pass. Those are the basics. The bigger difference a coach can make in a player's life comes through a caring and loving approach.

LOVE AND RELATIONSHIPS

As we journey through a season, or a player's four- or five-year career, our desire is to see the relationships between players and coaches deepen. We want every player to come to a place where he can share anything that's on his heart. In order for him to do that, we as coaches have to prove ourselves in the tough times as well as in the good.

As with the other Big Ten Fundamentals, this philosophy also works outside the sports arena. Of the people you have worked for, how many can you honestly say cared about you as a person and not just as another cog in the corporate machine? My guess is that if you've had a boss or a manager who was truly interested in you and your goals in the work environment and cared about you personally, you will never forget their kindness.

The wonderful thing about showing genuine concern for other people is that the giver gains as much as the receiver, if not more. There is a by-product of love for both giver and receiver that can't be quantified on a spreadsheet.

We teach our players that everyone on the team plays a role in our winning or losing. From the starting quarterback to the player who may not see much, if any, playing time, we are all one team. That means we try to treat everyone on the team the way the "stars" are treated. We have to train the whole team, just as we train the whole person through the Big Ten Fundamentals.

HER NAME WAS DOROTHY

During my second month of college, our professor gave us a pop quiz. I was a conscientious student and had breezed through the questions, until I read the last one: "What is the first name of the woman who cleans the school?" Surely, this was some kind of joke. I had seen the cleaning woman several times. She was tall, dark-haired, and in her fifties, but how would I know her name? I handed in my paper, leaving the last question blank. Just before class ended, one student asked if the last question would count toward our quiz grade.

"Absolutely," said the professor. "In your careers, you will meet many people. All are significant. They deserve your attention and care, even if all you do is smile and say, 'Hello.'"

I've never forgotten that lesson. I also learned her name was Dorothy.

As our guys fill out their goals in the Caring/Giving component, we really see inside their hearts. They may have a cousin who's autistic, and they want to have a chance to work with autistic kids. They may have had an experience with someone who had leukemia or another disease, and now they want to reach out to someone who's going through treatment. When we show our guys the truth about the ways they have been blessed and about how fortunate they are, they truly get it. Reaching out and touching the lives of others is not only a responsibility they take on; it's also a response to their desire to try to make a difference. And it winds up being a vital part of who they are. They feel good about outreach.

Loving others is not easy. You have to make time for it in your busy schedule. It has to be an intentional part of your plan, one that you put in writing. And love's schedule is not always convenient. It's easy to say you want to show love, but it's something else to truly commit yourself to doing it.

As coaches, we like to give our players opportunities to do what we know they like to do. It can be as simple as being courteous to the people who serve them in the dining hall. But it has to come from the heart and be genuine, because people can tell when you're just going through the motions. Our guys enjoy reaching out to little kids in elementary schools and reading to them, because that's a big deal to those kids. You should see their faces light up when they see a real Ohio State football player walk into their classroom to sit down and read with them. Those are important opportunities, and we're fortunate to be able to do things like that.

> **When you help someone up a hill, you get that much closer to the top yourself.**
>
> AUTHOR UNKNOWN

Ohio State has some great medical facilities on campus. There's the James Cancer Hospital, where our guys visit patients and try to encourage them. We also have Nationwide Children's Hospital, one of the top children's hospitals in the country, so our players go there to visit the kids. These are the types of things we would innately like to do, but sometimes we have to be given some structure and opportunity to accomplish it. Perhaps the desire just needs to be awakened deep inside.

LOVE AND COMPASSION

One of the strangest things that happened to me just before we played the 1993 national-championship game against Marshall University also involved Doc Spurgeon. The team had gone through an incredible crucible, playing through the stress and strain and agony of that particular season. I had taken some time to be alone and had walked down a series of steps to get to the field where we would play the game. I thought about the team we were up against and all the talent they had, and it seemed like such an uphill battle for us. To be honest, I was having a few doubts about my own ability.

Doc Spurgeon saw me, and I think he kind of sensed what was going on. He came up and asked what was wrong, and I was honest with him. "Doc, I'm not sure. This is such a challenge."

Without missing a beat, he looked straight at me and challenged me in his direct and eloquent way: "Wait a minute, Jim. Let me tell you something. If there were one play and I had to have one person call it, you're the only coach to whom I would say, 'Run that play.' Believe in yourself. You can do it!"

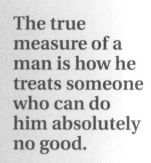

> The true measure of a man is how he treats someone who can do him absolutely no good.
>
> ANN LANDERS

I just smiled at him. There was such love in his words, and they came at just the right time for me, when I felt my resolve wavering a bit. We won that game 17-5.

The strange thing was that at the exact moment when Doc Spurgeon was speaking to me, someone took a picture of us. He still has that picture at his house in Statesboro, Georgia.

Doc gave me the same loving message when I arrived at Ohio State. He said, "There will be moments when you wonder if you will succeed; but know you can do it."

One of the helpful things I've either read or heard over the years is that we need to treat people as if they're hurting. You never know what others are going through. How many times have you found out later that someone you spoke with was dealing with a particular challenge, crisis, or heartache? Maybe you could have spent a few more minutes visiting with that person and didn't, and now you're kicking yourself. Or maybe you did take the time and treated the person as if he or she were hurting. Those opportunities may come up more often than we realize.

John Conroy, one of our outstanding seniors, and Anthony Gonzalez, who was a first-round pick for the Indianapolis Colts, had a request

A SIMPLE GESTURE

Mark was walking home from school one day when he noticed that the boy ahead of him had tripped and dropped all the books he was carrying, along with two sweaters, a baseball bat, a glove, and a small tape recorder. Mark knelt down and helped the boy pick up the scattered articles. Since they were going the same way, he helped to carry part of the burden. As they walked, Mark discovered the boy's name was Bill, that he loved video games, baseball, and history, that he was having a lot of trouble with his other subjects, and that he had just broken up with his girlfriend.

Mark went home after dropping Bill at his house. They continued to see each other around school, had lunch together once or twice, then both graduated from junior high school. They ended up in the same high school, where they had brief contacts over the years. Finally, the long-awaited senior year came. Three weeks before graduation, Bill asked Mark if they could talk.

Bill reminded him of the day years ago when they had first met. "Do you ever wonder why I was carrying so many things home that day?" asked Bill. "You see, I cleaned out my locker because I didn't want to leave a mess for anyone else. I had stored away some of my mother's sleeping pills, and I was going home to commit suicide. But after we spent some time together talking and laughing, I realized that if I had killed myself, I would have missed that time and so many others that might follow. So you see, Mark, when you picked up my books that day, you did a lot more. You saved my life."

JOHN W. SCHLATTER

for one of our chapel services. They asked if we could invite one of the priests from St. Ignatius High School in Cleveland to speak to the team. Every Buckeye fan knows about St. Ignatius, which has a storied history of producing good football players.

Anthony's priest brought in a special prayer that was written by Saint Ignatius Loyola, who lived from 1491 to 1556:

PRAYER FOR GENEROSITY

Lord, teach me to be generous.
Teach me to serve you as you deserve:
To give and not to count the cost,
To fight and not to heed the wounds,
To toil and not to seek for rest,
To labor and not to ask for reward,
Save that of knowing I am doing your will.
Amen.

LOVE AS A LIFESTYLE

Love is not something we can turn on and off at will; it has to be ingrained in our being. It's a vital ingredient in a winner's game plan. And, like every other fundamental, it has to be worked on every day. The people around us will know if what we're expressing is genuine or not. Love must be a lifestyle.

> You can give without loving, but you cannot love without giving.
>
> AMY CARMICHAEL

Doc Spurgeon has studied the topic of love for many years, and he believes the vast majority of people who use the word *love* use it as a synonym for "what gives me pleasure."

"I love strawberry ice cream," "I love Barry Manilow's music," or sometimes even "I love you," really means only that those things, or those people, give us pleasure. But love is much more than getting pleasure for ourselves. As we've seen in this chapter, love is a commitment, a purposeful giving of ourselves for the good of the group. In the context of a team, love shines through at some of the most incredible times.

At the same national-championship game where Reggie Lee stood up and gave his emotional message, Chris Sammarone, our center that year, also spoke. Doc Spurgeon had put together a crude red and white flag, representing our school colors. The cloths were really just rags that were stitched together. Chris held up that makeshift flag in front of the whole team. It represented everyone, from their different backgrounds and experiences, from different social and economic levels, and from different spiritual journeys.

"Look at this flag," Chris said. "People would say this is just a bunch of rags. But it's a beautiful thing to me. I'm putting this above the door tomorrow, and I'm going to touch it before we go out on that field."

Chris came up to Doc Spurgeon after that meeting and said, "I didn't know what love was until tonight."

Doc Spurgeon said that was the greatest night of his life.

I have a feeling there will be more nights like that for Doc, because he knows what love is. It can create miracles for a team. It can work its way deep into the lives of players and coaches. It's like a fountain that springs up in different ways—ways you can't predict but that you can count on.

There was an article written about Jon Heacock, one of my assistant coaches at Youngstown State who is now the head coach there. Jon was asked about his experience at the school during those years when Doc Spurgeon was with our team.

He didn't talk about defending against the wishbone or how to score once you're in the red zone. He said, "What I learned working at Youngstown State was how to love."

My guess is that Jon Heacock will have a stellar career as a head coach. And his players and coaches and everyone involved in the program will be richer because he knows that you can have a lot of important components of a winning program, but the greatest of them all is love.

QUESTIONS FOR REFLECTION

1. Do you think Doc Spurgeon is right when he says that we're experiencing an epidemic of a lack of commitment in our society? How do you plan to combat that personally?

_____

_____

_____

2. Loving and caring seem to be easier for some people than for others. Do you think that's true? Why or why not?

_____

_____

_____

3. If you had to pick the five most loving people you've ever known, who would they be, and why would they make the list?

_____

_____

_____

4. After reading this chapter, what new thoughts about love have surfaced for you? Has your definition of love changed at all?

_____

_____

_____

YOUR PERSONAL GAME PLAN

1. *Personal/Family:* Some people are easier to love than others. Is there a family member you can reach out to today to show the care and love talked about in this chapter?

_____

_____

_____

2. *Spiritual/Moral:* Loving others is an integral part of loving God. Is there someone in your life you feel is unlovable? Perhaps this is the very person God wants you to reach out to today.

_____

_____

_____

3. *Caring/Giving:* One of the main points of this chapter is that caring and giving to others has to have structure. It's not going to happen automatically. What kind of structure could you create in your life to help you accomplish this worthy goal?

_____

_____

_____

4. *Health/Fitness:* Loving and caring are not just directed toward team or family members. Loving yourself by caring for your body and making sure you have enough rest and proper nutrition is important as well. What can you do for yourself today that will make you better able to reach out to others?

_____

_____

_____

5. *Your Team:* If Doc Spurgeon is right that a winning team is both loving and disciplined, what steps can you take individually for your team to help make that a reality?

_____

_____

_____

6. *Academics/Career:* As you've read this chapter, perhaps you've seen how the axiom of love and caring can be put into action in your chosen career. How might you implement love in your workplace today? What small act of giving could help transform you and those around you?

_____

_____

_____

CHAPTER 10

RESPONSIBILITY

When in doubt, tell the truth.

MARK TWAIN

Even children are known by the way they act, whether their conduct is pure, and whether it is right.

PROVERBS 20:11

The whole art of government consists in the art of being honest.

THOMAS JEFFERSON

Most of all, my brothers and sisters, never take an oath, by heaven or earth or anything else. Just say a simple yes or no, so that you will not sin and be condemned.

JAMES 5:12

For most of our players, leadership is an important part of their role. They want to be thought of as leaders and looked up to as role models. You hear some athletes today say they don't want that pressure, that little kids shouldn't be looking to athletes as role models. Our guys *desire* that responsibility.

We talk a lot about the microscope they're under as players for Ohio State. In becoming Buckeyes, they've inherited a certain amount of responsibility. We don't assume they understand that fully, so we teach them the fundamentals of Doing Right and Accepting Responsibility.

In football, as in life, every small part of your craft is important. The minute you ignore a fundamental, you begin to lower your standards for your craft, and your work suffers.

Responsibility wasn't one of our original fundamentals when we started the Winners Manual back in 1986, but after several years, we came to the conclusion that we could no longer take certain things for granted.

When Vince Lombardi, the great football coach of the Green Bay Packers, wanted to get back to fundamentals, he didn't take anything for granted either. He is said to have held up a football as he looked intently around the room and then announced, "Gentlemen, this is a football." In the spirit of Lombardi, we felt that nothing was too basic to teach our players. We wanted to get down to the bedrock of our expectations for every player who was coming into our program.

> Associate yourself with men of good quality if you esteem your own reputation: for 'tis better to be alone than in bad company.
>
> GEORGE WASHINGTON

BE RESPONSIBLE AND DO RIGHT

When a prospective coach interviews for a position, people want to know what kind of standards he has for his players. They want to know the sanctions he'll mete out if a ballplayer breaks a rule. Administrators want to know the coach's approach to academics and whether he or she will require the players to be real students.

I'm the last one to have a long list of possible sanctions for players. I don't believe in it. But I do believe in telling each player what we're going to expect of him. It's simple: We expect each person on the team to "be responsible" and "do right." And if we're going to expect it, then it's up to us as coaches to teach the players how to do those two things. We need to talk about them often and keep them in the forefront of the players' minds. I'm not saying that players don't already have a sense of responsibility and a desire to do right when they arrive at Ohio State, because most have had great parents and/or mentors who have given them a wonderful foundation. But we want to review, talk about, and practice those qualities, so that they become even more ingrained in the players' lives.

It's interesting that when I talk with our seniors, or even with players

Toward the end of Mohandas Gandhi's extraordinary life, he listed the seven deadly sins he had encountered along the way:

Wealth without work
Pleasure without conscience
Knowledge without character
Business without morality
Science without humanity
Worship without sacrifice
Politics without principles

who have graduated and moved on to other careers, they say that this section on responsibility and doing right is one of the fundamentals they appreciate most. I say, "If I asked you to speak to the team about one fundamental, which one would you choose?" Responsibility and doing right are always at the top of the list. I think that's because the guys recognize that our society has a deep struggle with responsibility. The definitions of right and wrong keep shifting, and the line is fluid. Many people have no objective standard for judging what "right" is. So discussing what it means to "do right," and working through it and practicing it, become welcome disciplines for our players. It helps them define their own terms of right and wrong.

I've seen players make some very poor choices—things I couldn't believe they'd even consider doing. And that further emphasizes to us coaches the fact that we have to tackle these ideas head-on and not assume that our players have an inherent knowledge of what's right.

> **The reputation of a thousand years may be determined by the conduct of one hour.**
>
> **JAPANESE PROVERB**

Norman Vincent Peale said we all have sensors and that we really know whether or not we're doing the right thing. He said we have a little twinge inside that says, *No, I shouldn't do this.* But I don't take for granted that we all have the same "twinge level." So the idea of responsibility and doing right has become one of our most valuable fundamentals. Truly, no detail of this is too small to work on.

WITH TRADITION COMES RESPONSIBILITY

My Winners Manual has a large star next to this Japanese proverb: "The reputation of a thousand years may be determined by the conduct of one hour." When most people make a mistake in life, others may or may not notice. When a football player makes a mistake at Ohio State, the report explodes through the media. We're careful to explain the reality of media scrutiny to our players from the very first day, and every chance we get, we reinforce the reality of that scrutiny through current events and examples of people who had had good reputations but whose mistakes changed their lives in an instant.

As you walk up the steps to our game room, you'll see some old uniforms hanging on the wall to illustrate the historical evolution of the Ohio State uniform. These represent the great players of the past who are part of our heritage. In gigantic letters above those uniforms is this sentence: "With tradition comes responsibility."

That's a huge deal to us because we want our players to always remember what a privilege it is to play at Ohio State. And along with that privilege comes responsibility. In this fundamental we have the opportunity to explain *why* privilege and responsibility go hand in hand.

If I were to identify one of the biggest changes to occur in the relationship between players and coaches over the past twenty years, it would be the players' insistence on knowing *why*. When I began coaching, we told the players what to do, and they did it. Today, they want to know why they're doing what they're doing and what the ramifications are if they don't toe the line or do something properly. Knowing why deepens their resolve to do things right—whether it's a drill, a behavior, or an attitude—because they truly understand why it's important.

In discussing this fundamental, we cover a number of principles, such as the danger of a player ruining his reputation with "the conduct of one hour." And we not only try to get these fundamentals across to the players, but we also believe there are strategic times to present this material.

In 2007, the day we scheduled to have this discussion in our Quiet Time was Friday, August 24. That was a strategic day because we had been in training camp since August 5 and the players had basically been in "lockdown" day and night. The first part of camp is known as "eat, sleep, and meet," because that's all the guys do for three weeks. Finally, on the twenty-fourth, they got their first chance at freedom. They were off duty from noon on Friday until 4 p.m. on Sunday, which is when we would transition to our game-week preparation. That weekend provides a dangerous opportunity to err, because it's something like being on leave in the military. The guys say, "Hallelujah, I'm outta here!" So, before they go, we remind them of the fundamentals of taking responsibility and doing right.

> There is no pillow so soft as a clear conscience.
>
> FRENCH PROVERB

Later, just before school starts, we go over this subject again. At that point, the other students are returning to campus, and all the parties are starting. We feel we owe it to the players to constantly remind them, just as a mother would, "Be in by ten." If the kids were younger, their mother might say, "Stay away from the railroad tracks. It's dangerous down there."

It's all in the presentation, of course. Nobody wants to be talked to like a child. But, we know that, like children, young adults can forget about the importance of being responsible and doing right. In one impetuous moment, they can lose all they've worked so hard to achieve. So we tell them, "We know you already know this, but we want to remind you." We want them to know how to distinguish wrong from right, bad from good, and better from best.

CHARACTER OR CONSCIENCE?

I try to steer away from the word *character* when I'm dealing with young people, and I've had some good discussions with friends about this. But to me, addressing the idea of someone's character almost feels as if we're evaluating that person according to our own subjective standards: Does he have good character? Does she have good character? What does that really mean?

I prefer to use the word *conscience,* because I think what we're really asking is this: Is this young man aware of what's right? Does he have an intentional restraint at work in his life? Does he have a conscience? Does it bother him when he does wrong things? If you have a tender conscience, a functioning moral barometer that tells you when something is amiss, then you will automatically work toward living an upright life.

> When someone has been given much, much will be required in return; and when someone has been entrusted with much, even more will be required.
>
> LUKE 12:48

It's almost like trying to get clean water from a stagnant pool. It's not until you go back to the source of the water that you're going to get something pure.

I like to use the word *conscience* instead of *character* because it takes the focus off of our opinion and puts it on the actions of the other person. The book of Proverbs says, "Fear of the LORD is the foundation of true knowledge, but fools despise wisdom and discipline" (1:7). Reverence for God, a conscious desire not to disappoint him, is where it all begins.

To help our players put things in perspective, we show them examples of past players and others who have gone before us, whose lives and legacy we build upon. We tell them about the shoulders we all stand on, so that the new players can gain an understanding that they're not just out there playing for themselves or even for the current team but for all the teams and all the players who have worn the scarlet and gray.

Every time a current player gets into trouble, you know there's an Ohio State graduate in some office somewhere who is going to hear it from the Purdue grad he works with.

"I see your guys are having some problems," the Purdue grad will say.

Now, there's a problem with someone who would judge an entire school or program because of a mistake one person makes. That's not fair. But it does underscore our responsibility as coaches to talk to the players about doing right and the significance of the choices they make every day.

Doing the right thing can be a challenge on a college campus. When a new player comes in, a lot of people want to get to know him, be around him, hang out with him, and give him beer or even drugs. And then there are the agents, who are looking for the next star. They see a talented player as their meal ticket. They know right away who's going to be worth millions, and they want to get next to him. They'll entice him with their words and with an offer that sounds pretty good.

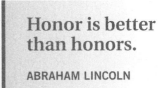

> ## Honor is better than honors.
>
> ABRAHAM LINCOLN

To be honest, we've emphasized this section more and more over the past few years at the request of the players. Every year we have the students evaluate the effectiveness of what we're doing, and we ask, "What can we do to help each other deal with all the negative influences and problems in our world?" I guess it's not very different from people who own a chain of restaurants and want to know how they can teach their employees not to steal from the cash register. Of course, the workers' rationale may be, "Hey, the owner of this place makes a ton of money, and I'm not getting paid enough. Nobody's going to miss a little cash here and there." But if the worker skims from the till to supplement his income, that reflects a problem of conscience.

INTEGRITY AND TRUTH

As I've listened to the players, I've become fired up more than ever to cover this section well. We can't scale back, because even though the culture of our team might be at a good level, society as a whole still has a lot of problems, and the players need to be prepared. In my opinion, we need to turn up the heat. For whatever reason, our society doesn't value honesty, and it doesn't value ethical treatment of employers. A lot of people sit at their desks and surf the Internet when they're supposed to be working. They steal from the company supply closet. They think these are just little, insignificant things that nobody will notice. Well, we need to turn it around and ask ourselves, "If I were the boss, would I want my employees playing solitaire when a report is due?"

There are so many examples of this kind of behavior in our society. Maybe we borrow a friend's CD and copy it because we like just one song and don't want to buy the whole CD. That's essentially stealing from the artist who created that song, but we tell ourselves it's okay because entertainers make so much money. We rationalize our behavior to the point that our conscience isn't even engaged. The same thing happens when we fudge on our tax returns or when we exceed the speed limit on the highway. Many times we do these things in front of our children. They see what Mom and Dad are doing, and the message comes through loud and clear.

> **Hold yourself to a higher standard than anyone expects of you. Never excuse yourself.**
>
> HENRY WARD BEECHER

A lack of integrity has a ripple effect. The actions of one person affect so many others. A friend told me a story about a house he bought. His family had lived there for a few years when they found a stain on the carpet in one of the bedrooms. The room was next door to the shower stall in one of the bathrooms, and when they traced the stain, they found that mold had been growing in the house for years.

As it turned out, the guy who built the house had installed the shower pan incorrectly. He had stapled the rubber membrane that was supposed to protect the stall from leakage; so every time the family took a shower in there, the water dripped out. That one little mistake affected all the contiguous rooms, cost the new owners a lot of money, and created a health concern.

That also reminds me of the story—I don't know if it's true—of the pilot who ejected from the airplane, pulled his rip cord, and made it safely to the ground. He had never thought about the importance of having a

There is a choice you have to make
In everything you do.
So keep in mind that in the end,
The choice you make, makes you.

JOHN WOODEN

working parachute, so when he got on the ground and was folding up his parachute, he looked at the name on the inspection tag. It was his own grandmother's.

You'd better be able to count on the airplane mechanic or the person who inspected your parachute or the guy who installed the brakes on your car. You'd better hope that person has integrity on the job and isn't just going through the motions. That's what responsibility is. Whatever your role, and no matter how small you think that role is, the team has to be able to count on you. You have to do your job and do it well, with all your heart.

To me, stay-at-home moms are good examples of commitment and integrity. Over the past few decades, many in our society have perceived stay-at-home moms as insignificant and have concluded that when women make the choice to stay home with their kids, they're throwing away their lives and wasting their talents. I want to say, "What? Are you kidding me? That's the most important thing a person could ever do." In society as a whole—as with a team—everyone's role is huge, because the success of the team depends on the hard work of each and every player. I'm thankful every day for my own mom's commitment to her role as a mother.

WHEN TEMPTATION COMES KNOCKING

I'm sure I can't imagine what our guys face every day and all the things they have to avoid or say no to. When I was in school, there were never any girls knocking on my dorm-room door. (I'll admit that may not be just a product of the era I'm from.) But it's a different society today, a much more difficult and complex world. These are not the good old days, when you went to church on Sunday and ate every meal at home with the family and talked about the lessons you'd learned. With the pace of life today, I don't know how many families still get to sit down together even once a week and have any kind of quality time. They're going through the drive-through and heading to the next practice, and the kids are either watching a video on the onboard DVD system or listening to music on their portable media players.

> ## Action springs not from thought, but from a readiness for responsibility.
>
> DIETRICH BONHOEFFER

If it's true that we're becoming more and more fragmented as a society and going whatever direction we see fit, I think it makes the Big Ten Fundamentals even more important. I know it fires our passion as coaches to equip our players and plant the seeds that will one day grow to maturity in their lives.

Class

> *Manners are like the zero in arithmetic; they may not be much in themselves, but they are capable of adding a great deal to the value of everything else.*
>
> DAME FREYA MADELEINE STARK (1893–1993)

We encourage our players to exercise responsibility and right living by having class. Class is the way you carry yourself; it's not a socioeconomic designation. It's not about how much money you make or don't make. It's not a way to pigeonhole people. Class is a way of life—a way of acting with confidence and style that reflects well on you and your team. It's having the freedom to do anything you want but choosing the right path.

You don't want to base how you live on what other people think of you. If you do, you'll always be struggling to live up to an image, trying to figure out what will make you look good in other people's eyes. Of course,

I think there's a place to ask yourself, *How do I want others to view me? If someone were to ask those people what kind of person I am, what would I want them to say?*

When our players treat the hotel employees well when we're on the road during bowl week, or when airline personnel compliment our guys on their courtesy, those players know they're acting with class, courtesy, and respect.

Some of our players come into the program with a healthy view of what the word *class* means. Others haven't had as many experiences, and they're at a different starting point. When those who have a little further to grow see how people react to their courtesy, politeness, or respect, they really like the positive feedback. Bringing a smile to someone's face or a warm feeling to someone's heart is rewarding.

> **It takes less time to do the right thing than to explain why you did it wrong.**
>
> HENRY WADSWORTH LONGFELLOW

Class is not arrogance. It doesn't put you above anyone else, and it doesn't call attention to itself; it simply treats people with respect.

CARRYING OURSELVES WITH CLASS

A good illustration of living with class happened in 2006 when we were playing the Texas Longhorns in Austin. Our general procedure when we travel to an away game is to go to the hotel first, change into sweats, and head over to the stadium. We walk around the locker room, see the sideline and the press box, and generally get a feel for the lay of the land. I like for our guys to see the venue and feel the atmosphere where we'll be playing the next day. We find out which end of the field we'll warm up on, where we'll go at halftime—the offense will be here, the defense there—and get a basic orientation to the game site.

When we arrived in Austin, we found that Texas is a top-drawer operation. They had a police officer there to provide basic security and make sure no autograph seekers would get to our players. We went into the stadium, did our walk-through, and then headed back to the hotel.

The next day was long, because it was a night game, but we made it through all the preliminaries, did our warm-ups, stayed focused, and in the end, won the game. I was the last guy out of the stadium for our team because I had media obligations. As I was leaving, the police officer who had been with us for two days stopped me.

> **Conviction is worthless unless it is converted into conduct.**
>
> THOMAS CARLYLE

"Coach," he said, "I just wanted you to know something. I've been at this post for about twenty-five years, and I've seen a lot of teams come in and out of here. I have to tell you, I knew on Friday that our team was in for a tough time. Your players were courteous to me, and I could tell they were courteous toward one another. Everything they did was very businesslike, as if they had a job to do and they were going to get it done. *They carried themselves with class.* I knew your guys were ready for this game. I just want you to know that I was really impressed, and you ought to be proud of the way they represented Ohio State."

I can't tell you how good that made me feel, and I made sure I told the team what the officer had said. It was motivation for them to do the same thing all the time, whether it was directed toward hotel staff, someone at the stadium, or on the airplane.

I met a man on a flight once who was interviewing prospects for the upcoming NFL draft. Later, we bumped into each other again at baggage claim, and I saw his college championship ring. I joked with him and said, "You're not here recruiting, are you? You stay out of Ohio. You've got enough recruits back in your home state."

He laughed and said he was just coming back from some interviews. "I want you to know, your guys get it," he said. "They understand what this is all about. And it's going to do nothing but help their draft status."

That was the year we had fourteen guys drafted, an NFL record since they went to the seven-round draft format. I think the scout was saying that our players had not only a concept of "team" but also an active conscience. They understood what doing right is all about. It makes you proud as a coach when, unsolicited, people who have nothing to gain by saying something nice will praise the conduct of your team. It makes you proud anytime your guys are seen as having class.

GUARDING YOUR TONGUE

It may be because of my upbringing that this principle is so ingrained, but the way you speak *about* others and the way you talk *to* others say so much about who you are. The book of Proverbs has a lot to say about the mouth and the tongue. A couple of verses in particular come to mind:

> *Watch your tongue and keep your mouth shut, and you will stay out of trouble.*
> **PROVERBS 21:23**

> *Spouting off before listening to the facts is both shameful and foolish.*
> **PROVERBS 18:13**

The words you use and the way you use them reflect the kind of person you are. So we've included a significant amount in the Winners Manual about guarding your tongue, because we give people impressions about us by what we say. Am I really a team player, or do I run people down when they're not around? Do I feel as if I have to criticize others to make myself feel better? Am I sensitive to the fact that my words really do affect how others feel?

Abraham Lincoln is often quoted as saying, "It is better to remain silent and be thought a fool than to speak and remove all doubt." I love that quote because it implies that keeping our mouths shut takes real discipline. I don't know how many times in my life I would have been better off just shutting my mouth and walking away rather than saying something I later regretted.

> *Those who exalt themselves will be humbled, and those who humble themselves will be exalted.*
> **LUKE 18:14**

We talked about the importance of humility in the chapter on attitude, but this quote from the Gospel of Luke indicates that those who are truly great will carry themselves with class. If you always have to be the one in the spotlight, the one getting all the honors; if you're always building yourself up at the expense of others, at some point life is going to humble you. It's better to help others up and give of yourself. Let someone else exalt you in due time. That's the path to true honor.

DO IT WITH CLASS

Class is respect for others. It is a deep and genuine respect for every human being, regardless of his status in life.

Class is having manners. It is always saying "thank you" and "please." It is complimenting people for any and every task done well.

Class is treating every other person as you would want them to treat you in a similar situation.

Class never makes excuses for one's own shortcomings, but it always helps others bounce back from their mistakes.

Class never brags or boasts about one's own accomplishments, and it never tears down or diminishes the achievements of another person.

Class does not depend on money, status, success, or ancestry. The wealthy aristocrat may not even know the meaning of the word, yet the poorest man in town may radiate *class* in everything he does.

If you have *class,* everyone will know it, and you will have self-respect. If you are without *class*—good luck, because no matter what you accomplish, it will never have meaning.

We talk a lot about this description of class. It's respect. It doesn't make excuses. It never brags. It's important for us to talk about these things, because when athletes play in a program like ours, there's no question they're going to be placed on a pedestal. And if there's even a hint of *attitude*—"I'm great, I'm a star"—it's going to be published or broadcast across the country. If a player is obnoxious and full of himself, people are going to pick up on that. However, if he's respectful of others, if he's nice to the staff who serve him when he sits at a team meal, if he thanks the bus driver when he's getting off the bus, all of those things create a general impression about him.

Another area of concern when it comes to class is the type of language a player or coach uses. This one strikes home for everybody, no matter what their age, because we've all been exposed to people who use four-letter words and can do it almost as an art form. The locker-room chatter and foul language can become second nature, because it's what many of our players have always heard. So we present a page in the Winners Manual that's meant to be humorous but gets the point across in a tongue-in-cheek way:

TEN REASONS WHY I SWEAR

1. It pleases my mother so much.
2. It is a fine mark of manliness.
3. It proves I have self-control.
4. It indicates how clearly my mind operates.
5. It makes my conversation so pleasing to everybody.
6. It leaves no doubt in anyone's mind as to my good breeding.
7. It impresses people that I have more than an ordinary education.
8. It is an unmistakable sign of culture and refinement.
9. It makes me a very desirable personality among women, children, and respectable society.
10. It is my way of honoring God, who said, "You must not misuse the name of the LORD your God."

We don't have a rule about swearing, or a penalty system for every foul word we hear. As coaches, we try to lead by example. If I'm in the locker room and I hear a guy spouting off, all I have to do is look at him and say his name. That look alone serves as a potent reminder. To me that's more important than putting a quarter in a cup for every swear word.

If a guy is running off at the mouth, I might say something like, "If your mom were here, would you talk that way?" Certainly he would rather do anything than disappoint his mother, because she's important to him.

> You can't slice up morals.
>
> JOHN STEINBECK

To me, that type of training is a lot more helpful than a bunch of rules. It's more relational.

And when you think about it, that's what the fear of God is. I don't ever want to disappoint God. I want him to be happy about the way I'm living my life, and I accomplish that with my commitment to finding out what "doing right" is and then doing it.

THE HONOR CODE

At the beginning of the year, we have our guys write an honor code. We enlarge it and make it into a sign that we hang in the locker room. Every one of us, coaches included, writes it in his Winners Manual, and then we all sign it and pledge to follow the honor code.

Here's the code the guys wrote for the 2007 season:

> The truth of the matter is that you always know the right thing to do. The hard part is doing it. As a member of the Ohio State football team/family, I will abide by this quote at all times in order to represent myself, my family, my teammates with the highest degree of class and dignity.

It's interesting to see how that code changes each year and the particular things the guys will highlight. These aren't my words or some assistant coach's idea of what the guys should do. This is what the honor committee—team members who hash out what's important—believes honor means to the team. This year, the team will once again write its honor code during preseason, and then we'll try to uphold those ideals every day, in every game and in every relationship.

QUESTIONS FOR REFLECTION

1. If you were to write an honor code for yourself or your team, what would it look like? Study the example of the Ohio State team honor code, and then write your own below.

_____

_____

_____

2. The responsibility of doing the right thing can weigh a person down when the focus is on rules and regulations. Do you agree with the approach of giving people expectations rather than a list of dos and don'ts? Why or why not?

_____

_____

_____

3. Who among your acquaintances has shown the most class? Tell that person about what you've read and compliment his or her behavior.

_____

_____

_____

4. If police officers, restaurant workers, cashiers at the grocery store, or those in any other service roles were to comment on your treatment of them, how would you measure up on the question of class? Is there anything you need to do to change that?

_____

_____

_____

5. Whose shoulders do you stand on in your career? What responsibility do you have to yourself, your team, and to those who have gone before you?

_____

_____

_____

YOUR PERSONAL GAME PLAN

1. *Personal/Family:* One of the most difficult places to tame the tongue is with your family. How can you be more considerate this week in your communication with those you love?

_____

_____

_____

2. *Spiritual/Moral:* What is your biggest struggle in choosing the right thing to do? Is there someone who could come alongside and help you make that choice? If so, ask that person today to do so.

_____

_____

_____

3. *Caring/Giving:* You will probably come in contact with someone today that you could simply walk past without speaking. Plan now not only to notice the person and speak to him or her but also to go out of your way to be kind, and see what happens.

_____

_____

_____

4. *Health/Fitness:* It may be more difficult for you to treat others with class when you don't treat yourself that way. What can you do for yourself in the next few days that will help you in the long run to give more to others?

_____

_____

_____

5. *Your Team:* If negative words or harmful speech can hurt those around you, how much can positive words do? How can you intentionally use your speech today to build up someone on your team?

_____

_____

_____

6. *Academics/Career:* What moral choices do you have to make on the job every day? Are there hidden temptations to slack off, take something that belongs to the company, or fudge in some way? Make a list of things that have been temptations or that could be considered compromising, and plan now how you'll handle each of those when they come up.

_____

_____

_____

CHAPTER 11

TEAM

Try to forget yourself in the service of others. For when we think too much of ourselves and our own interests, we easily become despondent. But when we work for others, our efforts return to bless us.

SIDNEY POWELL

Unity is the great need of the hour, and if we are united we can get many of the things that we not only desire but which we justly deserve.

MARTIN LUTHER KING JR.

Don't be concerned for your own good but for the good of others.

1 CORINTHIANS 10:24

Together
Everyone
Achieves
More

Each of the Big Ten Fundamentals affects every component of the Block O. But of all the tools we discuss with our players, the one that best allows us to understand and experience success is TEAM: Together Everyone Achieves More.

We talk a lot about the fact that winning is more than individual achievement or success. It's even bigger and broader than our team's success. In fact, in every area of life, I don't know if we're capable of accomplishing much without understanding that what we're working toward is much larger than we are as individuals *or* as a team.

In 1991, our Youngstown State team won the national championship in Division I-AA. When we arrived home after the game, ten thousand screaming fans met us at the Youngstown airport. The population of the city at the time was about ninety-seven thousand, so a crowd of ten thousand people represented a good percentage of the population, and there was great excitement about our victory over Marshall University.

When we stepped off the plane and tried to make our way through the throng to the bus that would take us back to campus, an older gentleman pushed his way through the crowd to get to me. I could see in his eyes the hardness of the years that had passed.

With tears streaming down his face, he said, "This is the greatest day in my life since V-E Day." This man had probably lived in Youngstown his whole life. After World War II, he'd probably worked in the mill, probably lost his job when the economy turned, and his family had no doubt struggled. It appeared that between the time of the Allies' victory in Europe and our team's victory on the football field, things hadn't gone very well for this man. But to know that our team had brought such joy to his heart, and to all of Youngstown, was a huge bonus for us.

> **The nicest thing about teamwork is that you always have others on your side.**
>
> MARGARET CARTY

Every great team I've ever been a part of has at some point come to the realization that our winning or losing affects more than just those of us in the room. It's easy to recognize that at Ohio State, with the throngs in the stadium and hundreds of thousands of alumni all over the country. ESPN declared the Ohio State/Michigan rivalry the greatest in all of sports. You have two great institutions in adjacent states; the history of the rivalry is legendary; the characters who have been involved over the years seem bigger than life; and many times when the two teams play, the league championship is on the line. Freshmen jump into Mirror Lake on the OSU campus—in November—to show their support, so you can see the magnitude of that one game.

But even if you don't have such history or rivalry, you must understand that *any* endeavor is a group journey. When you play for more than just the guys on the field, you can achieve the inner satisfaction and peace of mind that come from being part of something much larger than yourself.

GREAT TEAMS ARE UNSELFISH

Dr. Pat "Doc" Spurgeon, my good friend and mentor, has told me many times that every great team has two vital ingredients: love for one another and discipline. The great thing about that combination is that you don't have to worry about discipline if you have love. If the players really care about each other—not just for show but with a genuine love that is pure and giving— they will play their roles properly.

Chris Creighton, the head football coach at Drake University in Iowa, has always been one of my favorites. When he was still a young coach at Wabash College, he came up with the idea of asking coaches who had won a national championship what was the most important characteristic of their championship teams.

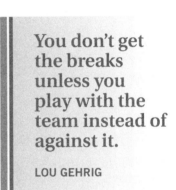

You don't get the breaks unless you play with the team instead of against it.

LOU GEHRIG

When he asked me that question, I thought about it a long time, and the word that popped into my mind was *unselfishness*. Every championship team I've been with has been unselfish. Guys weren't worried about their rushing stats, or how many tackles, interceptions, or catches they'd made, or how many points they'd scored. They were concerned primarily about the team. And because we had teams full of unselfish people, we were able to accomplish extraordinary things together.

My personal experience confirms Doc Spurgeon's point about the importance of love. If we have love, how can we be selfish? We can't. I believe that unselfishness is the number one quality exhibited by all great teams.

How does unselfishness work itself out in your business, your family, or your church? Spiritually speaking, people who are part of a church are part of a body of believers. How many times have you heard of someone making bad decisions that reflected poorly on their church or other Christians? That person has failed to see how interconnected he or she is to the whole body.

If you work for a business, are you more concerned about yourself or about the entire group? Do you care about the committee, the event being planned, your department, your individual goals, and the position you're striving for, or can you look at the entire company in an unselfish way? This takes us back to the definition of success we discussed in chapter 2, on the Block O of Life. If we really desire success, if we want the inner satisfaction and peace that come from knowing we did all we could for the group, then we'll begin looking at the teams we're part of in a healthy way.

Coming together is a beginning; keeping together is a process; working together is success.

HENRY FORD

This is absolutely one of the most difficult things to do in today's society. We are fragmented and individualistic. Our personal computers and iPods and TV screens isolate us in our own little worlds. In our churches, we can put up blinders and be more concerned about our congregation's particular distinctives than about the needs of the church down the street. It's easy to get caught up in thinking that "we're" right and "they're" wrong about some practice or point of theology and forget that we're all part of the same team.

Look at the Block O as it relates to the fundamental of Team. In the Spiritual/Moral area, are you doing things on your own, in your own strength, or are you part of a larger group, supporting and being supported? In your personal and family life, are you doing what you can for the team, keeping others in mind? Go to the bottom of the Block O and evaluate your health. Are you keeping yourself fit so that you can do a good job of loving your family? I know that I do a better job of coaching when

I'm healthier, when I'm well-rested, when I avoid putting things in my body that I shouldn't. That's a motivation to eat well, exercise, and keep myself in shape—not just for myself but for the good of everyone around me.

RELATING YOUR GOALS TO THE TEAM

If your career goal is to make a million dollars, that's fine. Some of our guys will list that on their goal sheets. That's not a bad goal. The question is, What are you going to do with that money when you reach your goal? Are you planning to benefit all of society, or are you thinking only about making money for yourself? Do you really believe that having lots of money and the things money can buy will make you happy?

Doc Spurgeon says that 99 percent of the people who say they love someone or something say it because that person or thing gives them pleasure. But the true measure of our love for someone or something is how much we give back to the object of our love. What are we contributing to our families, our churches, our jobs? Are we giving back to God?

> **Either we're pulling together or we're pulling apart. There's really no in-between.**
>
> KOBI YAMADA

Everyone who wins says, "Thank you, God. I love you." You see it after games or when people are being interviewed about winning the lottery. What they're saying is, "This gives me pleasure." Or maybe they're thinking, *We won the championship, so now I'll get a new contract,* or *I scored a touchdown. Thank you, God. Maybe now I'll get drafted in the first round.*

True success, however, comes from working in the opposite direction. True success is achieved when our main concern is the good of others and the building up of the team. That's why I don't mind passing along principles I've learned from other coaches. When Lou Holtz was coaching for South Carolina, he saw a copy of the Winners Manual we give to our players at Ohio State and asked if he could use it with his players. When Mike DeBord coached for Central Michigan a few years ago, he also asked for a copy. I teased him and said, "Now, this is for your use only—not for any other Michigan teams." Two years later, when he became the offensive coordinator at the University of Michigan, I said to him, "You're not going to use this stuff against me now, are you?"

A TEAM OF GEESE

When geese fly in formation, they travel about 70 percent faster than when they fly alone.

Geese share leadership. When the lead goose tires, he or she rotates back into the "V" and another goose flies forward to become the leader.

Geese keep company with the fallen. When a sick or weak goose drops out of the flight formation, at least one other goose will leave the formation to help and protect the weaker goose.

By being part of a team, we, too, can accomplish much more, much faster. Words of encouragement and support (honking from behind) inspire and energize those on the front lines and help them to keep pace in spite of day-to-day pressures and fatigue.

Finally, show compassion and active caring for your fellow man—a member of the ultimate team: humankind!

The next time you see a formation of geese, remember that it is a reward, a challenge, and a privilege to be a contributing member of a team.

PUTTING THE TEAM FIRST

It's human nature to be competitive and territorial. In a company, people can become so focused on their own success that they celebrate when someone in another department fails. Competition inside a company for goals and dreams isn't a negative thing; it can motivate employees to work harder. But when they get so focused on themselves and fail to work for the good of the team, everyone loses. Even minor victories will be hollow.

We're all human, and we all want to feel good about ourselves. That's why, when someone else doesn't do well, in a perverse way it can make us feel better about ourselves. That's an immature way of thinking, but it's a reality. I believe that God knows our frailty and that he wants us to recognize that foolish, selfish thinking and discard it. We have to repent of it.

We have to work on our team skills every day, because we're never entirely squared away in anything we do; growth is always a process, no matter who we are. People who say they don't have petty thoughts occasionally are either far better than anyone I've ever met, or they're not being honest.

A GOOD TEAM PLAYER . . .

1. Gives 100 percent
2. Shows courage *off* the field
3. Makes *no* mental mistakes
4. Cares about the team *above* all else
5. *Demonstrates* loyalty to all

Chris Gamble was a great wide receiver. His passion and dream were to play that position in the NFL. But in 2002, we were pretty solid at wide receiver—with guys like Michael Jenkins, an eventual first-round pick by the Atlanta Falcons; Bam Childress, who now plays for the Eagles; Drew Carter, currently an Oakland Raider; and Chris Vance—but we had a lot of injuries on defense. One of our defensive backs, Richard McNutt, had injured his ankle during his senior year in high school, and the surgery hadn't gone well. He was basically running bone on bone and playing through the pain. He had such a passion to help the team, and he was a fierce competitor, but he was taking so much medication for the pain that he began to have stomach problems. When the doctors finally said he

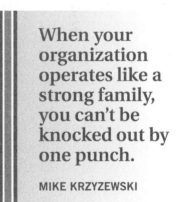

When your organization operates like a strong family, you can't be knocked out by one punch.

MIKE KRZYZEWSKI

couldn't play, it left us pretty thin at defensive back. In order to help the team in any way he could, Richard became a student coach, and he's now a defensive-backs coach for the Cleveland Browns.

218 THE WINNERS MANUAL

In practice, our receivers and cornerbacks work against each other. For fun, we'll sometimes flip them around and have the defensive backs run the routes and the wideouts try to cover them. When we did that, Chris Gamble was always the best cover guy. He was phenomenal. So after the third game with Richard hurting, I told our defensive coaches that when the ball was in the red zone (inside our 20 yard line) and the other team was getting close to scoring, they could utilize Chris as a cornerback and let him match up man-to-man. They wouldn't have to teach him anything about the defensive scheme, just let him go on his competitive instincts.

In one of those early games, against Cincinnati, Chris had an interception in the end zone that helped us continue our winning streak. As the season advanced and our record climbed to 7-0, we were still struggling in the defensive backfield. I talked to Chris and told him that we really needed his help at cornerback. His response was always the same: "I'm straight."

I told the defensive coaches, "When the ball crosses the 50, you can have Chris."

By the time we were scheduled to play conference rival Penn State, we were 10-0, one of the top-ranked teams in the nation, and closing in on a possible Big Ten championship. I told the defense they could have Chris for the whole game, and they decided to start him against Penn State.

> There is no delight in owning anything unshared.
>
> SENECA

"Chris, you okay with that?" I asked.

"I'm straight," he said.

In the final four games of the season, Chris averaged 125 plays per game. He not only played cornerback on defense and wideout on offense, but he also returned punts and kickoffs for our special teams. It took some real tenacity and fortitude for him to play that many downs.

Before the Michigan game, Chris was featured by a local news channel in a spoof of his workhorse performances. In the piece, he was shown as a sideline reporter, public address announcer, and drum major in the marching band. He sold concessions and tickets and wore the costume of Brutus, the Buckeye mascot. The feature ended with Chris sweeping up the stands after the game—and as he's working, the maintenance supervisor comes by, flips him the keys, and says, "Chris, can you lock up when you're done?" It was priceless.

We ended the season undefeated and prepared to play the Fiesta Bowl, that year's BCS national-championship game, against the University of Miami. Chris is from Miami, so he was looking forward to it, but I could tell he was a little tired from the season.

In the championship game, he was assigned to defend the Hurricanes' Andre Johnson, the best receiver in the country. The defensive guys said, "Wherever Andre Johnson lines up, you've got him, Chris."

To start the game, we called an offensive formation that didn't include Chris. We were trying to scale back a little bit and not use him on every play. But Chris was so excited about playing both offense and defense in the championship game against his hometown team that he went out anyway, and we ended up being penalized on the very first play of the game for having twelve men on the field.

> **A friend is always loyal, and a brother is born to help in time of need.**
>
> PROVERBS 17:17

"Chris, what are you doing?" I said, when he came off the field.

He just gave me a sheepish look and said, "I'm straight."

After that rocky start, Chris played a fabulous game. He stayed on Andre Johnson the entire night, and on offense he caught a sixty-yard pass. When it was over, Ohio State had won its first national championship in thirty-four years.

The next year, Chris was ready to play both sides of the ball the whole season, but because we had such a strong receiving corps, I told him I wanted him to play defense full-time and that we'd work him in part-time on the offensive side, which was not his dream.

"You all right with that?"

He thought about it a moment. "I'm straight."

Chris had a spectacular year on defense and attracted the attention of the NFL scouts. As the draft approached, he was projected as a first-round pick and was selected twenty-eighth overall by the Carolina Panthers, and all because he'd been willing to do whatever the team needed.

If he could have written his own script, he would have chosen to be a receiver, and he would have been a good one. But for the good of the team, he went over to the defensive side and then realized that though he could be a good receiver in the NFL, he could be a *great* cornerback. The moral of Chris's story is that if you do what the team needs and let your dreams and desires be shaped as you give to and support others, things will work out well for the team and for you. Chris is now entering his fifth year as a starter for the Panthers.

OLD WARWICK

A man became lost while driving through the country. As he tried to read a map, he accidentally drove off the road into a ditch. Though he wasn't injured, his car was stuck deep in the mud. Seeing a farmhouse just down the road, the man walked over to ask for help.

"Warwick can get you out of the ditch," the farmer said, pointing to an old mule standing in a field. The man looked at the haggard mule, and then looked back at the farmer, who just stood there nodding. "Yep, old Warwick can do the job."

The man figured he had nothing to lose, so the two men and Warwick made their way back to the ditch.

After the farmer hitched the old mule to the car, he snapped the reins and shouted, "Pull, Fred! Pull, Jack! Pull, Ted! Pull, Warwick!" With very little effort, the lone mule pulled the car from the ditch.

The man was amazed. He thanked the farmer, patted the mule, and asked, "Why did you call out all those other names before you called Warwick?"

The farmer grinned and said, "Old Warwick is just about blind. As long as he believes he's part of a team, he doesn't mind pulling."

YOU MUST BE WILLING TO LISTEN

Relationship coach Susan M. Campbell has said, "Teamwork is a constant balancing act between self-interest and group interest." We all have self-interest, and there will always be some players who have a hard time buying into the team concept—they're in it for themselves. If the majority of players care about the team, they can model that for the ones who don't quite get it. But if the majority are continuously self-obsessed, we will wind up with nothing but chaos.

One truth I've embraced in life is that you can influence people who will listen. And if you're open to being influenced, you can influence others. Sometimes we lack that openness in the Christian community. We don't want to hear other opinions. We say, "Don't talk to me about anything other than what I believe is true." Well, if that's your attitude, you're probably not going to be able to talk to the people you want to reach. If we could get past the issue of our differences and simply listen to each other, we'd be more likely to move forward. If people find us open and receptive, they're apt to say, "He's a nice person; I think I'd like to get to know him more. I'm going to see what makes him tick."

> **Teamwork is a constant balancing act between self-interest and group interest.**
>
> SUSAN M. CAMPBELL

Being part of a team means that you have to be willing to listen if you're ever going to be heard. I think that's very important.

Believing in the importance of the team was truly illustrated during the 2003 season at Ohio State. Coming off the 2002 national-championship season with a large class of returning seniors, we had high expectations as a team.

As it turned out, we had fourteen players selected in the 2004 NFL draft, the most ever from one school since the NFL adopted its present seven-round format. But despite all the talent on our team, we lost two tough ball games during the regular season, and our dreams of repeating as BCS champions didn't materialize.

You might think that when our team goals were no longer within

WHAT YOU MEAN TO ME

What you mean to me,
Words can't even explain,
Just know that without you,
My life would not be the same.

I'm going to miss you all,
When we go our separate ways,
I never thought I'd say this,
But, I'm going to miss two-a-days.

The hard work was fun,
For it brought out the very best,
And when it came to competing,
We were better than the rest.

We never gave up,
We always played with heart,
We made up with hustle,
Whenever we didn't play smart.

Our coaches were a little tough,
But it always made us better,
And more important than ever,
It brought us all together.

So as we look toward the future,
I can assure you of one thing,
We may not always play with each other,
But WE WILL ALWAYS BE A TEAM.

Thanks for everything.

NATE SALLEY, #21
OHIO STATE BUCKEYES, 2005

reach, the players' individual agendas would come to the forefront, especially with the bright futures that lay ahead for some of them. Instead, just the opposite happened. The 2003 seniors, which included Will Smith (currently with the New Orleans Saints), Darrion Scott (Minnesota Vikings), Ben Hartsock (Atlanta Falcons) and Michael Jenkins (also with Atlanta), committed themselves totally to the team. They pledged that they were not leaving Ohio State without a victory in the 2004 Fiesta Bowl against a Kansas State team that had just soundly defeated top-ranked Oklahoma in the Big 12 title game.

Because our guys put the team first, they were able to pull together and finish the season on an up note, defeating Kansas State 35-28.

QUESTIONS FOR REFLECTION

1. Have you ever experienced the chaos that results when the members of a team are self-absorbed rather than selfless? Looking back, is there anything you would do differently?

_____

_____

_____

2. Think of a time when you saw teamwork achieve something great. What did you notice?

_____

_____

_____

3. Chris Gamble saw his dream change because he participated in teamwork. Have you ever seen that principle at work in your own life?

_____

_____

_____

4. What is the larger goal of your team's success? In other words, how is what you're striving for about something bigger than yourself?

_____

_____

_____

YOUR PERSONAL GAME PLAN

1. *Personal/Family:* How can you better exhibit the fundamentals of TEAM in your personal/family life?

_____

_____

_____

2. *Spiritual/Moral:* Have you been a "team player" with others in your spiritual life? What specific thing can you do to improve in this area?

_____

_____

_____

3. *Caring/Giving:* Is there someone on your team that you can reach out to today?

_____

_____

_____

4. *Health/Fitness:* What can you do today to care for your body and thus become a better team member?

_____

_____

_____

5. *Your Team:* What can you do today that will make you a better member of your team?

_____

_____

_____

6. *Academics/Career:* Have you noticed someone who has exhibited unselfish teamwork? Write that person a thank-you note.

_____

_____

_____

CHAPTER 12

HOPE

Hope . . . is not the same as joy that things are going well, or willingness to invest in enterprises that are obviously headed for early success, but rather, an ability to work for something because it is good, not just because it stands a chance to succeed.

VÁCLAV HAVEL, *DISTURBING THE PEACE*

Live in your hopes and not in your fears.

JOHNNY MAJORS

There is no medicine like hope, no incentive so great, and no tonic so powerful as expectation of something tomorrow.

ORISON SWETT MARDEN (1850–1924)

I pray that God, the source of hope, will fill you completely with joy and peace because you trust in him. Then you will overflow with confident hope through the power of the Holy Spirit.

ROMANS 15:13

There are times in the game of life when it will seem as if things are not going very well. There are times when life departs from our familiar script and throws us something we had no idea was coming. It's tempting in those circumstances to lose faith in ourselves, in the people around us, and even in God. But if we've been planting the seeds of hope in our hearts, we'll be able to overcome the problems of life and use them not only to make ourselves stronger but also to produce something good for ourselves and those we love.

There's an old story in the OSU Winners Manual that's actually found in the section on Handling Adversity, but like many other stories, it could fit in multiple sections. It concerns a farmer whose mule fell into a dry well. The farmer heard the mule making noise and discovered the poor animal's misfortune. After assessing the situation, the farmer decided the mule wasn't worth the time and expense it would take to save it. Essentially, he lost hope in the old mule. So he called his neighbors together and asked them to help him haul dirt to bury the animal and put it out of its misery.

When the first shovelfuls of dirt came down, the mule became hysterical and began to kick. But as the dirt continued to hit his back, it dawned on the creature that he should shake it off each time and step up on the growing mound of dirt beneath him. Load after load of dirt hit him square in the back, but no matter how painful it was, he shook the dirt off and stepped on it.

Before long, the accumulation of dirt was such that the old mule, battered and exhausted, stepped triumphantly over the wall of the well. The dirt that had been meant to bury him had actually saved his life because of the manner in which he had responded to the situation.

> Hope is the feeling you have that the feeling you have isn't permanent.
>
> JEAN KERR

When we possess the hope and belief that ultimately we're going to be successful in our journeys, there's not much of what comes our way on a daily basis that we can't handle. When we see negative events as stepping-stones and have hope that our problems can actually propel us toward our goals rather than hinder us, then we are, of all people, truly blessed. If I could pass along one virtue to all of our players—and to every reader of this version of the Winners Manual—it would be the virtue of *hope*.

HOPE RALLIES THE TROOPS

Life is a series of ups and downs, peaks and valleys, wins and losses. When the bad times come, and they inevitably will, the seeds we've sown in our lives—what we believe in and hang on to and what we know is true and right—will help us maintain the hope that whatever stands before us is not permanent but only a temporary obstacle.

In the course of any football game, there are moments when the contest feels as if it's not going in the right direction. Someone makes a mental mistake or draws a penalty, the other team makes an incredible play, or we simply find ourselves on the wrong end of the score. By all objective standards—the score, the time remaining on the clock, the fact that the other team has the ball, or the yardage needed in order to score—the chances of pulling out a win seem pretty slim. That's when hope can rally the troops, and the other fundamentals—such as attitude, discipline, love, and knowing how to handle adversity—come into play to keep the team pursuing victory.

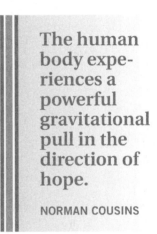

> The human body experiences a powerful gravitational pull in the direction of hope.
>
> NORMAN COUSINS

One example that comes to mind is our game against Michigan in 2005. With 7:49 to play in the fourth quarter, we were trailing 21-12 and had the ball on our own 33 yard line. We had scored only twelve points the entire game and were down by nine, which meant we would have to score twice in order to win. It was a situation in which we might have been tempted to despair or simply to play for pride, but I'll be honest: I really felt as if we still had genuine hope for a win. You could see it on our sideline. One look in our players' eyes told me that they felt they could still win.

Here's the reason for that hope: As a team, we had scrupulously prepared for that game. We had planted the seeds of physical training and had mentally worked through our opponent's strengths and weaknesses, and we believed in the plan we had set forth to come away with a victory. It wasn't a blind hope—one that simply believes the best and says, "Golly-gee, I hope this is going to come out okay." No, we had put a lot of sweat equity into that season, and we weren't about to let our opponent or ourselves off the hook by simply giving up.

As the clock continued to wind down, our quarterback, Troy Smith, took us down the field, hitting on a pass to Anthony Gonzalez, scrambling fourteen yards for a first down on a crucial third down play, and ultimately connecting with Santonio Holmes for a twenty-six-yard touchdown. All of a sudden the score was 21-19, and that nine-point deficit had been cut to two.

Our hope increased as our defense took the field. After a first down by the Wolverines, we forced them to punt and got the ball back on our own 12 yard line. We were eighty-eight yards from another score that could possibly win the game, but time was now definitely a factor, with just over four minutes to play. But you could feel the hope and the anticipation among our guys. If you see the video of that game, you'll see how alive our sideline was that day in Ann Arbor. Our players really believed that the problems of the first three quarters weren't permanent. They believed in one another. They held on to hope, because we still had four minutes on the clock, we still had all the preparation we'd gone through, and we still had belief in the team.

> **Learning is discovering that something is possible.**
>
> FRITZ PERLS

With less than a minute to go in the game, and after a series of great throws by Troy Smith and an unbelievable catch by Anthony Gonzalez, we scored the winning touchdown and went on to capture a share of the Big Ten championship for 2005.

Hope was an integral part of that game. Hope was the unseen factor that kept us believing in ourselves and in our mission. And that kind of hope isn't just for the football field; it's for every day of our lives.

HOPE PUTS FAITH TO WORK

I once read an interesting statement by psychiatrist Fritz Perls, who said, "Learning is discovering that something is possible." Every time I read that quote, I think about the young men and women who come to Ohio State and about the learning that takes place in their lives. But learning is not only for the young. People of any age can learn and grow if they'll stay focused and open to what's going on around them. As we learn and understand what it takes to achieve our goals—whether it's in our spiritual lives, our family lives, our other relationships, or any of the other components of the Block O of Life—academics or athletics—there's no doubt that our hope will grow stronger.

Knowledge is a wonderful thing. But *learning* means we take that raw knowledge and put it to work. When we learn and mature in knowledge, something takes place inside us that opens us up to a world of new possibilities.

There are scientists right now at The Ohio State University who believe they are on the right track to find a cure for some diseases that have killed hundreds of thousands of people. They base their belief on the evidence they see—the hard work they've done with state-of-the-art equipment. But all the best equipment in the world can't motivate a person to push forward through all the false starts, blind alleys, and other obstacles that stand between them and an eventual cure. Hope is an unseen ingredient in any successful endeavor.

As we go through the phases of our lives, we all need the kind of hope that puts faith to work. It's sometimes easier to doubt ourselves and not move forward. Others will question the goals of the group, their roles in the group, or their direction in life.

When we're tackling all the components of the Block O of Life, hope is a vital commodity. When hope is in place and is aligned with correct beliefs about ourselves, our team, and the plan, we are able to move ahead with confidence in whatever endeavor we're undertaking. We can go all the way around the Block O and see how hope affects each component.

> **Hope is putting faith to work when doubting would be easier.**
>
> AUTHOR UNKNOWN

For example, in our academic lives, if we're faced with a course that really challenges us and taxes our ability to comprehend, we have to have hope deep within that we're going to find the answers and get the job done. It will take preparation, diligence, the utilization of support systems, and the opportunity to ask questions to help us through the class, but at the core of it, we have to believe that the mission we're on will succeed. Hope is the by-product of acting on that belief.

FOLLOW MY VOICE

In the smoke and confusion that followed the 9/11 attack on the Pentagon, dazed employees looked for any way out. For many, all they heard was a booming voice, calling, "Listen to me. Listen to me. Follow my voice."

That voice belonged to Army Lt. Col. Victor Correa, who disappeared into a wall of smoke to look for his colleagues.

"Yours was the voice I heard," several people told him afterward.

"All of us had a different function," Correa said, "and I knew what mine was."

HOPE IS A CONSTANT BELIEF

When I was coaching Youngstown State in Division I-AA, if we were still close enough to the top sixteen teams that there was a chance we could still make the play-offs, you saw one group of players. Our teams had been to the play-offs a number of times, and we knew what it was like. But if we had a down season and had reached the point in the year where it was clear we weren't going to advance, you saw an entirely different group. You saw players who had less enthusiasm because they knew they weren't moving on. They had lost hope.

The type of hope I want to instill in my players is proactive and is based on reality, not on fantasy or wishful thinking. It's not the kind of hope a person might have when buying a lottery ticket with the last of the grocery money. Instead, it's a constant belief in the work that's already been done, the planning that's in place, and the potential that lies ahead.

We live in a skeptical world. News reporters are always looking for "change," and most of the time things change for the worse rather than for the better. But the constant negative drumbeat we hear about things not going well and people not doing the right things can wear us down as individuals and as a society. We tend to focus on the gloom and doom rather than on the wonderful things happening in our lives.

The quotation by Andrew Fuller—"Hope is one of the principal springs that keeps mankind in motion"—tells me that if I choose, I can be a carrier of hope. Leaders do that. They take hope with them and pass it on to others. We have to make sure that in everything we do, we exemplify hope with our lives—especially on those days when things aren't going well. Others should be able to look at our lives and see the guiding light of hope within us that turns into outward action. It's important for others to see that there's a different way to live.

Hope is one of the principal springs that keeps mankind in motion.

ANDREW FULLER

When people are devoid of hope, they're vulnerable to the traps of naysayers who think things can't be done and look at the world through negative lenses. A person who hopes says, "Sure, there are problems; yes, there are obstacles; but the future is bright—and with hard work, we can accomplish some great things."

Dr. Karl Menninger refers to hope as "an adventure, a going forward, a confident search for a rewarding life." I believe that every person needs to discover that perspective. We're all on an adventure, but some of us haven't fully embraced it. For example, it's been a lot of fun setting out on the adventure of putting together this book. Creating our Winners Manual years ago was a similar experience—it took a lot of work to put down a blueprint that would help us move forward and search for the rewarding life, but coming up with that game plan has helped thousands of players and coaches over the years, and now I hope this book will expand that number.

THE CONFIDENT SEARCH FOR A REWARDING LIFE

I have great hopes that the end result of your reading this book will be a boost in the direction of the adventure, the confident search for a rewarding life. The power is not in my words or in the principles we've discovered; the power is in the opportunity you have to reflect on your life and evaluate your own purpose and goals. I've often said of our goal sheets that it's the thought process they provoke that makes the difference.

Moving forward and gaining confidence in our search for true success will be a lifelong endeavor. If we begin when we're young, we'll be able to see the changes we consciously make over the years, and we'll be better equipped to evaluate our progress. But even if we're not so young anymore, we can begin today to develop our purpose and set our goals for the years still to come.

> **Hope is an adventure, a going forward, a confident search for a rewarding life.**
>
> KARL MENNINGER

After the players finish their goal sheets, I photocopy them and give them back their originals, telling the guys to put them in a place where they might bump into them occasionally. I don't want them to keep their goal sheets out in the open—on an end table or in their cars for public consumption—but maybe in their sock drawer or some other secluded place where they will likely be the only ones to encounter them every once in a while. I hope the goals and dreams the players write down will be part of them for the rest of their lives. I trust they will be reminders that the quest for a rewarding life is a daily process they need to pursue.

WHEN HOPE IS TESTED

When I read Dr. Menninger's quote about the search for a rewarding life, one experience I think about is the relationship between Ohio State football and former player Maurice Clarett. If you follow Ohio State football, you may recall that Maurice was an outstanding football player and an integral part of our national-championship team in 2002. He had a fantastic season, and his future looked bright.

Maurice's story is complicated, and it would probably take an entire book to detail all the hardships he's been through, but the bottom line is

FOCUS ON A HOPEFUL FUTURE

On August 22, 2005, I had the opportunity to speak before the OSU Buckeye football team and coaches. I shared the story about my spinal cord injury. I also shared lessons to live by to help them cope with change and deal with adversity, on and off the football field. . . .

One of the lessons I explained during my presentation was to focus on a hopeful future, not on self-pity. That lesson was taught to me by Christopher Reeve.

One year before my injury, I was in the audience at Reeve's presentation in Columbus. Reeve spoke about the loneliness of his nights in the rehabilitation center and his thoughts of hopelessness. I remember him explaining how self-pity is a trap that leads to deep depression.

When I was at Dodd Hall [OSU's rehabilitation center], I had a photo of Christopher Reeve, taken during his speech, mounted on the wall at the foot of my bed. I looked at it often during many lonely nights and tried to focus on how my life would have value again. As I focused my thoughts on a hopeful future, I began to feel encouraged about my recovery.

ROSEMARIE ROSSETTI

that he made some poor decisions along the way and is now paying the consequences. He is currently serving a prison sentence in Ohio.

Maurice was a great kid with a wonderful sense of humor. He came to Ohio State after graduating from Warren G. Harding High School in Warren, Ohio. I remember that when he first filled out his goal sheet, he said that he liked football a lot but what he really wanted to do was become a minister. As I did with the other players, I told him to put that on his goal sheet and we'd talk about how we might help him reach that goal.

After he distinguished himself in the first couple of games, I called him into my office and showed him a list of about fifteen things that I knew would happen to him as a result of his visibility on the team. I said,

"Just so you know and can be prepared, these are some things that are going to happen."

I told him that women would be knocking on his apartment door. Gamblers would try to get next to him. The media were going to focus on him. The students in every class were going to watch his every move and tell everyone they knew everything he did, good or bad. I listed all the things I'd seen happen to other players in his situation and warned him that he needed to be prepared to handle himself properly.

He looked over the list and then looked back at me. I could see the wheels turning in his head.

After one season at Ohio State, Maurice left the team and tried to gain early entry into the NFL draft—an endeavor that didn't work out for him. Eventually, he got into some real trouble and wound up in prison. So why am I including his story in this book, and specifically in this chapter about hope? I'm still hoping that Maurice's story will have a happy ending and that what has happened to him will serve a good purpose in his life and result in a greater good for him and for others. I believe he still may become the person we talked about when he wrote his first set of goals as a college freshman.

> **If there were not hope, the heart would break.**
>
> *ANCRENE WISSE*
> (CA. 1250)

Now, I wouldn't be talking about Maurice if I hadn't heard from him over the past few years. His senior season would have been 2005, so all those players who were drafted in the first round by the NFL—A. J. Hawk, Donte Whitner, Bobby Carpenter, Santonio Holmes, and Nick Mangold—were guys Maurice came in with. I got a long letter from Maurice about how proud he was of them and about the things he was learning—and learning the hard way.

I think it's healthy to talk about Maurice to Ohio State fans, as well. Many of our fans have a great deal of bitterness about what Maurice put the school through. They'll never forgive him for the way he mistreated the university and abused the privilege of being a player here. My perspective is that Maurice was a young man when he came to us. He was a kid. He made some bad decisions because he was acting like a kid. It doesn't excuse what he did, but it does put things in perspective. And I'm still hopeful that Maurice will be able to turn things around in his life.

I had a chance to speak with him recently, and I told him I wanted to include his story in this version of the Winners Manual. I let him know first and foremost that we're still thinking about him. I still pray for him. There's an ache in my heart every time I think about him and all that's happened. I wish I could have done more to help turn the situation around. But just as God forgives us every day for the things we've done and the mistakes we've made, it's our responsibility to forgive others.

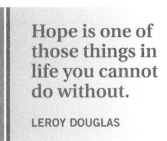

> Hope is one of those things in life you cannot do without.
>
> LEROY DOUGLAS

In talking with Maurice recently, it was neat to hear about the exercises he's taken during his incarceration. He really is seeking a rewarding life. He carries hope that things are going to be different, and I pray that he carries the hope we have for him as well.

He mentioned to me that he's used the tools of Proverbs and the Psalms. He's done extensive reading about positive living and about other topics, such as integrity, character, having a conscience, and all those buzzwords we use to remind ourselves about what it takes to go forward and what it takes to have a rewarding life. He said, "I may not ever be able to give Ohio State another yard—but if possible, maybe I can create an avenue where I can share some of the wisdom I have gained."

I have great hope for former Buckeye Maurice Clarett. It's not a blind hope; it's a hope built on a firm foundation that says with God, it's never too late to start over and head in a new direction. It's never too late to seek and find that rewarding life. Maybe you, too, have gone

> I know the plans I have for you. . . . They are plans for good and not for disaster, to give you a future and a hope.
>
> JEREMIAH 29:11

in a direction that was destructive to you for years. Maybe someone you love is going in that direction now. You can change. Your loved one can change. There is hope.

BECOMING DEALERS OF HOPE

I think Jeremiah 29:11 is relevant to all of us: "I know the plans I have for you. . . . Plans for good and not for disaster, to give you a future and a hope." That's certainly relevant to Maurice Clarett. It's relevant to me. God has plans for all of us that are good plans, not plans for disaster; and as long as we search for that rewarding life and carry that hope with us, we have a chance to end up leading winning lives.

Recently, I was speaking at a YMCA fundraiser in Ohio, and Gene Smith, who now runs the largest and most comprehensive athletic program in the country at Ohio State, gave what is probably the most rewarding introduction I've ever had. When he introduced me, he didn't rattle off statistics about how many games we've won; he didn't talk about coaching awards, national championships, or any of those fleeting things. He simply said, "Coach Tressel is a dealer of hope. He's creating the atmosphere and the culture of hope among student-athletes."

I like that phrase, *a dealer of hope.* I think it sums up the fundamentals we've been talking about. It's more meaningful than any statistic, any award, or any earthly accolade. And if we can grasp the power of hope and then give that hope to those around us, we will see great things happen in our lives and in the lives of people we touch.

QUESTIONS FOR REFLECTION

1. Do you see yourself as a hopeful person, or do you tend to rely more on dogged persistence? How have you seen hope at work in your life—either in a positive sense, when you had hope, or in a negative sense, when you lost hope?

_____

_____

_____

2. How did you relate to the story about the mule that had fallen into the well? Would you say that you allow your troubles to bury you, or do you look for ways they can become stepping-stones that help you to move closer to where you want to be in life?

_____

_____

_____

3. What are the characteristics of a person who has hope and one who does not?

_____

_____

_____

4. How do you respond to the promise of Jeremiah 29:11 that God has a future and a hope for you?

_____

_____

_____

YOUR PERSONAL GAME PLAN

1. *Personal/Family:* There is perhaps no more powerful force in a person's life than hope. Maybe someone you know has chosen a "hopeless" path. What can you do today to help him or her choose hope?

_____

_____

_____

2. *Spiritual/Moral:* If God has a plan for your future and wants to give you hope, do you feel as if you're part of that plan or working against him? Spend some time today asking God to show you his plan and to give you the strength to embrace it.

_____

_____

_____

3. *Caring/Giving:* Being a "dealer of hope" is one of the most life-changing things one person can do for another. What would it take for you to become a dealer of hope?

_____

_____

_____

4. *Health/Fitness:* Hope can help change a person's outlook on life. Do you live a hopeful life in regards to your health? If not, what can you do to change that?

_____

_____

_____

5. *Your Team:* Is there someone on your team who needs a bit of hope today? Reach out and give them some encouragement today.

_____

_____

_____

6. *Academics/Career:* How have you seen hope at work in your career? Would you be able to accomplish your goals without it?

_____

_____

_____

CHAPTER 13

HEROES AND WINNERS

Let me win, but if I cannot win, let me be brave in the attempt!

SPECIAL OLYMPICS PRAYER

I've got things to do with my life.

PAT TILLMAN

Keep your eye on your heroes, not on your zeroes.

ROBERT H. SCHULLER

He's added a great deal of inspiration to all of us. Because of the quality of the man, first of all, and because of what he has sacrificed and given up so all of us can sleep under the blanket of freedom. This is a man who has led soldiers in combat, who has sacrificed a great deal for all of us. We call him a part of the team, and he is a part of our team.

COACH TOM COUGHLIN, DESCRIBING NY GIANTS HONORARY CAPTAIN, WOUNDED WARRIOR LT. COL. GREG GADSON

One of the ways to live out the fundamentals you've just studied is to focus on people who emulate those values and principles. In a way, this is our eleventh fundamental, and because there are eleven teams in the Big Ten Conference, it's a subtle way of tipping our hat to that fact.

If you can find people who embody some of the things you've read about in this book, if you know people whose attitudes exemplify gratitude, or people who show class in what they do, people who have handled adversity with grace, or people who exemplify any of the other fundamentals we've talked about, get to know those people, and thank them for their influence.

In this chapter, I want to mention a few of my heroes as examples for us to follow.

LEE TRESSEL

The Big Ten Fundamentals in this Winners Manual have been included in every edition of the manual since 1986 and are directly linked to my father, Lee Tressel. The one fundamental in particular that stands out to me about my dad is the way he loved and cared for his players. I saw him model those attributes year after year, and it's one of my fondest memories.

When I was a kid, players sometimes lived at our house. If they didn't behave and needed a little closer supervision, they'd stay with our family. Picture a small college campus with a huge, brick house built in the 1920s or 1930s. Hardwood floors. Creaky furnace in the basement. That was our house. We had an attic that was kind of an apartment of its own, and at times players would live up there.

Right next to our place was a fraternity house where a lot of football players lived, and right behind the fraternity house was the stadium. Across the street from our house was the gymnasium where the basketball team played and where my dad's office was, so I got to see him in action with his players and his work, and I suppose a lot of that rubbed off on me.

The great impact my father had on his players was readily apparent to me. It wasn't just in watching him with the team he was coaching each year; it was also the number of former players who came back year after year seeking counsel on some life issue or wanting just to sit in our living room and talk. They valued my father's opinion. Many looked up to him as the father they never had. That was something that really made me feel good about his contribution, and I could see how rewarding a career in coaching might be.

Dad was the head football coach, the athletic director, and the head of the physical education department. He did everything. Yogi Berra once said, "You can observe a lot by watching," and that's what happened with my dad and me. It was much like the carpenter's son who gets to go into the shop every day and learn something as an apprentice. Being around sports and the coaching profession and picking up different ways to teach a fundamental or come up with a new play charged me up.

My father coached at Baldwin-Wallace for twenty-three seasons, from 1958 until 1980. He died of lung cancer in 1981. What many people don't know is that he dreamed of playing at Ohio State.

In 1942, my dad was high school player of the year in the state of Ohio. Paul Brown, the Ohio State coach, as well as one of the major figures in the development of the NFL, recruited him to go to Ohio State. Dad graduated early from high school and started at OSU in January. In the spring game, he scored two touchdowns and threw for another touchdown, and Paul Brown had all kinds of glowing words to say about this great young back, Lee Tressel. The other running back at that time was Les Horvath, who ended up winning a Heisman Trophy at Ohio State.

In the aftermath of Pearl Harbor, and with the escalating war effort, my dad was conflicted. I still have the postcard he sent to my mother that spring, in which he wrote that he'd talked with the Ohio State coaches and that he wasn't sure what he was going to do. "I'm going down to the recruiting station this afternoon. I'll see you on Tuesday and let you know."

It seems so matter-of-fact now, but when you think about it, my father was trying to decide whether to follow his dreams or serve his country. I'm sure that a big part of him wanted to stay in school and play football, but later that spring, after the term ended, he decided to enlist in the navy, and he eventually went into the V-12 program, which was designed to develop more naval officers during World War II. It's said that Paul Brown recruited one of the best freshman teams in college football, but nearly all of them went into military service. My father was one of them.

After enlisting, he was ordered to the V-12 program at a little college called Baldwin-Wallace, about three hours from his house. He'd never heard of it. The navy let him do his course work and go through training there. He became a navy lieutenant and played fullback for the Yellow Jackets in 1943–1944, and then again in 1946–1947, serving in the South Pacific in between.

My dad was a living example of someone who based his success not on personal goals but on evaluating the good of the group. And how many thousands of Americans in that generation set aside their dreams for the good of the country?

It was obvious to me, watching my father coach, that his love of the sport went way beyond the *X*s and *O*s. That's a great start in a relationship between a teacher and a student or between a coach and a player. If you know that the person who is over you cares about you, in some ways more than you care about yourself, and if you know that person has been down the same road you're traveling, that's a great comfort. You know there's someone in your corner who is willing to help you and guide you. Sometimes such a person will even carry you.

My dad wasn't the touchy-feely type. He was a man's man. But he knew how hard he had to be. I never saw him crush the spirit of a player, but I often saw him being very demanding on guys when they weren't putting their all into their craft. He wanted them to be the best they could be.

When I talk to companies about motivation, I usually don't know anything about their business; I don't know anything about what it takes to sell their product; I don't know what good sales figures are compared with bad sales figures. But I do know one thing: If the people know you care about them, that's a great start. That's probably the biggest thing that I took away from my relationship with my father, as a player and as a son. He cared deeply about everything. Whether it was about the player's parents or the player's academics or the player's behavior, he was fully there, present and engaged. I guess, inevitably, when I decided to be a coach, it was a lot like a pastor whose son decides to go into the ministry. I saw my father's devotion to his work, how much fun it was, and how much he loved doing what he did, and I thought, "He's making a difference in so many people's lives, and he's having fun doing it! He loves it so much he's never here!"

I was proud of my dad for throwing himself into that lifestyle, and although it was true that he wasn't at every performance or game I had, I understood that he was making a difference. I remember hearing Robert Kennedy's children talk about their father and answering the question,

"Were you angry that he died so young?" They were so proud of their father's courage and what he was trying to do. They said they felt that he was trying to make a difference, and therefore, his death didn't lead to anger but rather was an inspiration to them to follow in his footsteps.

The biggest thing I learned from my dad was how much caring for others could change not only their lives but also my own.

The other thing that makes my dad a hero to me is how unselfish he was. He coached at a small college and made very little money. He had opportunities to move up the ladder to bigger schools and earn bigger paychecks, but he was committed to his school and to his family. When you're a child, you never want to move. You want to hold on to that sense of stability and the feeling of being grounded. My dad was committed to that priority for us. He loved the community he lived in. He thought it was a great place to raise a family. He was loyal to the people he worked with, he was invested in the students, and he was just a very devoted person.

He told us boys—and this could also have come from my mother— that wherever we were employed, we should work as if we were going to be there for the rest of our lives. He said, "Even if at some point you end up leaving, you will have given everything to that place. And if you stay until you retire, you also will have given everything to that place." That's the pattern he set before us.

My older brother, Dick, coached at Hamline University in St. Paul, Minnesota, for twenty-three years before he moved to Ohio State to become a member of our staff. My other brother, Dave, just finished his thirty-fifth year of teaching in the Berea City School District.

Dad was not a talkative guy. He was quiet. So when he did talk, his players really listened. He was mild mannered and always tremendously prepared. His work ethic was legendary, and as a player, you knew he was doing the best he could for you and the team every week.

When I was home from college during the summers, I used to joke with him about his work ethic. If I got up before he did in the morning, I'd go into his room, shake him a little, and whisper, "Coach Mauer over at Wittenberg is up and in the office already."

The next morning, I'd wake up to see his big face in front of mine. "That quarterback over at Wittenberg has been working out for two hours. Better get up, Son."

At night, he came home from the office, and we ate dinner as a family—every single night for as long as I can remember. When he was finished, he'd lie down on the couch, and every night he'd say, "Now if I should happen to fall asleep, wake me up in a half hour."

Boom—he'd be out like a light. Every night, without fail, he'd just conk out; but a few minutes later he would be up and heading back to the office. Every night. I'd look across the street at the gymnasium, and you could see his office light on. Division III coaches didn't go out and recruit back then; it was all done by telephone. And the drive at Division III schools was to attract students. Small colleges needed a football program for enrollment. So Dad would make fifty to seventy-five calls every night.

My father knew how to create a team and pull people together. And he did that in our family as well. One of my most vivid memories is the year he went to the University of Indiana to finish his doctorate. He had to establish a residence there in order to finish. To do that, he had to take a leave from Baldwin-Wallace, because he wasn't just getting paid for coaching; he was also a teacher.

Mom didn't work outside the home, so money was tight. We couldn't even afford to call Dad on the phone, which sounds pretty strange now. We would send audiotapes back and forth in the mail.

I remember when Christmas came that year, it was a hard time for us. For his present, my oldest brother received a tie tack, which probably cost about fifty cents. My middle brother got a book, because he always wanted to be a teacher. It was a book he already had. And I got a pair of football pants that I'm sure the sporting goods salesman gave to my dad.

I don't tell you that to garner sympathy for our family, because we felt so proud that we were on our dad's team. We were sacrificing for him. There were other Christmases when we received a lot of toys and great presents, but out of all of them, that's the one I remember most vividly.

Prior to the years of Division III play-offs, Dad's season ended in early November, and we got to see him in the light of day. I can still see him sitting on the couch watching the Ohio State-Michigan game, and I remember the warm feeling of having my dad finally home and not preoccupied.

The next biggest day of the year was January 1, because of all the bowl games that were on TV. We'd borrow TV sets from our neighbors and watch all the New Year's Day bowl games—and there was Dad, right there with us. Those are some great memories.

When I was going into my senior year, the 1974 season, my dad said to me, "You know what? If you guys win the national championship, I think I'll get out of the coaching end and just be the athletic director. Then I'll be able to spend more time with your mom." It wasn't a big proclamation; we were just chitchatting.

Well, we had a good year and made it to the conference championship. If we won, we'd be in the final four for the national championship. However, in the game, I threw an interception that cost us, and we ended up losing and being eliminated. It was devastating at the time, but life goes on and you have to shake it off.

Four seasons later, Dad's team won the Division III national championship. He and I are still the only father and son in NCAA history to have won national championships.

Two months after that championship season, he was diagnosed with lung cancer. He coached two more years, but he wasn't in good shape. In the late 1970s, the cancer treatments weren't as effective as they are today. He was only fifty-six when he died, about the same age I am now.

In the years since he died, I've heard from countless former players of his, who write and tell me what my father meant to them.

I've often thought about my dad's comment before the 1974 season, and I wonder what would have happened if we had won the championship. Maybe he would have relaxed and gotten a physical. Maybe they could have caught the cancer earlier and he'd still be around. Losing a hero like that makes you think about those things. I wish he were here to see all that's happened. You can bet I'd phone him at seven o'clock some evening and tell him to wake up because Coach Mauer's still at it over at Wittenberg. And he'd do the same for me.

By the way, I don't think much about that interception. I don't have to. My buddies from that team remind me of it every chance they get.

CHUCK CSURI

I have such great respect for the men and women who have protected the freedoms of our country. As I stated earlier, my father enlisted in the navy during World War II. He and others like him were willing to put their personal goals and dreams aside to protect our country and liberate Europe from the stranglehold of the Nazis.

One such hero was Charles Csuri. His family was from Hungary, and during the Depression, his father mined coal in West Virginia. After a mining accident in which his father lost a leg, the family moved to Cleveland, Ohio.

Chuck became interested in art and football, an interesting combination. He became so good in the sport that after his senior year in high school, he was invited to attend The Ohio State University. He was a member of the 1942 team that won the university's first national championship, and Chuck was named to the All-America team.

Chuck's future looked bright, both in football and in his artistic endeavors. He was chosen as captain of the 1943 team, but he decided, like so many in that great generation, that he owed it to his country to serve in the war effort. He enlisted, and in December 1944 found himself in the middle of one of history's bloodiest battles, now known as the Battle of the Bulge. More than one million men, from both the German and Allied sides, fought in the bitter cold of one of the snowiest winters on record in the Ardennes Forest in eastern Belgium. With little food, subzero temperatures, heavy snow, and even heavier casualties, the American forces repelled the German advance in one of the more significant and strategic battles of World War II.

In one segment of that huge battle, Charles Csuri volunteered for a mission that would reestablish communication between his company and the rest of the Allied forces. He played a critical role, breaking through enemy lines, getting his helmet and his belt pack shot off, and delivering vital information that allowed the Allies to alter their strategy.

For his bravery in combat, Charles Csuri was awarded the Bronze Star. He served his country until 1946 and then returned to Ohio State. He finished his master's degree in art in 1948, and a year later joined the Ohio State faculty in the art department.

But Csuri's amazing story wasn't finished. He used his love of art and the new technology of computers to become a pioneer in the field of computer graphics, computer animation, and digital fine art. Much of the computer animation you see in today's movies, and many of the graphics you've seen on television over the years, are the products of technology first developed by Charles Csuri. His innovation and talent have won numerous awards, and his students have worked on such films as *Jurassic Park*, *Ice Age*, and many others.

Chuck Csuri is an amazing man, perhaps the greatest hero who ever played football at Ohio State. He's still active and is an inspiration to those who are privileged to know him. I suppose there are entire groups of people who won't come close to accomplishing what Chuck Csuri did as an individual before he was thirty. Yet he has an enduring humility that's refreshing. He cared so much about the teams he was on that he was willing to sacrifice for them. He embodies all of the fundamentals we've been talking about.

A few years ago, as a team we read *Expanding Your Horizons*, the story of the 1942 Ohio State national champions. And it was a special treat to have Chuck Csuri speak to our team in 2002 before our game against Texas Tech. Our guys were enthralled to meet him. It was dead silent as he spoke. He talked about the importance of focusing on the task ahead and having the discipline you need to succeed. If there's a man who knows that subject, it's Chuck Csuri.

TYSON GENTRY

In the chapter on Work, I mentioned an exceptional young man named Tyson Gentry. A third-year sophomore walk-on from Sandusky, Ohio, Tyson was both a punter and a wide receiver for us in 2006. During spring practice, Tyson went up for a pass and sustained an injury to his neck, fracturing his C4 vertebra.

There's an interesting side story to his injury and the recovery he's currently attempting. In August 2005, before he got hurt, Tyson was among those in the audience when motivational writer and speaker Rosemarie Rossetti spoke to the team about her spinal cord injury. At the end of her talk, she handed out sheets of paper and asked the guys to write something to new patients at the OSU Dodd Hall rehabilitation center. Each player wrote something and signed it.

After the meeting, my wife, Ellen, and I, along with Rosemarie and her husband, Mark Leder, read what some of the guys had written. I was so proud of the heartfelt emotion they expressed. It was clear that Rosemarie's message had gotten through to them.

Now, fast-forward eight months. Tyson Gentry is lying in the intensive care unit of the OSU medical center. A Dodd Hall staff member copied the get-well letter that Tyson had written eight months earlier and brought it to his bedside. The encouragement that he had hoped would help someone else was actually waiting for him when he needed it.

Tyson is an amazing young man, and his teammates were there for him every day. Our fans sent letters and cards and told him they were praying for his recovery. Other teams and players who have been through similarly devastating injuries have gotten in touch with him, which shows what a caring fraternity you can have in football.

Tyson has an unbelievable attitude. He has inspired and motivated us as a team the past couple of years. Our guys wear his number on the backs of their helmets. He has been tenacious about his schoolwork and his physical rehabilitation, and he is a constant reminder to our guys of what a real hero is.

His dreams of being an Ohio State player were curtailed by an unfortunate injury on a routine play. He simply went up for a pass, as he'd done a thousand times before, and the next thing we knew, after a seemingly routine tackle, he was lying motionless on the field.

But Tyson has shown us that it's not what happens to you that counts in life. It's how you handle it. And he has a committed family around him and some wonderful friends. I ask God to give me more of Tyson Gentry's attitude every day.

There is no question in my mind that Tyson Gentry is a hero, but so are the members of his family. The countless drives they've made from Sandusky to Columbus, to make sure all of his needs are being met, demonstrate their sacrifice and commitment. Mr. and Mrs. Gentry have been an inspiration and models of parental love for their son.

Tyson's sister, Ashley Gentry, graduated from nearby Capital University shortly after Tyson was injured. She has put her own plans on hold and has moved in with Tyson to take the lead in his recovery. In fact, she has become so passionate about the need for caregivers that she is seeking an additional degree from the local nursing school at Mount Carmel Hospital. In my eyes, Ashley, too, is truly a hero.

This past spring, we had the wonderful opportunity to have Mike Sullivan, the wide receivers coach of the New York Giants, speak at our annual coaches clinic. Mike was an assistant coach for us at Youngstown State in the 1990s.

Accompanying Mike, and also sharing with the coaches, was LTC Greg Gadson, one of Mike's teammates at West Point, who lost both legs to a roadside bomb in Iraq. You might recognize his name, because he became the honorary captain and inspirational leader of the New York Giants on their amazing Super Bowl journey.

LTC Gadson shared with the coaches, and later with our team, that he had no regrets about losing his legs in combat as he served our country and the cause of freedom in Iraq. He emphasized that the group, the team, the cause, is what his life is all about. He said, "My heart and my mind survived. I want to be a soldier, and they will allow me to continue to serve."

On that spring weekend in 2008, here at Ohio State, we were able to honor LTC Greg Gadson, along with other wounded warriors from Walter Reed Medical Hospital—SFC Matthew Miles, CPL Adam Poppenhouse, and SPC Michael Dinkel, all from Ohio. Each of these men lost limbs in the service of our country. None of them had regrets; all are true heroes.

FINAL THOUGHTS

Sometimes we miss the boat when we think about what really makes a hero. It's not the great, over-the-shoulder catch to win the game, the crunching sack by a linebacker to shut down a drive, or winning the championship. Most of the guys who talk about heroes in their winner's speeches don't talk about anyone famous. When they were kids, they may have idolized Michael Jordan, or Tom Brady, or any number of other outstanding athletes. But those people aren't their heroes. Their heroes are people who have served. People who have loved. To them, it's usually their mother or father or grandmother, who sacrificed a lot in raising them. Their heroes are often people that others have never heard about, and that's what makes such an impact on the other players.

We don't try to tell our guys, "Here's a great person; choose him or her as your hero." Heroes just naturally rise to the surface. People like Joe Daniels, our quarterbacks coach at Ohio State. He's battling cancer, and things have been tough. We're in the meeting room; it's 9:30 at night and we've been at work since 6:00 a.m. Everybody's tired. Everybody wants to go home. And here comes Joe, who's taking a new drug to shrink his tumor. They operated on his cancer, and then he had a heart attack after the procedure. He and his family have been through so much, but he's right there, on task, ready to go. Over the past seven years, he's had three different quarterbacks—and three different types of quarterbacks—take us to the national-championship game. But he's the kind of coach who can bring out the best in people. He's an unbelievable inspiration for us all.

Rex Kern is another man who comes to mind when I think of heroes. I was a sophomore in high school when he was the sophomore quarterback at Ohio State. He took that team to the Rose Bowl and won the national championship. I vividly recall reading about him in the Cleveland *Plain Dealer.* He was the Most Valuable Player in the Rose Bowl, and there was a picture of him holding the Rose Bowl ball in one hand and his Bible in the other. That was all I needed to know.

At school, I carried around one of those notebooks with all the subject dividers, and on the front cover was a full-size picture of Rex Kern from *Sports Illustrated.* He was my guy, but not just because of his abilities on the field. He was my hero because I saw what he was really about. He was willing to take a stand for Christ and serve by leading. To this day, he's one of Fellowship of Christian Athletes' biggest proponents and has spoken all over the country. Our Legend Award in the Central Ohio chapter of FCA, our most important award, is named after Rex Kern. He's the epitome of the Christian athlete.

Regarding heroes and winners, my hope for your personal game plan is that you'll find someone who exemplifies the fundamentals outlined in this book. Perhaps you know a person who models several of the fundamentals through his or her life. Maybe someone immediately comes to mind. If not, try to find people who are serving and giving, and see if they can motivate you to develop those qualities in your own life so that you become a hero to those around you.

EPILOGUE

"If the game of life ended tonight, would you be a winner?"

We began the book with this question, and it's a good way to end it as well, because of the way it has motivated me throughout my life. You've read much of the philosophy I've picked up from mentors, friends, coaches, and other thinkers who are included in the Winners Manual. I've tried to include as much of the heart of that resource as possible, and I hope it has been helpful to you. The final area to consider is my own faith journey and the answer I found to this important question.

I'm very thankful for the opportunity that came my way when my high school coach, Tom Madzy, asked if I wanted to go to a sports camp. The Kiwanis Club in Berea, Ohio, sponsored me, and I set off for Valparaiso, Indiana. It seemed like a world away from Berea, and I was excited.

Coach Madzy said that it was an FCA camp, which he explained stood for Fellowship of Christian Athletes. I had read something about the group a month earlier in the Cleveland *Plain Dealer.* The article said that Rex Kern, the great national-championship quarterback at Ohio State, was involved with FCA.

Like any young athlete, I was interested in pleasing my coach. Whatever he wanted me to do, I was happy to oblige. But when I heard about Rex Kern, I was sold. I wanted to *be* Rex Kern. He was a hero of mine when I was young. I remember the Rose Bowl between USC and Ohio State in January 1969, when Rex led the Buckeyes to victory, protected their undefeated season, and won the national championship.

When I went to the camp, I thought I was going there to become a better athlete, meet coaches and other athletes, and get exposed to different ideas about football. As the week went on, it became apparent that the issues weren't only athletics and football. I was hearing more about life—the big picture—and I had the feeling that I should pay attention. Something I couldn't explain was going on inside of me that week.

On Thursday evening, when we got together for our evening meeting, Bobby Richardson spoke. He had played second base for the New York Yankees from 1955 to 1966, and he was an amazing athlete. He was a consistent fielder and hitter and had played in several World Series, and I looked up to him.

It had been two years since he'd retired, but as he walked to the podium, he still had the look of a major leaguer. For four days we had been learning a lot about our chosen sport, but we'd also been hearing about the importance of living for God. That wasn't a foreign concept to me; I'd heard about God since I was a kid, but the speakers at the camp seemed to have something different. They approached life in a different way from what I had seen before. In a sense, we had been prepared all week for what was about to transpire. Everything culminated with Bobby Richardson's message.

It was probably the simplicity of the question that drew my attention. I'm a simple guy, and Richardson's question made a lot of sense to me. He said, "If the game of life ended tonight, would you be a winner?"

As I've said, my dad was a coach, and I knew the difference between winning and losing. I had a competitive edge to me, and I didn't like to lose. Even when I was playing pickup games in the backyard, I hated coming up short. Losing was just so permanent. Once the last second had ticked off the clock, you could never get that game back. It was gone.

There were more than three hundred campers there that night, but it felt as if Bobby Richardson were talking specifically to me. I was sixteen years old, and I didn't have a good answer to his question. If my life had ended right there and then, I didn't know whether I would be deemed a "winner" or a "loser." I was a confident young man with a lot of blessings, but my confidence ebbed away as I pondered Bobby Richardson's words. In my head, I was answering, *I don't know.*

Richardson paused for what seemed like a long time after the question, and then a bit of relief washed over me when he said, "If you're not sure how to answer that question, I can help you answer *yes.* Let me tell you how you can assure victory."

If you think I was listening closely before, I was on the edge of my seat now. I wanted to hear his perspective.

Richardson said that we needed to ask God into our hearts and give him total control of our lives. We needed to let God direct everything we did. He said that was all we needed to do to make sure we were winners in the game of life. He didn't say it was easy. And he didn't say that if we did it, everything from that point on would be a bed of roses. But he did say that if we would simply pray and ask God to come in and to forgive our sins, and let him take over, that would assure victory.

We weren't asked to raise our hands or come forward or anything like that. When the meeting was over, I'm not sure where everyone else went, but I slipped out the back door of the assembly hall, the weight of the question still on my mind, and walked down to the softball field. It's interesting now, looking back, that this significant event would happen on an empty field, with me sitting on a bench. I felt as if God were calling me to be on his team, and that was a very humbling prospect.

I'm grateful for Bobby Richardson and how his question affected my life. I'm grateful for his example and his willingness to ask the question and give the answer. I haven't lived a perfect life since that moment, and I've gotten a lot of mail that proves it. It's well documented. My wife, Ellen, thank goodness, is patient with me. The people who are closest to us always see the truth.

But living a perfect life isn't the point. We can't live perfect lives. We need God's forgiveness. Inner peace—what the Bible calls the peace that passes all understanding—is a true gift of God. It's something that we're given, so that in any situation we can know we have a purpose that we haven't manufactured on our own but that comes from a loving God who created us and loves us.

You can put the principles found in this book to work in your life, and they will help you. No question about it. If you begin to work hard at your craft, have a good attitude about the task ahead, persistently tackle problems, and persevere, you're going to get ahead. But the irony of the

Winners Manual is that you first must admit you're not able to win on your own. You need help.

The game of life is an inside job. So much of our success comes from inner strength, inner awareness of our weaknesses and strong points, and inner resolve. But ultimately, when we strip away all the things we use to salve our souls with—striving for awards and honors—we come away empty if there's not something bigger to live for.

Purpose is a gift from God. Without him, I would still be searching for purpose in my life. Lasting goals are also from God, and they affect the people around us for good. And every component of the Block O of Life can be traced back to principles discussed and fleshed out in the Bible. Of course, they also work outside of any religious arena, but the point is that they work.

So, my approach with players is to take them from whatever background they're from, whatever moral and ethical roots they have, and whatever religious upbringing they've experienced, and try to help them move further down the road. I've never had a player tell me he felt uncomfortable with my approach or that I jammed religion down his throat. I respect our players too much to do anything like that. I would never be unfair to anyone, whether in recruiting, in practice, or during the season.

In fact, I've heard just the opposite from my players. They appreciate my position and the team rules that derive from it. When guys commit to playing for us, they already know where I'm coming from spiritually, and many sincerely desire a deeper walk with God. But even if they don't feel that desire, I'm going to love them, help them get better at what they do, and make them vital parts of the team. That approach comes directly from my faith, which teaches me that I should treat others as I want to be treated.

In the OSU edition of the Winners Manual, we print the state motto of Ohio, which reads, "With God all things are possible." That's really what it's all about for our state, our nation, and our place in the world. It's not about me.

Perhaps you picked up this book because you've heard of the success of Ohio State football. Maybe you just like red sweater vests. But whatever success I've achieved, whatever goals I've been privileged to reach on the field of play, I want you to know that everything I've shared with you is the result of God's work in my life and in the lives of others around me.

I'm very grateful to have had the chance to learn from some wonderful people. One particular day at Youngstown State, our team was getting ready for a very important game, and we didn't know what the outcome was going to be. It was an uncertain time. I had invited Bishop Thomas Tobin, the bishop of the Roman Catholic diocese in the Youngstown area, to come and talk to our team, and it turned out to be one of the most concise and interesting messages I've ever heard about what the future holds. I'll paraphrase what Bishop Tobin said, and perhaps you'll also find it helpful.

> I don't pretend to know the future. The fact that I'm the bishop doesn't mean I know the future. But here are three quick things I believe are true about the future:
>
> 1. The future for each and every one of us is going to be a mixture of good and bad. Some things we'll enjoy, and some things we won't. And the same will be true in this game you're about to play. It's going to be a mixture of some good things that happen and some things you'd really rather not have happen.
>
> 2. The ratio of positives and negatives that happen to us in the future are going to be most affected by the decisions we make. We are going to have an impact on the highest percent of the ratio. In this game you're getting ready to play, the amount of good and the amount of not-so-good that happens is going to be mostly affected by what you do—not by what

your opponent does, not by what the referee does,
not by what the crowd does, not by the way the ball
bounces, but by what *you* do.

3. No matter what happens in the future, no matter
what the percentage of good and bad, I really believe
it's true that God will never leave us. He will always
be there for us. And the same thing is going to be true
in this game. No matter what happens in the course
of this game, God will be there at the conclusion.

That's a lesson I've never forgotten, and I think our players felt the same
way. And, of course, that lesson isn't just for football. I've experienced the
truth of it countless times in my life. I thought it was a tremendous blessing that Bishop Tobin shared his wisdom with us that day.

GOD'S HALL OF FAME

The Hall of Fame is only good as long as time shall be,
But keep in mind, God's Hall of Fame is for eternity!
To have your name inscribed up there is greater more by far,
than all the praise and all the fame of any man-made star!

The poem "God's Hall of Fame" helps give me perspective each day.
In athletics, election to the Hall of Fame is supposedly the ultimate
achievement. If we can make it there, we've made it to the top in the
world's eyes.

But football (or any other sport) is a man-made star. Whatever business you're in is a man-made star. It's something that human beings have
decided to create, and we have decided to make it important. We all have
things in our lives that we deem important, and we all spend a lot of time
doing what we do. But perspective is so important.

For example, I can tell you right now how many days it is until the

Ohio State-Michigan game. As you may know, Buckeye coaches can be officially pronounced dead if they don't take that game seriously and win it more often than they lose. But really, whether it's the Michigan game, the Hall of Fame, the Million Dollar Sales Club, the physicians' Hall of Fame—whatever it happens to be—those are man-made stars. Our perspective needs to be that we seek to be in God's Hall of Fame.

The beauty of it is that we can all make God's Hall of Fame. The NFL elects five or six guys each year; in baseball, they can vote not to elect anyone in a given year. I'm glad God doesn't do that. In God's Hall of Fame, everyone who is willing to admit he needs God's help can have a place. And it's so simple. We simply need to ask God to direct our lives.

Now, I'm not pretending that's easy. It won't be without its ups and downs, just like what Bishop Tobin told us about the future. But it's a simple, trusting relationship that says, "God, I want to be part of your plan. Work through me to touch other people."

The bulk of this book is about the fundamentals. As a coach of young people, I know that certain fundamentals will make the difference on and off the field. Every team spends a lot of time and energy talking about the intricacies of the game and what it will take to win against this team or that, but really, it comes down to a few basic things. Likewise, in the game of life, God has a few fundamentals that he knows will make the difference for us.

GOD'S FUNDAMENTAL #1: KNOW HIM.

At the bedrock of our faith must be a desire to know God. Not just to know *about* him, though that's important, but to know *him* personally. To experience him.

How do we know him? Of course, we read about him in Scripture. We talk to him in prayer. You'd be amazed how much you can learn about him if you will just sit quietly with him in prayer.

We come to know God better by being in relationship with other people who know him. Interaction with others who are seeking to master the same fundamentals is vital if we want to cultivate a deeper relationship with God. He desires our fellowship. He wants us to know him.

GOD'S FUNDAMENTAL #2: LOVE HIM.

God also wants us to master the fundamental of loving him. If you're a parent, you know that some of the happiest moments of your life are when your children come and want to sit on your lap, just to be with you. That's more important than whether they achieve in the classroom or score a touchdown or make a big sale or invent something. Those accomplishments are nice, but the thing we like most as parents is for our children to love us and want to be with us. To come sit in our laps. That means more than anything.

God covets our love, as well. He wants us to be with him. To communicate with him. To share our feelings with him. To share our concerns with him. Or just to listen to him. And it's from that close relationship of our knowing God and spending time with him that his love is poured out through our lives. If we love God, we'll love the people he has created. We'll want to act with kindness and compassion toward those around us.

In these uncertain and competitive times, it's easy to be divided. It's easy not to love others. But God loves everyone, and he wants us to love everyone as well. Whether we agree with them or not isn't the point. God will take care of that. And he will take care of us.

God wants us to love and be patient and forgive. And sometimes it's hard to forgive. He wants us to be caring, even when it's difficult to reach out or when what comes back in our direction is tough to take. Love is not just a gushy feeling; we have to work hard at it and master the fundamental of loving God and people.

GOD'S FUNDAMENTAL #3: SERVE HIM.

When we truly understand that the purpose of our existence is all about God, not about the national championship or making the bottom line at work or any of the other things we lift up as important on a human level, then we can begin to master the fundamental of serving him.

We can try to serve God in our own strength, but that kind of living keeps the focus of our lives on ourselves. The point is not to try to score points with God so he'll bless us; the point is to submit ourselves completely to what he wants and allow him to work through us. If we have God in our hearts, it will be easier to listen closely to what he wants. It will be easier to serve his people and serve those in need. That could mean something as little as giving a smile or giving thirty seconds to someone when you don't have thirty seconds to spare. Serving God means serving all of his people.

Knowing him, loving him, and serving him all begin with *gratitude*. If we understand that we're blessed, and if we're grateful for what God has given us, it will motivate us to know him, love him, and serve him more.

At Ohio State, our players know that they're blessed, but sometimes it's helpful to remind them to actually list their blessings in comparison to whatever it is they're struggling with. The negative things pale in comparison to all they have to be thankful for. If we're honest, our blessings will always create a much longer list.

I'm reminded each day of the brevity of life and the fleeting nature of fame. A time will come when no one remembers our names. The legacy we leave will be our service to God. And we leave that legacy one day at a time by practicing the fundamentals. Work hard on those important things. The fundamentals will make the difference in our lives.

The last thing that we say together as a team before we leave the locker room for a game is a simple poem. We have it on a big sign in our locker room, and the players don't even have to look at it anymore because they know it so well. It's a poem by Edward Hale, and it's a final motivation for us as we head onto the field to see how we're going to do:

> *I am only one. But I am one.*
> *I can't do everything, but I can do something.*
> *And that I can do, I ought to do.*
> *And what I ought to do, by the grace of God, I shall do.*

That's all we can ask of our teammates and coaches. In good times and bad, we need to make sure that whatever we *can* do, we *will* do. And we need to understand that it is only by God's grace that we shall do whatever he has called us to do.

I'm truly humbled by the fact that you have chosen to take the journey through this book. I'm grateful to God for the opportunity to share some of the things I've learned from some great friends and colleagues. May you be encouraged by these fundamentals and live a life of purpose. May God help you achieve goals you can't even dream of right now. May you truly be a winner at the game of life.

CREDITS

ABOUT THE AUTHORS

JIM TRESSEL is the head coach of the Ohio State Buckeyes football team. Since taking over the reins in 2001, he has guided the Buckeyes to seven bowl appearances, including five BCS games; five ten-win seasons; four Big Ten titles; and one national championship. Prior to coming to Ohio State, Tressel spent fifteen seasons as the head coach at Youngstown State University, where he was selected four times as the Division I-AA National Coach of the Year. Entering the 2008 season, Coach Tressel has an overall coaching record of 208-72-2 and is ranked twelfth all-time in Division I coaching victories.

In the course of his coaching career, Tressel has been named the Chevrolet National Coach of the Year ('93, '94, and '97); the American Coaches Association National Coach of the Year ('91, '94, and '02); the Eddie Robinson National Coach of the Year ('94 and '02); and the AFCA Regional Coach of the Year ('87 and '93). He has also been selected seven times as Ohio College Coach of the Year.

Coach Tressel is actively involved with the American Football Coaches Association, the Fellowship of Christian Athletes, Alpha Tau Omega, The Ohio State University Medical Center, and the William Oxley Thompson Library.

He and his wife also work on behalf of the Alzheimer's Association of Central Ohio, the Columbus Children's Hospital, the Tressel Family Fund for Cancer Prevention Research, Ronald McDonald House, the Youngstown State University Minority Student Endowment, the Mount Carmel School of Nursing, and the Jim and Ellen Tressel Athletic Scholarship Fund.

Coach Tressel and his wife, Ellen, live in Upper Arlington, Ohio. They are the parents of four children: Zak, Carlee, Eric, and Whitney.

CHRIS FABRY is the host of *Chris Fabry Live!* on Moody Radio and the author of more than sixty books. His first novel for adults is *Dogwood* (Tyndale, 2008). Chris and his wife, Andrea, have nine children and live in Colorado. They now cheer for Ohio State. Find out more about Chris at www.chrisfabry.com.